Bankocracy

Éric Toussaint

Resistance Books
IIRE
CADTM

First English edition published in 2015 by
Resistance Books and IIRE
www.resistancebooks.org
www.iire.org

Originally published in French as *Bancocratie*
by Les Editions Aden, 1060 Brussels, Belgium, 2014

Bankocracy is Issue number 58
of the IIRE Notebooks for Study and Research

© Co-edition CADTM
2 place de Bronckart
4000 Liège
Belgique

ISBN 978-0-902869-37-0

Translated, revised and refined by Snake Arbusto,
Vicki Briault Manus, Adam Clark-Gimmig,
Mike Krolikowski, Charles La Via
and Christine Pagnoulle.

Edited by Fred Leplat, Susan Pashkoff
and Terry Conway.

Designed by Pierre Gottiniaux.

Printed in the UK by Lightning Source,
Milton Keynes, MK11 3LW

Bankocracy

"What's breaking into a bank
compared with founding a bank?"

Berthold Brecht, *The Threepenny Opera*

Governments of the most industrialised countries have dramatically increased their public debt to bail out the private banks after the most disastrous economic and financial meltdown in capitalist history since the 1930s. Paying debts and reducing fiscal deficits have become the perfect pretexts to enforce austerity measures everywhere. The Troika (European Commission, ECB and IMF) and all EU governments have launched an unprecedented attack on the social and economic rights of their peoples. This book will enable the reader to understand how the crisis developed: the consequences of deregulating the banking system, the logic underpinning private banks' responses, and the crimes they perpetrate on a daily basis with the collusion of governments and central banks. It argues for socialisation, rather than 'nationalisation', of the banking sector so that it becomes a proper public service under citizen control and monitoring. It argues for the cancellation of illegitimate public debt that largely results from bank bail-outs. It uses simple straightforward language to make it possible for anyone to understand the current crisis and see coherent alternatives to current policies.

This book is dedicated to those who wish to better understand our struggle for empowerment, wherever they are; to the refugees who are shamefully denied access to our Western countries; to all those who have lost their jobs or their homes because of the irresponsible behaviour of banks; to those who fight injustice and all forms of oppression.

Éric Toussaint

Éric Toussaint is a historian and political scientist with a PhD from the universities of Paris VIII and Liège. He is spokesperson for the CADTM (Committee for the Abolition of Third World Debt) international network, of which he is one of the founding members. He sits on the Scientific Council of ATTAC France. He took part in the process that launched the World Social Forum in 2001 in Porto Alegre (Brazil).

For more than twenty years his economic analyses have been widely read in the press and on the Internet. He is the author of numerous books, of which the most recent are: *Bankocracy* (2015); *World Debt Figures 2015* co-authored with Pierre Gottiniaux, Daniel Munevar and Antonio Sanabria (2015); *The Life and Crimes of an Exemplary Man* (about Jacques de Groote, former Executive Director of the IMF) (2014).

Several of his books have been published in more than a dozen languages and have become reference works on questions of debt and international financial institutions: *Debt, the IMF and the World Bank: Sixty Questions, Sixty Answers* (2010); *The World Bank: A Critical Primer* (2008).

Toussaint took part in Ecuador's Debt Audit Commission appointed by the Ecuadorian President Rafael Correa in 2007. In the same year he advised the President of Ecuador and the Minister of Finance on the creation of a 'Bank of the South'.

In April 2015, Éric Toussaint took on the role of Scientific Coordinator of the Truth Committee on the Greek Public Debt set up by Zoe Konstantopoulou, the President of the Hellenic Parliament.

Éric is the author of: *The Life and Crimes of an Exemplary Man*, CADTM, Liège, Belgium, 2014, http://cadtm.org/The-Life-and-Crimes-of-an ; *Glance in the Rear View Mirror. Neoliberal Ideology From its Origins to the Present*, Haymarket, Chicago, 2012;

Debt, the IMF and the World Bank: Sixty Questions, Sixty Answers, Monthly Review Books, New York, 2010; *The World Bank: A Critical Primer*, Pluto, London, 2008; *Your Money [or] Your Life – The Tyranny of Global Finance*, Chicago: Haymarket, 2005. He has co-authored with Damien Millet, *The Debt Crisis: from Europe to Where*, VAK, Mumbai, 2012, http://cadtm.org/The-Debt-Crisis-From-Europe-to; *Who owes Who? 50 Questions about World Debt*, London: Zed Books, 2004. See also Éric Toussaint in *Capitalism – Crisis and Alternatives*, Ed. Fred Leplat and Özlem Onaran, Amsterdam-London: IIRE-Resistance Books, 2011.

Contents

Foreword and Acknowledgements

This book is intended to help those who do not belong to the inner circles of banking or political institutions to understand what is going on in the world of private banking, central banks and the European Commission, i.e. the places where crucial decisions are made that impact on the living conditions of the vast majority of the world population.

Chapters 1 to 3 trace the development of the capitalist system, and of the banking sector at its heart, since the 1970s-1980s. How the banking system in the US and Europe has evolved over the past twenty years to cause the 2008 meltdown is analysed in Chapters 4 to 7. The cynicism behind banking regulation is described in Chapters 8 to 10. Chapters 11 to 16 examine the state of banking in 2011-2014, while the manipulations and crimes that banks resort to are described in Chapters 17 to 25. The impact of governments, central banks and the IMF on the class struggle are studied in Chapters 26 to 34. Chapter 35 covers the development of banking over the past two centuries; and to conclude, Chapter 36 outlines a consistent set of alternatives and proposals.

I have tried to provide keys to understanding the various decisions that were made at top level. I also wanted to show that there are alternatives that are within reach if we act together. Social and political democracy has to be fought for on a daily basis. Collective action is a vital instrument of self-empowerment. Writing this book took almost two years. I read thousands of documents on the world of finance to achieve an in-depth understanding of how it works. Readers will understand that the very situation I attempt to describe here is changing from day to day. It is far more difficult to analyse an on-going process than to explain past events.

The book was written in several countries (Greece, France, India, Ecuador, Brazil, Haiti, Tunisia, Morocco, Belgium, Spain, Portugal...) while I took part in the CADTM's many activities. It could not have been completed without the invaluable help and support of many people, whose contribution I wish to acknowledge.

For eight months, Patrick Saurin kindly read one chapter after another and commented on the banking world, which he knows from the inside. I wish to thank him heartily. My thanks also go to François Chesnais, Aline Fares, Jean-Marie Harribey, Michel Husson and Antonio Sanabria, who read parts of the book and gave advice. Pauline Imbach and Damien Millet provided precious help during the difficult early stages. Daniel Munevar, Claude Quémar, Virginie de Romanet, Antonio Sanabria, Nacho Álvarez, Daniel Albaracin, Jean-Denis Gauthier, Stéphanie Jacquemont and François Sana were unstinting with their time when I needed help with research. The CADTM team devoted two whole days of workshop to the finished manuscript in February-March 2014. For this, I owe a debt of thanks to Myriam Bourgy, Jérémie Cravatte, Robin Delobel, Chiara Filoni, Pierre Gottiniaux, Cécile Lamarque, Emilie Paumard, Claude Quémar, Virginie de Romanet, Antonio Sanabria, Christine Vanden Daelen and Renaud Vivien, as well as Alice Minette. We all worked through the text in order to make it more accessible. I also benefitted from the comments and support of Brigitte Ponet.

The close collaboration of Claude Quémar, Patrick Saurin, Robin Delobel and Damien Millet in March 2014 was essential for the realisation of this book. I am also grateful for the support of the Walloon branch of the public services union CGSP (*l'Interrégionale Wallonne de la Centrale Générale des Services Publics*).

I also extend my gratitude to the publishers *Editions Aden* who published the original edition in French in June 2014 and to Icaria in Barcelona, who published the first edition in Spanish in November 2014. The current edition in English would not have been possible without the support of the International Institute for Research and Education (Amsterdam) and the assistance of Susan Pashkoff, Fred Leplat and Terry Conway of Resistance Books. Snake Arbusto, Vicki Briault Manus, Adam Clark-Gimmig, Mike Krolikowski, Charles La Via and Christine Pagnoulle spent months of hard work translating the book into English as well as revising and fine-tuning it.

The illustrations are by Pierre Gottiniaux (CADTM), with whom I enjoyed long chats about how various banking devices might be represented. Rémi Vilain helped with the referencing of all tables. And of course, I am entirely responsible for any mistakes or errors.

Notwithstanding the number of pages, there was not enough time and space to do full justice to some issues, such as how money is created, or an in-depth analysis of the euro. More work is needed, to probe deeper into the banking system and to motivate people to take action. The CADTM team is eager to take up the challenge.

Éric Toussaint, September 2015

Author's preface

From the twelfth century to the beginning of the fourteenth, the Knights Templar, who were present in much of Europe, had become bankers for the powerful and been involved in financing several crusades. At the beginning of the fourteenth century, they were the main creditors for the King of France, Philip the Fair. Faced with a debt burden that was straining his resources, the wily king rid himself of both creditors and debt in one fell swoop by demonising the Knights Templar, accusing them of many crimes.[1] Their Order was outlawed, its leaders executed and its assets seized. Its 15,000-strong army, including 1,500 knights, its property and its credits to rulers failed to protect it from the power of a state set on eliminating its main creditor.

During this same period, Venetian bankers were also financing the Crusades and lending money to the powerful of Europe, but they were cleverer than the Knights Templar. In Venice they took control of the state by establishing the Venetian Republic. They financed the transformation of the Venetian city-state into a proper empire, which included Cyprus, Euboea (*Negroponte*) and Crete. Their strategy to gain a permanent source of wealth and to ensure the repayment of their loans was to drive the Venetian state into debt with the banks they owned. They set the terms of the loans and became both bank owners and rulers of the state.

While Philip the Fair had an interest in eliminating his creditors to free himself from the debt burden, the Venetian state reimbursed its bankers on the nail. The latter came up with the idea of creating public debt bonds that could circulate between banks. This was the first step towards the establishment of financial markets.[2] This type

---

1 David Graeber, *Debt: The First 5,000 years*, New York: Melville House, 2011; Thomas Morel and François Ruffin, *Vive la Banqueroute !* (Long live bankruptcy!), Paris: Fakir Éditions, 2013.
2 Fernand Braudel, *Civilisation matérielle, économie et capitalisme. XVe-*

of loan was the forerunner of the major form of state debt as we know it in the twenty-first century.

The national states and the contemporary European Union pro-to-state may be more complex and sophisticated than the Venetian – or Genoese – Republics in existence from the thirteenth to the six-teenth centuries, but they are nonetheless mere instruments in the hands of the ruling class – that is of the 1% holding sway over the 99%. Mario Draghi, a former managing director of Goldman Sachs in Europe, is at the head of the European Central Bank. The private bankers have placed their representatives or allies in key positions in governments and institutions. Members of the European Commission are very attentive to the interests of private finance while the banks lobby European MPs, regulators and magistrates with fearful efficiency.

Seven centuries after Philip the Fair crushed the Knights Templar, today's European bankers, just like their Venetian or Genoese prede-cessors, clearly have nothing to fear from governments in place.

If a handful of major capitalist banks have occupied the centre stage in recent years, this should not distract us from the role of major cor-porations in industry and commerce, who use and abuse their close links with state structures just as deftly as the bankers do. The maze of interconnections and overlapping interests among states, govern-ments, banks, big companies and major private communications groups is as characteristic of capitalism in its current phase as it was in earlier times. What has changed, however, is how capital has be-come embedded in the financial system. Before, it was easy to distin-guish between financial capital and industrial capital. One part of the capitalist class controlled finance and another, industry. Over the last thirty years the financial sector has transformed the industrial sector: corporations' financial investments have even more influence on their behaviour than their investments in the productive sphere itself. Cap-ital has become dominated by finance. Its parasitic and destructive character has persisted and is even more evident than in the previous two centuries; what has changed is its appearance.

XVIIIe siècle (see also *Capitalism and Material Life*, 1400-1800), Paris: Armand Collin, 1979; David Graeber, op. cit.

Indeed, ever since capitalism became the dominant mode of production and of social relations, the representatives of major capitalist groups and their allies have continuously exercised power. Looking back in history, the New Deal launched by President Roosevelt in 1933 and the thirty years following the Second World War were merely an interlude during which the ruling class had to make real concessions, albeit limited ones, to the working class.

In the 1980s, the ruling class again became utterly uninhibited in the all-out exploitation of people and of nature, cynically boasting of their profits. Margaret Thatcher's notorious slogan, 'There is No Alternative', still echoes around the political, economic and social arena, with continued attacks on social rights and gains. Mario Draghi, Angela Merkel, Silvio Berlusconi and José Manuel Barroso have become emblematic figures of the continuation of Thatcher's plan. The active complicity of socialist governments (e.g., Schröder, Hollande, Blair, Brown, Papandreou, Zapatero, Socrates, Letta, Di Rupo and more) shows the extent to which they have become parties to the logic of the capitalist system, just like Barack Obama on the other side of the Atlantic. As US billionaire Warren Buffett famously stated, 'There's class warfare, all right, but it's my class, the rich class, that's making war, and we're winning.'[3]

The public debt system as it functions in capitalism is a permanent mechanism for the transfer of wealth produced by the people to the capitalist class. The crisis which began in 2007-2008 reinforced this mechanism because the losses and debts of major banks were transformed into public debt. On a very large scale, governments socialised bank losses so that banks could continue to make profits, which are then redistributed to their capitalist owners.

Governments are the direct allies of the big banks and they use their powers and public funds to serve them. There is a constant revolving door between major banks and governments. The number of Ministers of Finance and of the Economy or Prime Ministers coming directly from major banks or joining them when they leave government has increased steadily since 2008.

---

3   Ben Stein, 'In Class Warfare, Guess Which Class Is Winning?', *New York Times*, 26 November 2006.

The banking profession is too essential to the economy to be left in private hands. Banks must be socialised (this means expropriating them) and put under citizen control (of bank workers, customers, associations and representatives of local public institutions) so that they become a public service and their income is used for the common good.

Public debt incurred on the pretext of saving banks is definitely illegitimate and should be cancelled. A citizens' audit should determine other illegitimate and/or illegal debts and play a part in mobilisation to shape an anti-capitalist alternative.

Socialisation of the banks and cancellation/repudiation of illegitimate debt[4] should be part of a broader programme.[5]

In this book we examine how banks work and the complicity they receive from governments and big corporations. The agendas behind the discourse demanding lean government, sharp competitiveness and debt repayment will be discussed. We expose one of the characteristics of capitalism – 'bankocracy' – that shows itself in the way financialisation has developed since the 1970s to this day, by focusing particularly on the European Union.

The on-going financial crisis has revealed the weaknesses of the capitalist system, but this is far from being the first crisis in history. Crises are an organic part of the system. The 99% do have the means to bring about change, to face up to the challenge, to reverse the balance of power and defeat this oppressive system. This book takes a fresh look at the enemy to better understand its methods and motives and the reasons behind the policies that it enforces. It also reflects on which choices are possible and necessary to build a better world that works for the wellbeing of the people and the planet.

---

4   The definitions of illegitimate, illegal, odious and unsustainable debt can be found in Section VI of Chapter 36, 'Alternatives'.
5   Damien Millet and Éric Toussaint, 'Europe: What emergency programme for the crisis?', http://cadtm.org/Europe-What-emergency-programme, 1 July 2012; Thomas Coutrot, Patrick Saurin and Éric Toussaint, 'Cancelling debt or taxing capital: why should we choose?', http://cadtm.org/Cancelling-debt-or-taxing-capital, 2 November 2013; 'What to do about the debt and the euro?' http://cadtm.org/What-to-do-about-the-debt-and-the, 5 May 2013.

1.
2007-2008 - the explosion of private debt

The roots of the current international crisis that began in the United States in 2007-2008 go back to economic and political activities in the 1990s. First, there was overproduction in the real-estate (property) market and other sectors of the economy, particularly the automobile industry. Then there was the overdeveloped financial sector, especially the banking sector, and its deregulation. Next came the way bank CEOs acted, and the massive increase in private debt. Finally, the US Central Bank (the Federal Reserve, often known as 'the Fed') and government policy encouraged the development of a speculative bubble in the real-estate sector for economic and political reasons. Indeed, George W. Bush championed the ownership society in his 2004 re-election campaign:

> We're creating [...] an ownership society in this country, where more Americans than ever will be able to open up their door where they live and say, welcome to my house, welcome to my piece of property.[6]

In his memoirs, written just after the crisis that erupted in 2007, Alan Greenspan confirmed that there had been a policy strategy underlying the attitude adopted by the Federal Reserve, which supported Bush's policies:

> I was aware that the loosening of mortgage credit terms for subprime borrowers increases financial risk, and that subsidised

6 Naomi Klein, 'Disowned by the ownership society', *The Nation*, February 18, 2008, www.thenation.com/article/disowned-ownership-society.

> home-ownership initiatives distort market
> outcomes. But I believed then, as now, that
> the benefits of broadened home-ownership
> are worth the risk. Protection of property
> rights, so critical to a market economy, re-
> quires a critical mass of owners to sustain
> political support.[7]

As we will see, the Bill Clinton and George W. Bush administrations gave systematic support to the big banks, which wanted to do away with the disciplinary constraints imposed on them by Roosevelt in the 1930s that prevented them from doing business exactly as they pleased.

The crisis was triggered by a speculative real-estate bubble. Before it burst, it had driven up the price of real-estate,[8] and brought about an excessive increase in the construction sector compared to solvent demand. The number of new housing units built each year surged from 1.5 million in 2000 to 2.3 million in January 2006. A growing proportion of new housing units went unsold, even though the banks were offering easy lending conditions to potential buyers, and despite the encouragements of the US authorities.

This overproduction ultimately caused a sharp drop in real-estate prices. The expectations of households that had taken on subprime[9] mortgages were shattered by this radical change of circumstances. In the US, households generally refinance their home loans every two or three years when real-estate prices are rising in order to obtain a lower-interest loan. For subprime loans, the interest-rate for the first two or three years was low (about 3%), while as of the third or fourth year, not only did the rate increase substantially (up to 8 or 10%), but it also became variable, and in many cases reached 14 or 15%.

---

7   Alan Greenspan, *The Age of Turbulence*, New York: Penguin Books, 2007, p. 258.
8   From 2001 to 2007, the price of real-estate doubled in the US.
9   'Subprime' designates mortgages that are riskier for the lender (but with a higher yield) than prime loans.

In 2006, when the price of real-estate started dropping, households with subprime loans could no longer refinance their mortgages on favourable terms.

As Paul Jorion writes in *La crise du capitalisme Americain* (The Crisis of American Capitalism), subprime loans were really aimed at

> [...] seizing the savings of the unfortunate, who aspired to the 'dream' but did not really have the financial means to achieve it. The first of these were the Black and Latino populations. There were many clever tricks, ranging from written agreements that differed from the verbal agreements to offers that drove the beneficiaries to bankruptcy so that their homes could be repossessed, and refinancing agreements presented as favourable, whereas they were in reality catastrophic.[10]

A few years later, lawsuits filed by the hundreds of thousands of families that had been illegally evicted by the banks would show that the bankers had massively defrauded their clients. In over 500,000 cases examined by the US Department of Justice, banks were found to have deliberately misled the people who had signed mortgage contracts. As we will see in Chapter 21, after long negotiations relating to the crimes and offences they had committed involving mortgages, the leading US banks finally agreed to pay fines amounting to approximately $86 billion (for 2008-2013).[11] By paying these fines, the banks were able to avoid legal sanctions, but the payments are proof that they played a role in the crisis.

---

10   Paul Jorion, *'Inédit : les 3 premières pages de 'La Crise du capitalisme Americain'* (Unpublished: the first three pages of *La Crise du capitalisme Americain* - The crisis of American capitalism), 23 February 2012, http://www.pauljorion.com/blog/?p=34264 (in French).
11   'Credit crisis and mortgage-related settlements for select bank holding companies', *SNL Financial – ABA Banking Journal*, http://www.ababj.com/images/Dev_SNL/CreditCrisis.pdf, accessed 22 February 2014.

A *Wall Street Journal* study shows that the high-rate subprime mortgage market touched not only low-income Americans, but also affected the middle class. For example, the WSJ writes about a photocopy shop owner who had bought a house in Las Vegas for $460,000 in 2006. In 2006-2007, she had to make monthly instalments of $3,700 with an interest-rate of 8.2%, but in 2008, the monthly payments rocketed to $8,000 with an interest-rate of 14%. Meanwhile, because of the crisis, her home dropped in value to $310,000 (the value of real-estate dropped by 30% in 2007).[12] She stopped paying her mortgage and lost the home of her dreams.

In early 2007, an increasing number of households started defaulting on their loans. Between January and August 2007, 84 mortgage companies in the US went bankrupt. The companies and wealthy households that had speculated on rising real-estate prices, making juicy profits in the process, suddenly withdrew from the market, which made prices drop even more dramatically. Those banks that had invested their mortgage claims in structured products and sold them on a large scale (in particular to major European banks craving for high-yield products) were at the heart of the crisis.

The giant edifice of private debt began to collapse when the speculative bubble burst in the US real-estate sector. This event was followed by similar crises in the real-estate sector in Ireland, the UK, Spain and Cyprus, as well as in several countries in Eastern and Central Europe, and since 2011-2012 in the Netherlands.

In France, Nicolas Sarkozy[13] followed George W. Bush's example when he suggested that French people should take on more debt. In the April 2007 issue of *Revue Banque*, he wrote:

> Today, French families are the least indebted in Europe. But an economy with insufficient debt is an economy that lacks confidence in the future and doubts itself. That is why I would like to open up more opportunities for mortgages, with state

12   Éric Toussaint, B*ank of the South. An Alternative to IMF-World Bank*, Mumbai: Vikas Adhyayan Kendra, 2007.
13   President of the French Republic from 2007 to 2012.

> guarantees in case of illness. [...] If home loans were easier to get, the banks would be less concerned by the credit quality of the borrowers, and would pay more attention to the value of the mortgaged property. (Translation CADTM.)

It is easy to imagine what would have happened in France if the subprime mortgage crisis had not broken out in 2007-2008, and if Sarkozy had continued promoting the model being applied in the US.

The interpretations generally given by the major media outlets in 2007-2008 when the crisis erupted in the US were inadequate or patently deceitful. They constantly repeated that the economic chaos was due to the irrational behaviour of poor Americans who had taken on too much debt to buy homes that were beyond their means. These explanations failed to mention the overwhelming responsibilities of US authorities and bank CEOs.

After Lehman Brothers went bankrupt in 2008, the dominant discourse focused on the pariah of the financial world, Bernard Madoff, who had organised a $50 billion scam, and Richard Fuld, the CEO of Lehman Brothers, who were supposedly undermining the righteous functioning of capitalism.

The current crisis erupted when the speculative real-estate bubble burst; however, our analysis should not stop there, as Karl Marx reminds us:

> The years 1843-5 were years of industrial and commercial prosperity, a necessary sequel to the almost uninterrupted industrial depression of 1837-42. As is always the case, prosperity very rapidly encouraged speculation. Speculation regularly occurs in periods when overproduction is already in full swing. It provides overproduction with temporary market outlets, while for this very reason precipitating the outbreak of the crisis and increasing its force. The crisis

itself first breaks out in the area of speculation; only later does it hit production. What
appears to the superficial observer to be the
cause of the crisis is not overproduction but
excess speculation, but this is itself only a
symptom of overproduction. The subsequent disruption of production does not appear as a consequence of its own previous
exuberance but merely as a setback caused
by the collapse of speculation.[14]

Inspired by Marx's succinct analysis made more than 150 years ago, the chain of events leading up to the current economic crisis in the US may be outlined as follows: low growth in the 1980s and a stock-market crash in 1987 (Reagan Administration) followed by growth in the second half of the 1990s (Clinton Administration), which was boosted by a speculative bubble on the stock market mainly driven by new technology (IT) and energy brokerage companies like Enron. The bubble burst in 2000, and was followed by an aggressive low interest-rate policy implemented by the Federal Reserve to jump-start the economy without cleaning it up. As a result, a real-estate bubble emerged (as desired by the George W. Bush Administration and the Federal Reserve for economic and political reasons).[15] All of this took place in a context in which the derivatives market was exploding, and with banking and stock-market euphoria that hid the overproduction in the real-estate and automotive sectors in the US for a while. When the real-estate bubble burst in 2006-2007, the house of cards of private debt held by banks collapsed.[16] Central banks and governments then decided to implement a policy based on massive cash injections and low interest-rates, which started new speculative bubbles. Banks

---

14   Marx-Engels, 'Review: May-October 1850,' *Neue Rheinische Zeitung*,
https://www.marxists.org/archive/marx/works/1850/11/01.htm
15   Alan Greenspan recognises that by radically lowering interest-rates
to get out of the crisis, 'We were willing to chance that by cutting rates we
might foster a bubble, an inflationary boom of some sort, which we would
subsequently have to address'. He adds that: 'Consumer spending carried the
economy through the post-9/11 malaise, and what carried consumer spending was housing.' Greenspan explains that the government encouraged the
development of the subprime market. Alan Greenspan, op. cit., p. 229.
16   At the same time, speculation increased, first on raw materials and food
staples (see Chapter 17).

and companies in general did not clean up their financial practices, and started a massive reduction of jobs, resulting in a major increase in unemployment. The policies put in place also contributed to attacks on wages and social rights. Finally, governments engineered the explosion of public debt destined to help the major private banks and implemented policies that favoured big capital.

To return to the crisis that started in 2007-2008 in the United States and Europe, the collapse of the edifice of subprime loans and structured products created since the mid-1990s had very serious effects on production in various sectors of the real economy. Austerity policies then plunged the economies of the most industrialised countries into a period of prolonged recession and depression from which they have not yet emerged.

The impact of the US real-estate crisis and the banking crisis that followed had an enormous effect, because many European banks had invested heavily in US structured products and derivatives. As these products had been developed, sold and bought by the same major international banks, this connected them, exposing them to the same risks and making them vulnerable to the same impacts. From the mid-1990s, the huge quantity of these products, on and off the banks' balance-sheets, caused a local crisis (a US real-estate bubble) to develop into an international financial and economic crisis.

Starting in the 1990s, growth in the US and several European economies was sustained by overdevelopment of the private financial sector and a formidable increase in private debt (household debt[17] and debt from financial and non-financial corporations). At the same time, there was a downward trend in public debt from the mid-1990s to 2007-2008.

---

17   Household debt includes debts incurred by American students to pay for their studies. Student debt reached $1 trillion in 2011. By way of comparison, this colossal sum is higher than the total external public debt of Latin America ($460 billion), Africa ($263 billion) and southern Asia ($205 billion). For the size of the debts of these 'continents', see Damien Millet, Daniel Munevar, Éric Toussaint, *World Debt Figures 2012*, CADTM, 2012, Table 7, http://cadtm.org/2012-World-debt-figures.

US household debt by income quintile
2000 - 2008

in billions of $

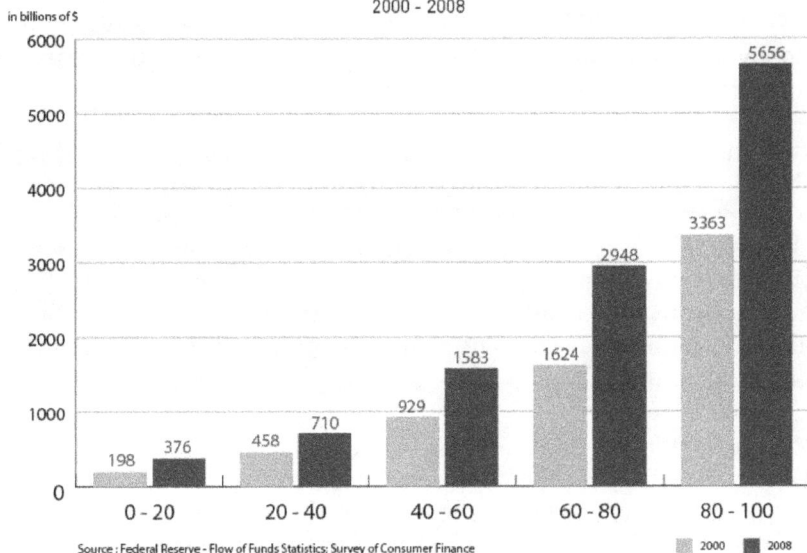

Source : Federal Reserve - Flow of Funds Statistics; Survey of Consumer Finance   2000   2008

This chart shows very clearly that not only are the poor indebted, but rich households are responsible for much of the increase in debt, to which we should add the debts of both non-financial and financial corporations (banks, investment funds, etc.), which have become gigantic (see table below). Low-income households increasingly financed their consumption through debt to compensate for the stagnation or drop in their wages. The debt of the poorest 20% of households rose by 90% between 2000 and 2008, making them the natural target of the subprime lenders.

Yet if we look at the mass of loans, the richest 20% contributed half of the increase in household debt recorded between 2000 and 2008. The debt of the richest 20% rose by nearly $2,200 billion, whereas the increase for the poorest 20% was only $178 billion, or only a twelfth of that of the richest 20%. This is very instructive: the rich became indebted in order to speculate, mainly on the stock market and in the real-estate sector by buying housing and commercial premises that they did not live in or use.[18] These rich households (and the companies they controlled) speculated on the rise in real-estate prices. Alan

---

18   Unlike low-income families, who took out loans to buy their homes.

Greenspan implicitly recognises this himself. He wrote in his memoirs that 25% of house purchases in 2005 were made by investors, not by 'subprime' families,[19] which contributed greatly to the creation and bursting of the speculative bubble.

It is important to bear in mind the unequal distribution of wealth in the US as in other highly industrialised countries. In 2010, the richest 1% held 35% of the total wealth of the US. In broad terms, this corresponds to the capitalist class, which holds an impressive concentration of wealth. The richest 10% possessed 70% of total wealth. This additional 9% represents the entourage of the capitalist class, or their allies in the broad sense. The remaining 90% had to make do with 30% of the wealth, and the poorest 50% possessed only 5%.[20]

Private debt in the US constantly increased between 1980 and 2008. Households financed their expenses by borrowing more and more – the poor to compensate for the drop in their income, and the rich to make even more money from their increased income through the magic of 'leveraging' (see Chapter 4). The debts of banks and other financial corporations grew exponentially (an increase of more than 600% in 28 years). Public debt, which had risen considerably during the 1980s after the Fed increased interest-rates in 1979 and the Savings and Loan banks were bailed out,[21] fell during the 1990s (during the Clinton Administration) and started to increase again between 2000 and 2008 during the George W. Bush Administration. At this point, public debt represented less than one sixth of total debt and less than one fifth of private debt.

---

19   Alan Greenspan, op. cit.
20   Éric Toussaint, 'What can we do with what Thomas Piketty teaches us about capital in the twenty-first century?', CADTM, 24 February 2014, http://cadtm.org/What-can-we-do-with-what-Thomas.
21   In the 1980s, the Savings and Loan associations (S&L), American financial institutions specialising in savings and housing loans, multiplied their high-risk investments in real-estate and invested heavily in junk bonds (in particular with Drexel Burnham Lambert). In all, more than 1,600 banking institutions and S&Ls went bankrupt. The bail-out cost American taxpayers more than $250 billion.

United States: Total debt and debt by institutional sector 1980-2008 (as a percentage of GDP)

Sector	1980	1990	2000	2008
Households	49	65	72	100
Non-financial corporations	53	58	63	75
Financial corporations	18	44	87	119
State	35	54	47	55
Total	**155**	**221**	**269**	**349**

Source: Michel Aglietta using the Fed Flow of Funds statistics[22]

Meanwhile, in Europe, commensurate with the overdevelopment of the private financial sector, the volume in assets of private European banks surged excessively in the 1990s to reach €42,100 billion in 2007 (more than three times the GDP of the 27 EU member countries).[23] In 2007, the debt of Eurozone private banks (accounted for in the volume of liabilities) was also three times the GDP of the 27 member countries.[24]

---

22   François Chesnais, *Les dettes illégitimes* (Illegitimate debt), Paris: Raisons d'Agir, 2011, p. 70.

23   Damien Millet, Daniel Munevar and Éric Toussaint, *2012 World Debt Figures*, CADTM, 2012, Table 30, p. 23. This table is based on the data of the European Banking Federation, http://www.ebf-fbe.eu/index.php?-page=statistics. See also Martin Wolf, 'Liikanen is at least a step forward for EU banks', *Financial Times*, 5 October 2012.

24   A bank's debts must not be confused with its assets. Debt is part of a bank's 'liabilities'. In an accounting balance-sheet – a document that summarises at a given moment what the company owns, its 'assets' (land, buildings, etc.) and its resources or 'liabilities' (capital, reserves, credits, etc.) – the assets and liabilities must be equal. A company's money comes from somewhere (liabilities), and goes somewhere (assets). Hence, assets are always equal to liabilities.

The gross debt of the Eurozone member states was 66% of their GDP in 2007.[25] Specific information for Spain and Greece is given below:

	Gross debt of financial sector in % of GDP in 2007	Public debt in % of GDP in 2007
Greece	239%	108%
Spain	162%	37%
Eurozone	309%	66%

The pump was primed for the private debt crisis to become a public debt crisis.

This is clear in the following table and the charts that illustrate it. The table shows that public debt in the Eurozone had started to fall between 2000 and 2007. The reduction in public debt was particularly significant in Spain. On the other hand, the debt of financial corporations (banks) continued to grow, in the Eurozone as a whole but especially in Spain, Portugal and Greece. The same was true of the debts of households and non-financial corporations. Everywhere, the increase in public debt was significant and sudden after 2007, due to the crisis and government bank bail-outs.

---

25   Damien Millet, Daniel Munevar and Éric Toussaint, *2012 World Debt Figures* (op. cit.), Table 24, p. 18. Sources: Morgan Stanley research database: http://www.ecb.int/stats/money/aggregates/bsheets/html/outstanding_amounts_index.en.html, and Bank of Greece, 'Aggregated balance-sheets of monetary financial institutions (MFIs)', http://www.bankofgreece.gr/Pages/en/Statistics/monetary/nxi.aspx.

Debt by sector as % of GDP

	2000	2007	2011
Eurozone			
Gross Public Debt	68	66	82
Household debt	49	54	61
Non-financial corporations' debts	76	87	96
Financial corporations' debts	232	309	333
Spain			
Gross Public Debt	58	37	62
Household debt	46	83	81
Non-financial corporations' debts	60	116	118
Financial corporations' debts	137	162	203
Portugal			
Gross Public Debt	49	63	96
Household debt	59	84	93
Non-financial corporations' debts	97	112	123
Financial corporations' debts	349	266	306
Greece			
Gross Public Debt	104	108	162
Household debt	14	42	56
Non-financial corporations' debts	42	53	58
Financial corporations' debts	200	239	311

Source: Morgan Stanley Research Database
http://www.ecb.int/stats/money/aggregates/bsheets/html/outstanding_amounts_index.en.htm; http://www.bankofgreece.gr/Pages/en/Statistics/monetary/nxi.aspx

Debt by sector as a percentage of GDP

Greece

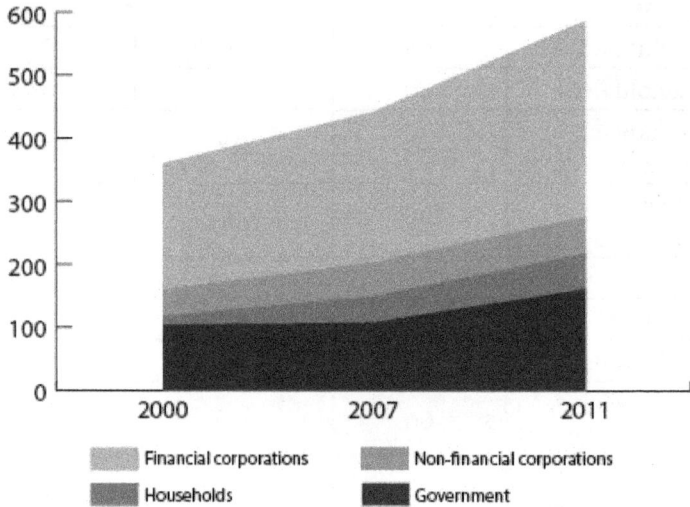

Legend:
- Financial corporations
- Non-financial corporations
- Households
- Government

Portugal

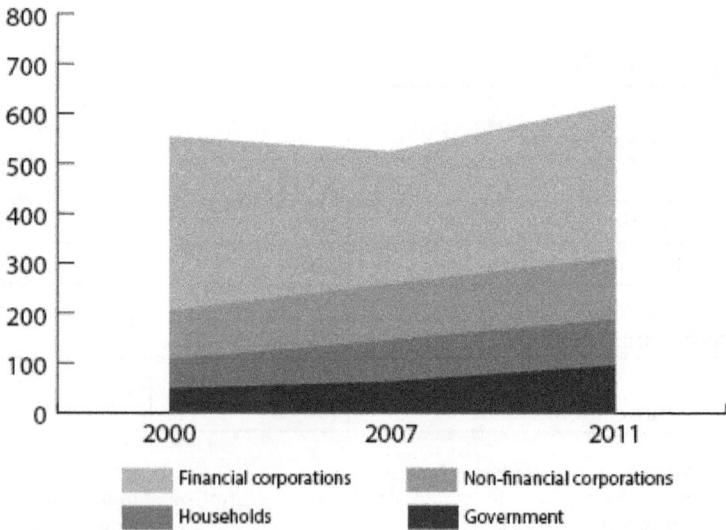

Legend:
- Financial corporations
- Non-financial corporations
- Households
- Government

Spain

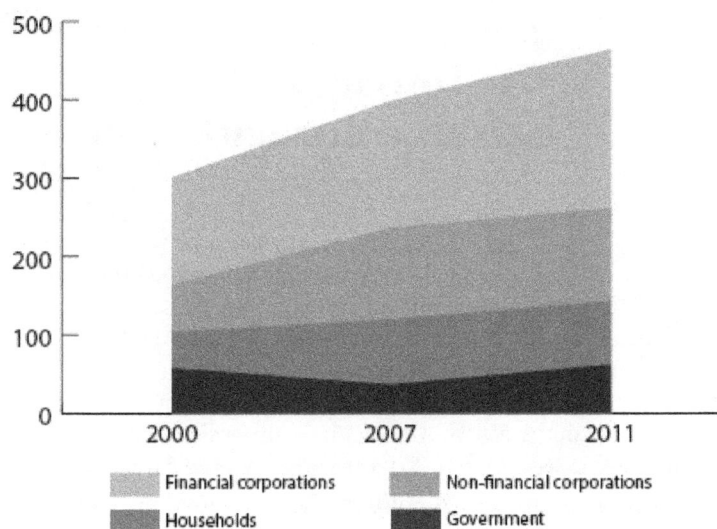

Financial corporations Non-financial corporations
Households Government

Euro Zone

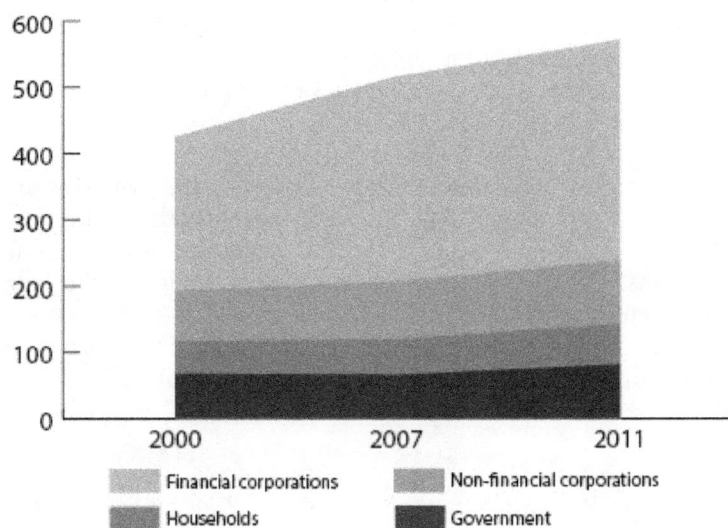

Financial corporations Non-financial corporations
Households Government

2.
The impact of banking deregulation

The Wall Street Crash in October 1929, the enormous banking crisis of 1933 and the prolonged period of economic crisis in the US and Europe during the 1930s caused President Franklin D. Roosevelt and the European governments of the time to regulate the financial sector strictly so as to avoid the repetition of serious stock-exchange and banking crises. As the North American neoliberal economists Carmen M. Reinhart and Kenneth S. Rogoff show in *This Time is Different: Eight Centuries of Financial Folly* ,[26] these political measures drastically reduced the number of banking crises in the thirty years after the Second World War. Kenneth Rogoff was the chief economist of the International Monetary Fund (IMF) and Carmen Reinhart, a university professor, was advisor to the IMF and the World Bank. According to their analysis (which is very much in line with the dominant discourse), the much smaller number of banking crises is mainly explained by the regulation of domestic financial markets (to different degrees), and then by massive recourse to capital control for many years after the Second World War.

One of the major measures taken by Roosevelt and West European governments (in response to popular pressure after the Second World War) consisted of limiting and strictly regulating how banks used public funds. This principle of protecting deposits led to the separation between commercial banks and investment banks, best known in the form of the US's Glass-Steagall Act, although it was also applied with certain variations in European countries as well.

---

26   Carmen M. Reinhart, Kenneth S. Rogoff, *This Time Is Different: Eight Centuries of Financial Folly*, Princeton (NJ): Princeton University Press, 2009.

With this separation of banking activities, only the commercial banks could receive state-guaranteed deposits from the general public. In parallel, their field of activities was reduced to granting loans to private individuals and companies and excluded the issuing of securities, whether in the form of shares or any other financial instruments. Investment or trading banks, on the other hand, had to obtain their resources on the financial markets in order to issue securities, shares and other financial instruments.

In Europe after the Second World War, the strict regulation and in some cases nationalisation of the banking sector[27] should be seen in the context of social struggles expressing the desire for a society different from that of the 1930s and their rejection of the financial magnates who had supported or collaborated with the Nazis and fascists and while doing so, greatly increased their fortunes.

INVESTMENT
BANK

FINANCIAL MARKETS

PURCHASE/SALE
OF SECURITIES AND DERIVATIVES
(BANKS, INVESTMENT FUNDS,
INSURANCE COMPANIES, INDIVIDUALS)

ISSUANCE
AND HOLDING
OF SECURITIES

PROPRIETARY
TRADING

£
$
€
¥

LIABILITIES
(INVESTORS, CREDITORS)

CAPITAL (SHAREHOLDERS)

---

27 In France, the government nationalised the Banque de France in 1945 (with shareholder compensation), together with the four largest commercial banks: Crédit Lyonnais, Société Générale, Banque Nationale du Commerce et de l'Industrie, and Comptoir National d'Escompte de Paris. The British government nationalised the Bank of England in 1946.

The neoliberal shift of the late 1970s called these regulations into question. Some twenty years later, bank deregulation and general financial deregulation had made giant steps. As Kenneth Rogoff and Carmen Reinhart show, banking and stock-exchange crises began multiplying in the 1980s, and became more and more severe.

In the traditional banking model, inherited from the long regulation period, banks assess and assume credit risk. In other words, they analyse credit requests, decide whether to grant them, and once loans have been made, keep them on their balance-sheets until they are paid off. This is called the 'originate-to-hold model'. Financial deregulation enabled banks to abandon originate-to-hold in order to increase their Return on Equity (see Chapter 5: What is Return on Equity (ROE)?).

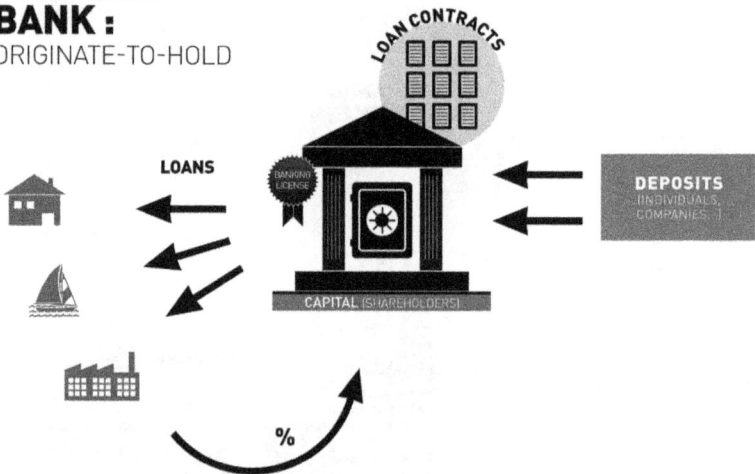

COMMERCIAL
BANK :
ORIGINATE-TO-HOLD

LOAN CONTRACTS

LOANS

BANKING LICENSE

DEPOSITS (INDIVIDUALS, COMPANIES...)

CAPITAL (SHAREHOLDERS)

%

Banks then made massive use of securitisation,[28] which consists of transforming the bank loans they have granted into financial securities, which they then resell. In this way they broaden their activities and increase their profits without keeping the loans, and the attached risks, on their books. Banks thus transformed loans into securities

28   The first wave of securitisation on a massive scale was in the period following the outbreak of the Third World debt crisis in 1982.

in the form of structured financial products, which they sold to other banks or private financial institutions. This new banking model is called 'originate-to-distribute' or sometimes 'originate, repackage and sell'. The system has a double advantage for banks: when things go well it reduces credit risk by removing the loans they have made from their assets, and it gives them additional resources for speculation.

A GROCERY SHOP

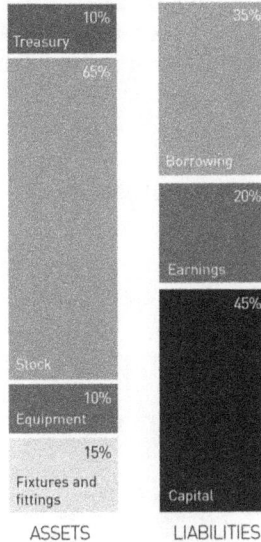

ASSETS	LIABILITIES
Treasury 10%	Borrowing 35%
Stock 65%	Earnings 20%
Equipment 10%	Capital 45%
Fixtures and fittings 15%	

What is a bank balance-sheet?

A company's balance-sheet lists its assets and how those assets are financed at a particular point in time. For a company that produces or distributes goods – for example a grocery shop (see diagram) the balance-sheet is broken down, broadly speaking, into its stock, equipment (cash desk, shelves, fridges, etc.) and cash, all of which are listed on the assets side. This is what the grocery shop owns. On the liabilities side, indicating how the shop is financed, there is capital (the money invested by the owner to finance the business), accumulated profits kept within the company to finance its development (for example updating equipment or redecorating the shop), a bank loan and debts in the form of due dates granted by suppliers to enable the grocer to finance part of the stock.

At any given time, ASSETS = LIABILITIES. In other words, it should always be possible to identify the source of financing for a given asset, and in the other direction identify how a given financial resource is used.

The same principle applies to a bank, but obviously with very different types of assets and liabilities. The assets of a traditional (commercial) bank are the loans granted to its customers and the investments made by the bank (see the 'Securities' part of the balance-sheet in the Banque Martin Maurel diagram). These credits are in fact contracts, or promises to repay, which makes them assets for the bank. The bank's assets also include reserves deposited at the central bank and loans to other banks.

Martin Maurel Bank (Deposit Bank)

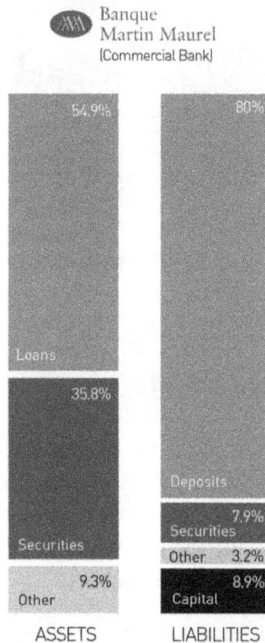

Banque
Martin Maurel
(Commercial Bank)

Source: Olivier Berruyer, Le « modèle français de banque universelle », 2011, Les-crises.fr. Available at https://www.les-crises.fr/modele-de-banque-universelle/

Liabilities are credits partly financed by the bank's equity capital (money invested by its shareholders) but above all by customer deposits, which are in fact debts owed by the bank to its customers. Given that the bank's equity capital is just a few per cent of the loans granted, it will also have to use interbank financing (borrowing from other banks) and market financing (borrowing from financial markets by issuing bonds, for example).

This description applies to a simple commercial bank, which only operates as a deposit and credit bank (see Banque Maurel diagram). When a bank is involved in traditional investment-bank activities, other categories appear on the balance-sheet. Deposits are replaced by financial securities (bonds issued by the bank to finance itself) and borrowings on the interbank market. Loans to customers are replaced by trading activities.

If the bank combines deposit, credit and insurance activities, it becomes a 'universal bank' and its balance-sheet changes once again (see the diagrams of the balance-sheets of BNP Paribas, Barclays and Deutsche Bank). The assets now include financial securities held as a result of various trading activities (mainly shares, bonds and derivatives) and activities on the capital markets more generally.

Barclays, Deutsche Bank & BNP Paribas

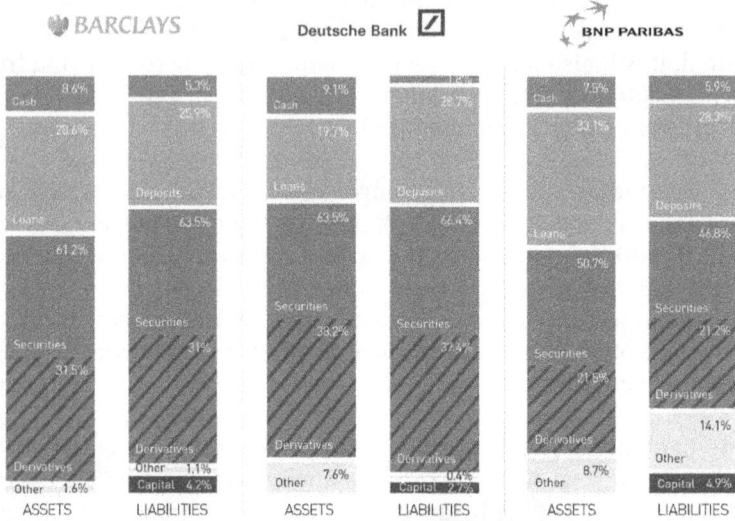

Sources: Olivier Berruyer, Le « modèle français de banque universelle », 2011, Les-crises.fr, Available at https://www.les-crises.fr/modele-de-banque-universelle/; author's calculations from Deutsche Bank Annual Report, 2012, available at https://www.db.com/ir/en/download/Deutsche_Bank_Annual_Report_2012_entire.pdf

To finance this part of its business, the bank will borrow from other banks (very short-term loans, no more than a few days) and from the financial markets, by issuing bonds, for example (short and medium-term – a few months or years). A universal bank, like an investment bank, is highly dependent on market financing. It is exposed to major variations in both its assets (the value of securities can suddenly change) and its liabilities (for example, the 'contraction' of the financial markets in 2008 cut off the financial resources of many banks; loans granted to banks – by other banks or other lenders – decreased in value considerably overnight).

As we saw above, the liabilities show the origin of the bank's resources, i.e. the funds collected by the bank. The assets show how those funds are used. Some say, 'Tell me what you eat and I'll tell you who you are'. One might say, 'Bank, tell me what your liabilities are and I'll tell you what kind of bank you are'. If the proportion of your borrowings in the form of securities exceeds your customers' deposits (that is, the loans your customers make to you), then you are taking extravagant risks at their expense. As for assets, if the portfolio of securities (held in your own account or for a third-party account) exceeds the volume of loans granted to your customers, that means you prioritise the financial markets more than your traditional activity of intermediation (collecting deposits and lending).

The website of the French Ministry of Economy and Finance provides edifying data indicating just how much the composition of bank balance-sheets has dangerously evolved as banks have developed speculative activities:

> If we look at the balance-sheet of all French banking establishments, deposits accounted for 73% of liabilities in 1980, but just 26% in 2011. Loans accounted for 84% in assets in 1980, but only 29% in 2011. This is the consequence of the banks' activities on the financial markets where they play a major role, investing either on their own account (direct holding of securities), or for third-party accounts, or as financial-product providers, or as market-makers. On the balance-sheet, this trend is shown by the growing importance of securities and interbank loans, which accounted for 19% of the liabilities of French banks in 1980 and 54% in 2011.[29]

---

29   French Ministry of Economy and Finance website, 'Les comptes d'une banque. Le bilan d'une banque', (The accounts of a bank. A bank's balance-sheet), *La Finance pour tous* study, Institut pour l'Education Financière du Public, http://www.economie.gouv.fr/facileco/comptes-dune-banque.

BANKS' BALANCE-SHEET EVOLUTION BETWEEN 1980 AND 2011

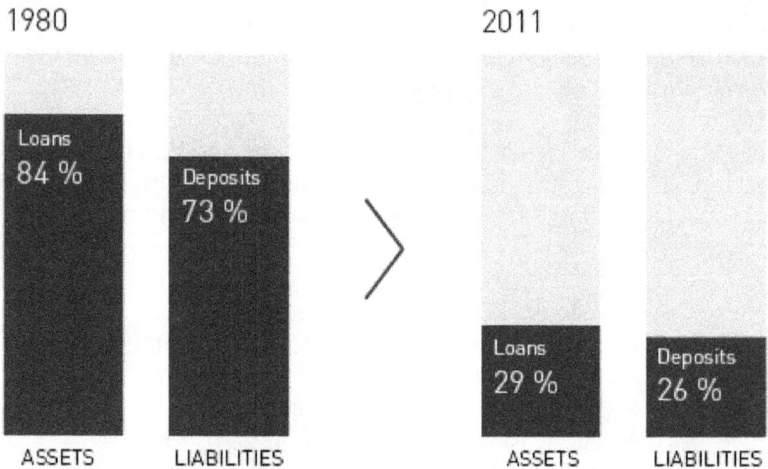

1980   2011

Loans 84 %   Deposits 73 %   Loans 29 %   Deposits 26 %

ASSETS   LIABILITIES   ASSETS   LIABILITIES

Source: Ministère de l'Économie et des Finances, « Les comptes d'une banque. Le bilan d'une banque », 2013, available at http://www.economie.gouv.fr/facileco/comptes-dune-banque

In 2011, the volume of derivatives held by French banks was 'eleven times the total value of their balance-sheets.'[30]

The development of the inappropriately named 'universal bank'

Another very important change was thus the removal of the separation between commercial and investment banks during the 1980s or 1990s, depending on the country. This gave rise to the universal bank, as we now know it. Universal banks (also called 'full-service banks') are large financial structures grouping and practising all the different banking professions – commercial banking, finance and investment banking, asset management, insurance agents ('Bank Assurance'). The whole package of services is made available nationally and abroad through subsidiaries. The main danger of this banking model is that the losses of the high-risk activities of the finance and investment bank must also be borne by the commercial bank, which is part of the

---

30   Ibid. We will come back to this figure again in the Off-balance-sheet section below.

universal bank, thus jeopardising the money of small and medium savers, shopkeepers, small and medium enterprises (SME) and public administrative bodies that deposit their funds at the bank. In addition, because savings deposits are covered by a state guarantee which, since 2008, has protected deposits of up to €100,000 in Europe, and because commercial banking (dealing with credit, savings and payments) is essential for the economy to work, the state is obliged to intervene when there is a risk of a universal bank failing. All the major banks[31] have transformed themselves into universal banks and have become too large for states to allow them to fail ('Too Big to Fail'). The development of their activities on the financial markets has been encouraged by the implicit state guarantee accorded to all universal bank activities, even the riskiest and most speculative ones!

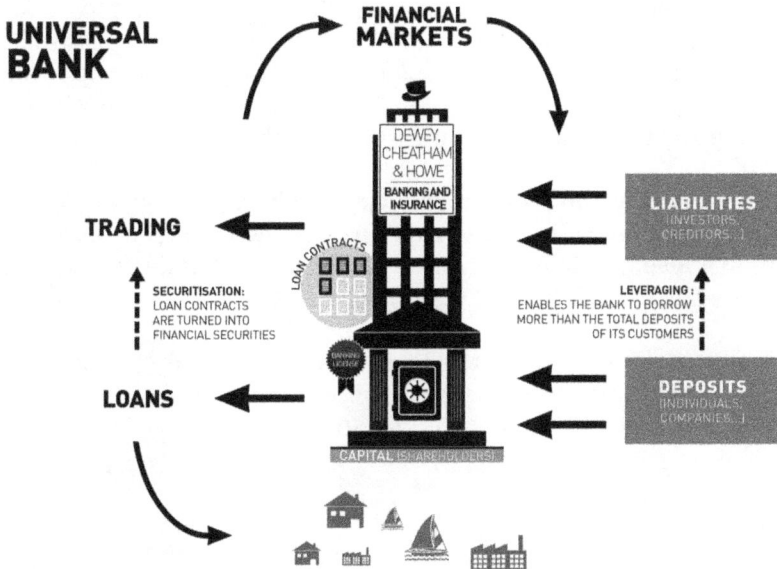

UNIVERSAL BANK

FINANCIAL MARKETS

DEWEY, CHEATHAM & HOWE
BANKING AND INSURANCE

TRADING

LOAN CONTRACTS

SECURITISATION: LOAN CONTRACTS ARE TURNED INTO FINANCIAL SECURITIES

LOANS

LIABILITIES (INVESTORS, CREDITORS...)

LEVERAGING: ENABLES THE BANK TO BORROW MORE THAN THE TOTAL DEPOSITS OF ITS CUSTOMERS

DEPOSITS (INDIVIDUALS, COMPANIES...)

CAPITAL (SHAREHOLDERS)

---

31   After the US government allowed the Lehman Brothers investment bank to fail in September 2008, Goldman Sachs and Morgan Stanley (also investment banks) took the necessary steps to change their status and become universal banks, so that the government would provide financial assistance in the event of a problem. See Andrew Ross Sorkin and Vikas Bajaj, 'Shift for Goldman and Morgan Marks the End of an Era,' *The New York Times*, September 21, 2008 http://www.nytimes.com/2008/09/22/business/22bank.html

3.
Thirty years of
financial deregulation

This book analyses the banking crisis and its management by government ministers. However it is important not to isolate an analysis of the banking crisis and its possible solutions from the evolution of capitalist society as a whole and the global alternatives that should be pursued. The banking crisis that broke out in 2007-2008 should be situated in a more general context, that of a new phase of finance-dominated capital accumulation that started in the late 1970s. This new phase underpins the neoliberal shift that began in Western Europe and the US and then spread all over the planet.

To put it simply, the neoliberal policies that have become widespread since the 1980s have enabled capitalists to increase their portion of national income while the fraction paid in wages has decreased. Employers have thus increased their rates of profit.

The graph of wages as a percentage of GDP shows a drop of 8 points in the US between the early 1970s and 2012. In Europe it also fell by 8 points between the mid-1970s and 2007.

Share of wages

Source : Michel Husson, http://hussonet.free.fr/

The graph of the evolution of profit rates as a percentage of GDP shows a rise in profits in both the US and Europe starting from the neoliberal shift of the early 1980s.

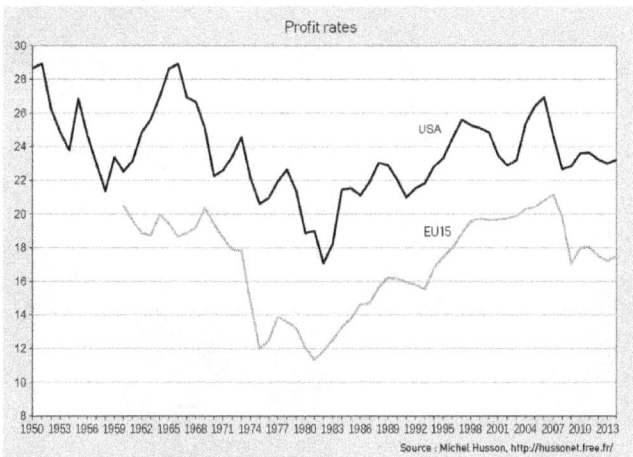

Profit rates

Source : Michel Husson, http://hussonet.free.fr/

However, private consumption continued to increase in the 1990s until the crisis started in 2007-2008 because it was largely supported by loans, as shown by the two 'Consumption and Wages' graphs for the EU and US.

Wages and consumer spending - EU 15

Consumer spending as a % of GDP (left scale)

Share of wages (right scale)

Source : Michel Husson, http://hussonet.free.fr/

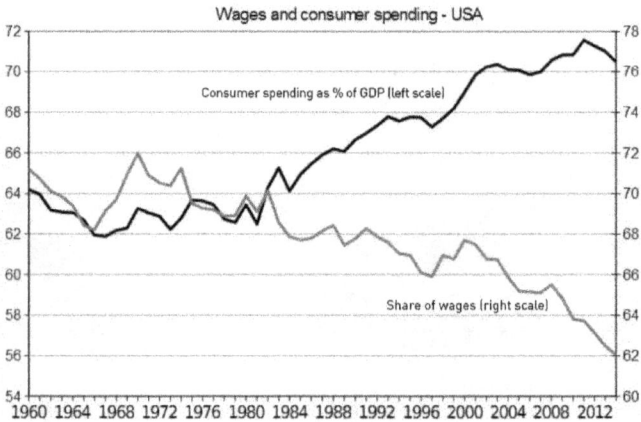

Wages and consumer spending - USA

Consumer spending as % of GDP (left scale)

Share of wages (right scale)

Source : Michel Husson, http://hussonet.free.fr

The following graph, for Spain, shows very clearly that the fall in wages as a percentage of national income is counterbalanced by the rise in household indebtedness up to 2007.

Percentages of wages in national income and of household debt in available income

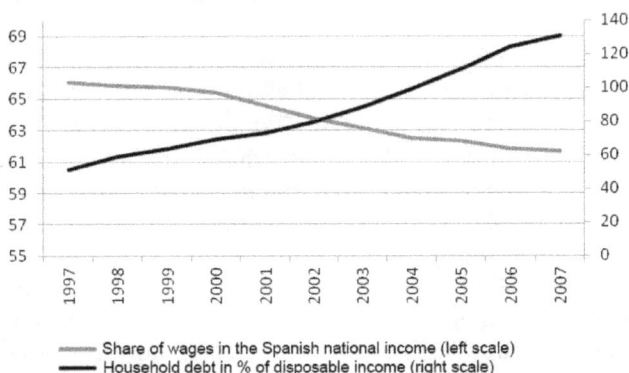

Share of wages in the Spanish national income (left scale)
Household debt in % of disposable income (right scale)

Source: *Nacho Álvarez, Fernando Luengo, Jorge Uxó*, Fractura y crisis en Europa, *Madrid: Clave intelectual, 2013, 342 p., Chapter 4, graph 4.15.*

Household debt rose considerably in the US and much of Europe (UK, Ireland, Spain, Greece, Portugal, Italy, Netherlands, Central and Eastern European countries).

Capitalists invested an ever-smaller proportion of their profits in production, preferring instead to distribute them as dividends to shareholders,thus reinforcing the power of the financial markets.

Since the 1980s, the growth of the financial markets has been largely fed by the profits that the major industrial groups have not reinvested in production but distributed to their shareholders. According to a study published by Lille 1 University:

> We see that in the space of about thirty years, the sums companies devote to remunerating shareholders have increased to at least double the amount devoted to extending and improving their production capital, whereas

43

the reverse was true in the early 1980s, when
the profits distributed amounted to only half
the sums devoted to accumulation.[32]

The spectacular growth of the financial markets is also the result of
an enormous edifice of debt, the vast majority of which is fictitious
capital corresponding to no productive activity.

From the 1980s until today, the large-scale siphoning off of the value
created by the process of mass production of fictitious capital shows
that we are at the opposite extreme from J. M. Keynes's wish for 'the
euthanasia of the rentier'.[33] The workforce and production cycle are increasingly mobilised to satisfy the demands of interest-bearing capital
represented by banks, pension funds and other financial companies.

The large industrial groups (such as Arcelor Mittal, Siemens or Peu-
geot) see their actual production as simply one way amongst others of
developing their capital. The adjective 'global', now used to describe
the strategy of these multinational groups, thus has two complementary meanings. It denotes that they work on a planetary scale and also
that their strategy is clearly based on an assets development policy
that is at least as financial as it is industrial. Many firms traditionally
involved in production now operate like financial groups that make
decisions based on the profitability of the capital invested in their
different activities and subsidiaries. Indeed the largest groups quite
simply have their own banks.[34]

32   CLERSÉ, *Le coût du capital et son surcoût* (The cost of capital and its
extra cost), Lille: Lille 1 University, 2013, p. 63. For a complementary study,
see Michel Husson, 'Un essai de mesure de la ponction actionnariale' (An
attempt to measure what is siphoned off by shareholders), *Hussonet*, 7 November 2013, http://hussonet.free.fr/ponctiona.pdf (in French).
33   John Maynard Keynes, *The General Theory of Employment, Interest
and Money* [1936], Amherst, NY: Prometheus Books, 1997.
34   Having their own banks enabled VW Bank and Mercedes-Benz Bank
to access ECB loans at 1 to 0.25% over three years in the framework of the
LTRO programme started in December 2011. Today they can access the
ECB's short-term loans at 0.05%, which has been the ECB's official market
rate since September 2014. (See 'List of abbreviations').

A growing proportion of the capital being accumulated from new profits is not invested in production. Up till the year 2000 this additional capital was poured into shares and what used to be called the 'new economy'. It provided the cash assets required to feed enormous operations involving mergers and acquisitions until 2001, the US stock exchange and real-estate until 2006-7, raw material commodities as of 2003 and foodstuffs in 2007-8. Speculation on currency-exchange rates, bonds, futures markets on materials and agricultural products and derivatives has increased unceasingly.

The overdevelopment of the financial sector, which is one of the characteristics of the current phase of world capitalism, can be measured in several ways. Between 1986 and 2004, Gross World Product increased by a factor of three and the export of goods and services by five, whereas the international issuance of securities (i.e. debts, shares and bonds) was multiplied by seven, international bank loans by eight, the volume of the currency market by nine and the derivatives market by 98.[35]

The stages of financial deregulation

Until the 1970s, financial and monetary systems were largely compartmentalised at national level. US president Richard Nixon's 1971 decision to end the Bretton Woods system by eliminating the convertibility of the dollar into gold led to the creation of floating exchange rates that opened up international exchange markets considerably.
From 1979, the measures taken by the government leaders of the main industrialised countries progressively ended the control of international movements of capital. They liberalised, or to put it another way, de-compartmentalised, national financial systems.

This happened in three phases: first, complete decompartmentalisation of the currency-exchange market; second, decompartmentalisation of the bond market; and finally, decompartmentalisation of the shares market (in 1986).

---

35   Pablo Bustelo, 'Progreso y alcance de la globalización financiera: Un análisis empírico del periodo 1986-2004' (Progress and scope of financial globalisation: An empirical analysis of the period 1986-2004), *Boletín económico de ICE, Información Comercial Española*, 2007, # 2.922 (in Spanish).

During the 1980s, all forms of administrative control of interest-rates, credit and movements of capital were progressively abolished. The main leaders of the most industrialised countries consciously chose this option. This led to a disorderly retreat by nation-states confronted with the power of financial integration. One after the other, states abdicated before the enormous mass of capital circulating in the world and resigned themselves to making do with the reality they had helped create. They competed with each other to attract capital and, in order to do this, abandoned most of the taxes on income from capital.

Tax rate on corporate profits

Countries	1986	2006	2012
France	45%	33.33%	33.33%
Germany	56%	26.37%	26.37%
Belgium	45%	33.99%	33.99%
Ireland	50%	12.50%	13%
Italy	36%	33%	33%
Netherlands	42%	between 25.5 and 29.6%	29% or 34%
United Kingdom	35%	30%	28%
Sweden	52%	28%	26.30%

Source: CADTM, World Debt figures 2012, 2012, Table 26, p.20.

European integration from the 1980s and 1990s until today has further aggravated the complicity and submissiveness of government leaders towards major private financial, industrial, commercial and communications companies. The successive treaties of the EU and the Eurozone set in stone the diktats of private capital.

The major players on the financial markets

There are not many players on the financial markets that really count: the large international banks (of which there are between thirty and fifty worldwide depending on the criteria used) are beyond any shadow of a doubt the major players. If we add up all the assets managed by the financial markets worldwide, we reach $225 trillion (i.e. three times GWP).[36]

The total international assets of the banks amounted to more than $100 trillion in 2013.[37] If we factor in what they manage through 'shadow banking' (see below), the figure will surely reach at least $140 trillion.[38] The fifty largest international banks alone counted for $66 trillion in assets in 2013.

The other major players in 2013 were:[39]

• Private pension funds, which managed $33 trillion;[40]
• Insurance companies, which managed $25 trillion in assets;
• Mutual funds, which managed $26 trillion (see box about BlackRock);
• Sovereign wealth funds of a certain number of 'emerging countries', which managed $5,200 billion;[41]
• Hedge funds[42] (which managed $2,500 billion in assets);
• And money-market funds (MMF),[43] also worth $2,500 billion.

---

36   This volume of $225 trillion does not include most derivatives. It is arrived at by adding up the assets declared by the companies concerned. By definition, everything off-balance-sheet, including the vast majority of derivatives, is not included in the calculation.
37   This estimation is based on the data provided by the IMF, the BIS and the *Liikanen Report* (see footnote below).
38   According to the G20, the funds managed through shadow banking amounted to more than $71 trillion in 2012. This figure does not include the vast majority of derivatives, as mentioned above.
39   Note that the total assets of the various players exceed $225 trillion because some MMF, hedge funds (via shadow banking), and mutual funds belong to banks.
40   The figures for pension funds, hedge funds, and sovereign funds come from the report published in 2013 by Deutsche Bank entitled *The Random Walk - Mapping the World's Financial Markets 2013*: Sanjeev Sanyal, Deutsche Bank, 13 February 2013, http://www.euromoney.com/downloads/3/DEUTSCHE BANK_RandomWalk_2013-02-13_0900b8c08653e545.pdf. The largest pension funds are based in the US, UK and other industrialised Anglophone countries (Ireland, Australia, New Zealand, Canada, etc.), the Netherlands and Japan. The private pension funds of the Latin, Germanic and Scandinavian countries are less developed.
41   Also the Norwegian sovereign fund, which managed $810 billion in 2013.
42   Some of them are directly controlled by the major banks.
43   Some Money-Market Funds are also created and directed by the major banks.

The BlackRock phenomenon

Among the mutual funds, two big and growing investment service corporations should be mentioned: BlackRock, which manages $4.1 trillion in assets,[44] that is more than all the hedge funds put together and as much as the biggest international banks,[45] and PIMCO (US), a subsidiary of the German insurance company Allianz, which manages nearly $2 trillion in assets.[46]

Before and during the banking crisis, BlackRock purchased major subsidiaries of Merrill Lynch and Barclays. It is the principal shareholder in JPMorgan Chase (the largest US bank), Apple, Microsoft, Exxon Mobile, Chevron, Royal Dutch Shell, Procter and Gamble and General Electric, with stakes ranging between 4.9% and 6.2%. It is the second-ranking stakeholder in Warren Buffet's Berkshire Hathaway (6.8%), Google, Johnson & Johnson, Wells Fargo (the fourth-ranking US bank), and PetroChina. It is the biggest stakeholder in Nestlé (3.7%), and also owns large stakes in Walmart, Roche and Novartis. The seventeen companies just cited hold dominant positions in their respective fields. They are among the largest

---

44 The figure of $4.1 trillion in assets managed by BlackRock is advanced by *The Economist*, whose principal stakeholder is the Pearson Group, which is in turn controlled by BlackRock (*The Economist*, 'The Rise of BlackRock', 7 December 2013, http://www.economist.com/news/leaders/21591174-25-years-blackrock-has-become-worlds-biggest-investor-its-dominance-problem). See also 'Le fonds d'investissement qui a la puissance d'un Etat' (The investment fund with the power of a state), *Le Point*, 9 June 2011, http://www.lepoint.fr/Économie/le-fonds-d-investissement-qui-a-la-puissance-d-un-État-09-06-2011-1342433_28.php (in French).
45 According to *Bloomberg*, the assets managed by JPMorgan Chase amount to $4.5 trillion. See explanation in Chapter 11.
46 'PIMCO', *Wikipedia*, http://en.Wikipedia.org/wiki/PIMCO.

in terms of ca-pital value on the world's stock exchanges. BlackRock possesses a risk management consultancy called Aladdin, which counsels companies holding more than $11 trillion in assets[47] and is a shareholder in Moody's and Standard & Poor's (via its owner McGraw Hill), two of the three most important international credit rating agencies.

To further illustrate BlackRock's influence: Tim Geithner, US Secretary of the Treasury from 2009 to 2013, made 49 telephone calls to Larry Fink, BlackRock's chairman, between 1 January 2011 and 30 June 2012. He called Jamie Dimon (JPMorgan Chase) only seventeen times, and Brian Moynihan of Bank of America and James Gorman of Morgan Stanley five times each.[48]

Finally it is interesting to note that BlackRock was commissioned by the Troika (European Commission, ECB and IMF) to audit the Greek banks in 2014.[49]

Financial and currency-exchange markets

The currency-exchange markets are the part of the global financial market which, along with derivatives markets, has grown the most. Between 1970 and 2013, the volume of currency-exchange transactions has increased by a factor of more than five hundred (going from just over $10 billion to $5,300 billion a day). Although in theory, the

---

47   See: *The Economist*, 'The monolith and the markets', 7 December 2013, http://www.economist.com/news/briefing/21591164-getting-15- trillion-assets-single-risk-management-system-huge-achievement.

48   Shahien Nasiripour, 'Geithner has phone friend at BlackRock', *Financial Times*, 12 October 2012.

49   Patrick Jenkins, 'Greece's plight offers clue to future of EU banking system', *Financial Times*, 25 February 2014.

main function of the currency-exchange markets is to facilitate international trade, in 2013 the total value of transactions linked to the exchange of goods was not even 3% of the total transactions on these exchange markets.

The following table compares the daily volume of currency-exchange operations with the annual volume of goods exports worldwide. In 1979, it took the equivalent of 200 days of currency-exchange market activity to attain the annual volume of world exports. By 2012, only four days of currency-exchange market activity were needed to attain the annual volume of goods exports worldwide. This shows the extent to which the activities of financial markets are disconnected from the productive economy and the trading of goods.

The growth of currency markets and exports

Year	Total of daily turnover on the currency market (in $ billions)	Annual world exports (in $ billions)
1979	75	1546
1984	150	1800
1986	300	1998
1990	500	3429
1994	1200	4269
1998	1800 (X 70)	5142 (X 12)
2001	1250	6155
2005	2100	10159
2007	3500	14023
2012	4600	18300
2013	5300	18800

Source: Author's calculations from UNCTAD

In 2013, four banks alone controlled 50% of the currency-exchange market (Deutsche Bank 15.2%, Citigroup 14.9%, Barclays 10.2% and UBS 10.1%). If we add six more banks (HSBC, JPMorgan Chase, Royal Bank of Scotland, Credit Suisse, Morgan Stanley and Bank of America), we reach 80% of the market.[50] Half of all the currency-exchanges take place on the London market.

In addition to speculation on currency-exchange markets, another activity has developed: the derivatives market.

The derivatives market[51]

In a world where relative currency values are in continual fluctuation, with movements considerably amplified by speculation, the advocates of derivatives explain that they enable companies to cover themselves against currency-exchange and interest-rate risks.

The mechanism is simple: if a company in the Eurozone wants to import a product denominated in dollars and be confident of the value of that dollar (covering themselves against a rise in the dollar, which would increase the purchase price), they buy an option (or make a 'call') to buy the dollar at a fixed price. To do this, they pay a premium to the issuer of the option. At maturity (a date determined by

---

50 Daniel Schäfer, Alice Ross and Delphine Strauss, 'Foreign-exchange: the big fix', Financial Times, 13 November 2013. We shall see below that in 2013 the financial regulatory authorities launched an in-depth inquiry aimed at fifteen banks accused of having manipulated exchange rates (including Deutsche Bank, Barclays, Citigroup, Goldman Sachs, HSBC, JPMorgan Chase, RBS, Morgan Stanley, UBS, and Credit Suisse). See the article mentioned above and the opinion (in French) of Georges Ugeux, 'Après le Libor, le marché des changes risque-t-il d'imploser ?' (After the Libor scandal, is there a risk of the foreign-exchange market imploding?), Le Monde, 1 December 2013, http://finance.blog.lemonde.fr/2013/12/01/apres-le-LIBOR-le-marche-des-changes-risque-t-il-dimploser/. See also (in French) 'Marché des changes: certaines banques sont dans le collimateur des régulateurs' (Forex Market: certain banks targeted by regulators), Finance-Banque, 2013, http://www.finance-banque.com/marche-change.html.
51 Some of the explanations were taken from Jean-Pierre Avermaete and Arnaud Zacharie, Mise à nu des marchés financiers. Les dessous de la globalisation (The bare truth about the financial markets. The hidden agenda of globalisation), Paris & Brussels: Syllepse, Vista, ATTAC, 2002 (in French).

both parties), there are two possible solutions: either the dollar has fallen, in which case the Eurozone importer prefers to pay less for the product and does not exercise their option (and the issuer pockets the premium); or the dollar has risen, in which case the importer exercises their option and the issuer has to provide the dollars at the predetermined price, i.e. cheaper than the real price.

Derivatives market

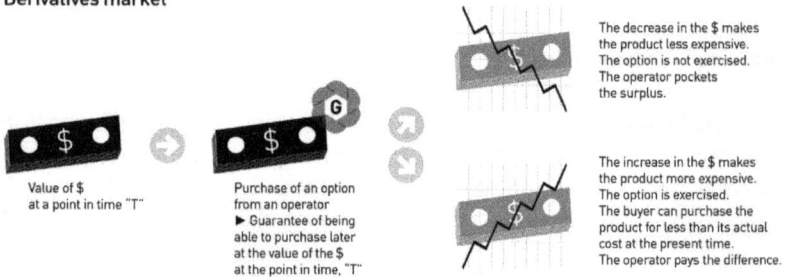

Value of $
at a point in time "T"

Purchase of an option
from an operator
▶ Guarantee of being
able to purchase later
at the value of the $
at the point in time, "T"

The decrease in the $ makes
the product less expensive.
The option is not exercised.
The operator pockets
the surplus.

The increase in the $ makes
the product more expensive.
The option is exercised.
The buyer can purchase the
product for less than its actual
cost at the present time.
The operator pays the difference.

Interest-rate swaps are by far the largest segment of the derivatives market (see illustration below). An interest-rate swap is a contract by mutual agreement to exchange interest-rate cash flows calculated from a fixed rate against interest-rate cash flows calculated from a floating rate, without really exchanging the amount. Consider a town council indebted at a floating rate (for example with Euribor 12-month bonds). To cover themselves against an increase in the interest rate, they agree to swap the Euribor 12-month rate against a fixed rate of 4.5%. At each fixed maturity date, the swapped rate is compared to the Euribor rate.

If the Euribor rate is 5%, i.e. higher than the fixed rate, the local authority pays interest on its debt on the basis of the Euribor rate (5%) but receives the difference between the two rates (i.e. 0.5%) from the bank with which it agreed to the swap. The real interest-rate on the loan is therefore 4.5%.

If the Euribor rate is 4%, i.e. lower than the fixed rate, the council pays interest on its debt on the basis of the Euribor rate (4%) and pays the difference between the two rates (i.e. 0.5%) to the bank. The real interest-rate on the loan is thus still 4.5%.

The French National Assembly's 2011 commission of inquiry into the high-risk financial products subscribed to by local public stakeholders, chaired by Claude Bartolone, highlighted the risks being taken by local authorities: 'In the case of structured swaps, the notional amounts judged to be high-risk come to €2,530 billion, i.e. 38.6% of the total.'[52]

It is the major banks who fix the reference rates and they have ways of manipulating them if they agree amongst themselves – as proved to be the case with the London InterBank Offered Rate (LIBOR – see below, Chapter 23). It is suspected that the ISDAFIX rate, a benchmark in a 380-trillion-dollar market, has also been manipulated. The Commodity Futures Trading Commission (CFTC), the regulatory authority in the US, has launched an investigation into the matter.

According to their defenders, derivatives serve to allow investors to cover themselves by transferring new fluctuations to another party who agrees to accept the risk: that is for a premium, the other party takes on the productive investor's risk as a form of insurance.

In the face of the growing instability caused by deregulation, derivatives are developing at lightning speed and taking on more and more varied forms. According to the ISDA (International Swaps and Derivatives Association), the private organisation that groups together the banks selling derivatives, 82% of derivatives are held by fourteen of the largest banks in the world.

According to the Bank for International Settlements, only 7% of derivatives have a non-financial counterpart. This means that the vast majority of operations on derivatives are totally speculative and disconnected from exchanges of goods. Take this example: two speculating banks agree on a derivative based on the correlation between the market prices of wheat and oil over a period of one month. If, for example, the correlation between the prices of wheat and oil remains within a margin of 3%, speculator A is the winner. If the correlation exceeds the margin of 3%, speculator B pockets the winnings. It can easily be understood that neither party could care less about the nature of the two assets. The only interest they have in wheat and oil is as variables on which to speculate for a month.

---

52   French Parliamentary Commission report, 6 December 2011, p. 38 (in French), http://www.assemblee-nationale.fr/13/pdf/rap-enq/r4030.pdf.

More than 90% of derivatives are sold by mutual agreement (over the counter – OTC), i.e. on a market that is not at all regulated or controlled. The volume of the derivatives market has literally exploded. It went from $94 trillion in 1998 (in notional value) to $650 trillion in 2007 and $700 trillion in 2011.[53] That is about ten times the Gross World Product! According to the ISDA, 94% of the 500 largest banks in the world use derivatives (in order of scale, on currency-exchange risks, interest-rates, raw materials and credit default swaps; see below). The vast majority of derivatives are produced and commercialised by banks. For them, it is a captive market. Hedge funds (some of which belong to banks) do not account for much on the derivatives market relative to banks. As we have seen, they only amount to $2.5 trillion, as compared with $100 trillion in the hands of the banks (without including the other players involved in shadow banking).

Four of these banks (Barclays, BNP Paribas, Deutsche Bank and Royal Bank of Scotland) hold derivatives that have a notional value of more than twenty times their assets and more than 300 times their equity capital in the strict sense.

Banks	Derivatives held by banks in notional value in relation to their assets
Royal Bank of Scotland	30 times
Deutsche Bank	28 times
Barclays	28 times
BNP Paribas	25 times
BPCE	7 times

Source: *Liikanen Report*. p.45, Chart 3.4.8.

---

53 For further details, see the Deutsche Bank report already cited above: http://www.euromoney.com/downloads/3/DEUTSCHE BANK_RandomWalk_2013-02-13_0900b8c08653e545.pdf, pp. 7–9. See also BIS quarterly report, December 2011, 'Principales tendances des statistiques internationales BRI' (Main trends in BIS international statistics) (in French), http://www.bis.org/publ/qtrpdf/r_qt1112b_fr.pdf.
For more on the *Liikanen Report*, see footnote 79 below.

Interest-rate swaps account for 74% of the total, currency-exchange derivatives 8%, credit default swaps (CDS) 5% and derivatives on shares 1%. The remainder includes a multitude of different products.

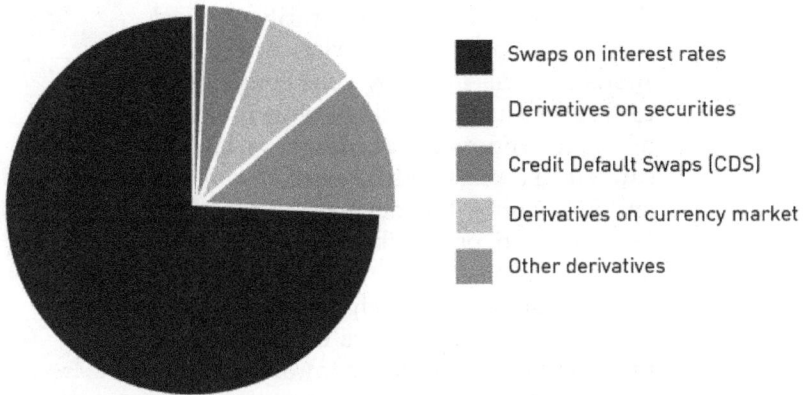

- Swaps on interest rates
- Derivatives on securities
- Credit Default Swaps (CDS)
- Derivatives on currency market
- Other derivatives

According to the Bank for International Settlements, London hosts between 40 and 50% of the derivatives market.

The myth of the fecundity of capital

It is essential to analyse the banking crisis and its management by government ministers within the framework of a more global understanding of the evolution of capitalist society as a whole. The analysis presented in this book is in line with that of economists such as François Chesnais, Michel Husson, Bibiana Medialdea, Nacho Álvarez, Özlem Onaran, Costas Lapavitsas and Jean-Marie Harribey, to name but a few. Harribey, in his book *La richesse, la valeur et l'inestimable. Fondements d'une critique socio-écologique de l'économie capitaliste* (Wealth, value, and the incalculable. Foundations of a socio-ecological critique of capitalist economics), perfectly summarises the transformations of the capitalist system and the intrinsic links between the evolution of that system and the current crisis:

The first transformation concerns the financialisation of the capitalist economy, usually euphemistically referred to as 'globalisation'. Three decades after the start of the process of liberalising the movement of capital, that is, after the re-establishment of the rate of profit that temporarily resolved the serious profitability crisis of the late 1960s and the 1970s by considerably distorting the sharing of added value in favour of capital and to the detriment of labour, capitalism reveals both its extreme violence and its fragility. Financial crises occur too frequently to be attributed to accidents, a lack of transparency in the markets or a deficit of moral principles amongst the players involved. They are the outcome of the evolution of capitalism towards its purest and at the same time most savage logic: give the value to the shareholders – the supreme goal of the circulation of capital, of deregulation, of the proliferation of financial products, and of the securitisation and depoliticisation of the central banks so that they can better serve operators on the financial markets. Against the backdrop of the restructuring of all activities to harness the possibility of producing value where profitability was highest and the changes brought about by information and communication technologies, the system encouraged the general public to believe that a 'new economy' was at work, bringing wealth within everyone's reach. The competition of the market would lead to the best choices and the stock-market boom was a promise of generalised prosperity. Money made money, and we could trust the pension funds to resolve the problem of ageing populations and to pay out pensions to the increasingly numerous retired people.

That was how the myth of the fecundity of capital took shape. Endowed with prolific virtues, it was capable of reproducing itself, of gaining value beyond any productive reality. At last, capital could dream of ridding itself of labour, of definitively doing without it in order to grow on its own. It is a myth as old as capitalism itself, but revived by sophisticated theoretical constructs: thanks to the magic of self-fulfilling prophecies, the valorisation of capital was no longer linked to the 'fundamental' indicators of the economy, that is, production, its growth and the profits made from selling goods. Even accounting rules were changed to evaluate the assets of companies not according to their real purchase or replacement value, nor their residual value, but according to the value that the permanently fluctuating financial market placed on them. Needless to say, the periodic bursting of financial bubbles shatters the myth of the fecundity of capital, with all the more force because we see every time that the holders of financial securities cannot all 'liquidate' their stock at the same time.

But the 'fetishism'[54] of money is always just below the surface. The most frequent comments when the bubbles burst are that 'billions have gone up in smoke' or 'evaporated'. Yet the thing that really disappears into thin air is the fiction of capital growing as the bubble rises.[55]

---

54   'Fetishism' is the term Karl Marx used in the third notebook of his 'Paris Manuscripts' (*Economic and Philosophic Manuscripts of 1844*, Moscow: Progress Publishers, 1959). He would develop this idea concerning the dual character of labour and goods in *Capital*, Volume I (Harmondsworth: Penguin Classics, 1993; online version https://www.marxists.org/archive/marx/works/1867-c1)

55   Jean-Marie Harribey, *La richesse, la valeur et l'inestimable. Fonde-*

In some cases this fictitious capital can have repercussions on the real economy, and therefore on working class people, by causing large-scale processes of destruction of productive capital. The result is that companies go bankrupt and create large-scale unemployment.

ments d'une critique socio-écologique de l'économie capitaliste (Wealth, value, and the incalculable. Foundations of a socio-ecological critique of capitalist economics), Paris: Les liens qui libèrent, 2013, pp. 8-9 (in French).

4.
Banking methods
at the root of the crisis[56]

Deregulation made it possible for the private financial sector, and banks in particular, to put into place, or to push to their limits, various mechanisms that were at the root of the banking crisis.

Leverage

Leverage is one of the main instruments of banking speculation. The Banque de France gives this definition of leverage:

> The lever effect measures the effect of indebtedness on the financial return for a given economic profitability. In agreeing to resort to indebtedness, the shareholders of a company or financial institution expect an even higher return due to the additional risk taken.[57]

Banks in particular take full advantage of this effect. Xavier Dupret describes the leverage phenomenon clearly:

> The banking world has accumulated large amounts of debt in recent years through

---

56   Two other banking methods – high-frequency trading and short selling— are discussed in a later chapter.
57   See Banque de France, *La Crise de la dette souveraine* (The Sovereign-Debt Crisis), Banque de France, *Documents et débats no.4*, May 2012, p. 112 (http://www.banque-france. fr/fileadmin/user_upload/banque_de_france/publications/Documents_Economiques/documents-et-debats-numero-4-integral.pdf (Translation CADTM).

what is called leverage, which works by borrowing in order to increase the profitability of one's equity. This means that the rate of return of the selected project needs to be higher than the rate of interest to be paid on the borrowed amount. As leverage increased over time, this caused problems. In the spring of 2008, the Wall Street investment banks had leverage rates between 25 and 45 (for each dollar of shareholders' equity, they had borrowed between 25 and 45 dollars). Merrill Lynch had a leverage rate of 40. The situation was explosive since an institution that is leveraged at 40:1 can lose its shareholders' equity with a drop of 2.5% (1/40th) in the value of the acquired assets.[58]

LEVERAGE

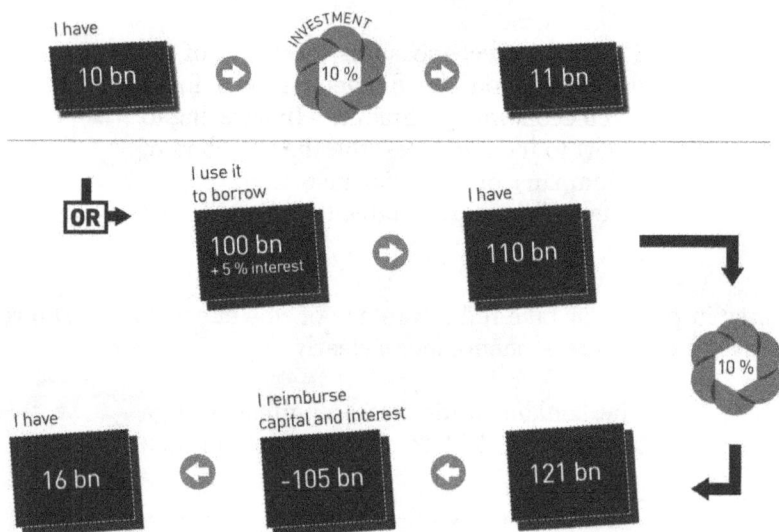

---

58 Xavier Dupret, 'Et si nous laissions les banques faire faillite?' (What if we let the banks go under?), Gresea, 22 August 2012, http://www.gresea.be/spip.php?article1048 (in French).

Off-balance-sheet practices

Thanks to deregulation, banks were able to develop activities that require huge amounts of financing (and therefore of debt) without having to declare them on their balance-sheets. Off-balance-sheet practices are used to account for a bank's activities which have not yet produced either a payment or the receipt of a payment, but which generate risks for the bank. These are usually on-going contracts concerning derivatives, *foreign-exchange* or signature commitments, and are perfectly legal. They have been used a great deal to hide the great risks banks have taken with their high-volume operations on the derivatives markets (see below).

According to the official website of the French Ministry of Economy and Finance, the off-balance-sheet position of French banks, in 2010 and 2011, is as follows:

	2010	2011
Financing commitments : - given - received	- 1,038.76 539.69	- 950.26 463.08
Guarantee commitments - of order - received	- 1,075.34 1,061.07	- 1,108.79 1,213.36
Securities commitments - securities to be received - securities to be delivered	- 220.27 220.53	- 184.98 188.60
Currency transactions - currencies to be received - currencies to be delivered	- 5,844.34 5,852.64	- 6,071.95 6,060.34
Commitments on forward financial instruments (= derivatives)	91,292.73	95,922.43
TOTAL In billion euros.	**107,145.37**	**112,163.79**

Source: Ministère de l'Économie et des Finances, « Les comptes d'une banque. Hors-Bilan», 2013, Available at http://www.economie.gouv.fr/facileco/comptes-dune-banque

Over the last few years, banks' off-balance-sheet accounting has increased continually.

Banks' largest off-balance-sheet entries are commitments on forward financial instruments such as derivatives transactions. In 2011, the total of these commitments of all banks together represented about €96 trillion, eleven times more than the total value of their balance-sheets. Interest-rate trading instruments make up the bulk of that amount – €84,739 trillion for the year 2011. This is 34 times the total amount of loans granted by banks to their customers. This figure is a striking example of the activity of banks in the financial markets.[59]

According to Laurence Scialom, in the United States:

> This massive commitment in off-balance-sheet positions is reflected in the growth of the share of the revenue gained by engagement in these commitments, and the trading associated with them, in banks' overall revenue.[60]

That share was 19% in the 1960-1980 period and had risen to 43% of net banking revenue by 1999.[61]

Given the huge volume of off-balance-sheet activities, any major financial accident that concerns them, including on derivatives, can endanger the bank. The big banks do not hesitate, however, to make massive use of them because, as Laurence Scialom also points out, they can produce significant revenue and can be used to screen risks from the eyes of the regulatory authorities.

---

59   See French Ministry of Economy and Finance, www.economie.gouv.fr/facileco/comptes-dune-banque, consulted 17 October 2013.
60   Commissions and trading revenues.
61   Laurence Scialom, *Économie bancaire* (Banking Economics), Paris: La Découverte, 2013, p. 22. (in French).

Shadow banking

Shadow banking is another vehicle created for speculation, which is also perfectly legal and permitted by the regulatory authorities.

Financial shadow-banking activities are mainly carried out on behalf of major banks by financial companies (money-market funds, hedge funds, investment funds, etc.) called Special Purpose Vehicles (SPVs) that the major banks themselves have established for this purpose. These companies do not receive deposits, and are thus able to operate without being subject to national or international banking regulations and/or regulatory authorities. Asset management companies like BlackRock and PIMCO are also active in shadow banking and have very close relationships with major banks. As we have seen, BlackRock is the largest shareholder in JPMorgan Chase and the second-largest shareholder in Wells Fargo, the two largest banks in the United States.

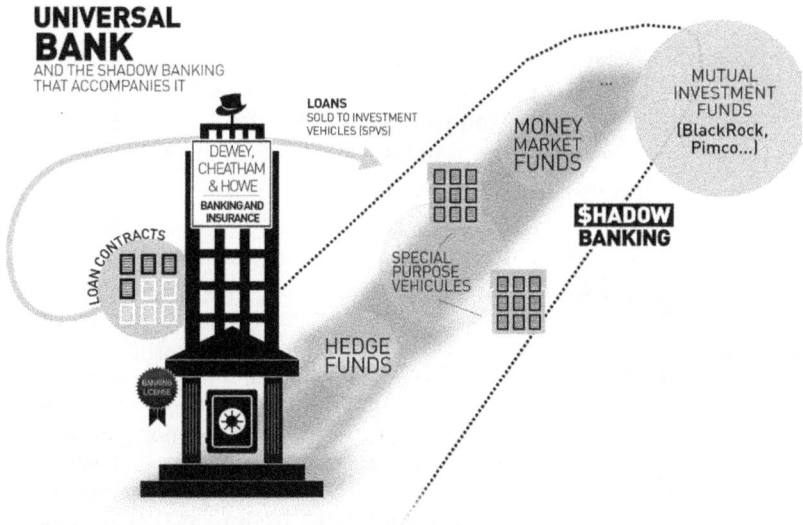

UNIVERSAL BANK
AND THE SHADOW BANKING THAT ACCOMPANIES IT

LOANS
SOLD TO INVESTMENT
VEHICLES (SPVS)

DEWEY, CHEATHAM & HOWE
BANKING AND INSURANCE

LOAN CONTRACTS

BANKING LICENSE

SPECIAL PURPOSE VEHICULES

HEDGE FUNDS

MONEY MARKET FUNDS

$HADOW BANKING

MUTUAL INVESTMENT FUNDS
(BlackRock, Pimco...)

In the 'shadow' of the bank are the companies it has created itself to avoid certain regulations or to create structured products using SPVs, for example, and other companies such as mutual funds, which also play a role in shadow banking.

Thus shadow banking and universal banks are complementary. The use of shadow banking enables the universal bank to dodge direct risk management more than ever.

The volume in assets managed in shadow banking has greatly increased. There was an upsurge before the 2007-2008 crisis, with the volume of shadow banking climbing from $26.375 trillion in 2002 to over $62 trillion in 2007. After a drop to $59.350 trillion in 2008, volumes rose again to $66.614 trillion in 2011.[62]

According to Richard Hiault, writing in Les Echos in 2012, 'This "parallel" sector alone represents half the size of the total assets of the banks.' The Financial Stability Board (FSB), the entity created by the G20 forum to oversee financial stability around the world, has issued revealing figures for 2011:

> 'The US has the largest shadow banking system, with assets of $23 trillion in 2011, followed by the euro area ($22 trillion) and the UK ($9 trillion).
> [...]
> Jurisdictions where NBFIs [Non-bank financial institutions] are the largest relative to GDP are Hong Kong (520%), the Netherlands (490%), the UK (370%), Singapore (260%) and Switzerland (210%).'[63]

In 2012, the volume of shadow banking assets approached $71 trillion,[64] approximately equivalent to the Gross World Product (GWP).

---

62   Source: Institut Numérique, 'Besoin ou non d'un financement alternatif – le Shadow Banking' (Do we need alternative financing? – Shadow Banking) http://www.institut-numerique.org/ii-besoin-ou-non-dun-financement-alternatif-le-shadow-banking-51bec7069258c (in French). See also Daniel Munevar, 'Les risques du système bancaire de l'ombre' (The Risks of Shadow Banking), CADTM, 21 April 2012, http://cadtm.org/Les-risques-du-systeme-bancaire-de (in French or Spanish). See also: Tracy Alloway, 'Traditional lenders shiver as shadow banking grows', *Financial Times*, 28 December 2011.

63   Financial Stability Board, 'Global Shadow Banking Monitoring Report 2012', 18 November 2012, p.4 http://www.financialstabilityboard.org/wp-content/uploads/r_121118c.pdf.

64   'Près de 71.000 milliards de dollars ont été brassés par le "shadow

The financial regulatory authorities made no effort to radically deflate the volume of shadow banking, let alone eliminate it. So great is the influence of the big banks and powerful investment funds such as BlackRock and PIMCO (see the section above 'The major players on the financial markets') that the authorities continue to turn a blind eye to the shadow banking activities that generate their profits and bolster their weight in the economy. Mark Carney, President of the FSB and Governor of the Bank of England, feels that shadow banking should be transparent and secure, providing a diversity of long-term sustainable funding sources. He says that the FSB will continue to observe shadow banking with a view to regulating it at some future date.[65]

Off-shore banking

In 2009, it was estimated that two thirds of OTC financial transactions involved off-shore parties. This estimation was the result of a study by Philippe Lamberts, (MEP – Green Party, Belgium) who probed the annual reports of many European banks. The award for biggest involvement goes to Deutsche Bank, which controls 974 companies and subsidiaries, of which 657 are outside Europe.[66] Other major banks involved are BNP Paribas with 280 companies, the Belgian bank KBC with nearly 100, Crédit Agricole with 95, Société Générale with 82, and BPCE with 81 companies.

Off-shore tax havens are characterised by the following five independent criteria:
- Bank secrecy and similar ways of protecting financial high-rollers;
- Low taxes, sometimes as low as zero for non-residents;

---

banking" en 2012' (Close to $71 trillion were handled by shadow banking in 2012), *La Tribune*, 18 November 2013, http://www.latribune.fr/entreprises-finance/20131118tribooo796286/pres-de-71.000-milliards-de-dollars-ont-ete-brasses-par-le-shadow-banking-en-2012.html (in French).
65   '70.000 milliards de dollars pour le 'shadow banking'' ($70 trillion for shadow banking), *Les Échos*, 17 November 2013, http://www.lesechos.fr/entreprises-secteurs/finance-marches/actu/0203131027751-70-000-milliards-de-dollars-pour-le-shadow-banking-630041.php (in French).
66   Philippe Lamberts and Gaspard Denis, 'The Seven Deadly Sins of Banks', The Greens/EFA, 2013, http://bankingsins.eu/en/.

- Easy regulations permitting the creation of front companies and no requirement that the companies actually conduct business in the territory;
- Lack of cooperation with the inland revenue services, legal authorities and customs and excise authorities of other countries;
- Slack financial regulation or none at all.

Switzerland, the City of London and Luxembourg receive the largest amounts of off-shore deposits. Other tax havens include the Cayman Islands, the Channel Islands such as Guernsey and Jersey, Hong Kong, and many more throughout the world. The very wealthy companies seeking to avoid paying due taxes and/or wishing to launder criminal money can have access to banking services that 'smuggle' money through a succession of tax havens in return for juicy commissions. The first stops are generally Switzerland, the City of London or Luxembourg. Then the funds transit through even shadier territories, in order to cover their tracks and hinder pursuit by the authorities, before settling back in Switzerland, the City of London or Luxembourg, where they are either recovered by their owners or managed by a wealth manager.

Le Monde provided us with an illustration on 25 January 2014: [67]

> The Chinese authorities admit that in 2010, $6.1 billion left China for the British Virgin Islands, $3.5 billion for the Cayman Islands, $3.2 billion to Luxembourg, and $1.3 billion to the US; only $27 million were bound for Switzerland. In fact only a small portion of these sums remain in tax havens. Most return to China or find their way onto accounts in Zurich, Paris, London or New York, held by foreign companies rather than Chinese nationals. (Translation CADTM).

---

67 In *Le Monde*, 25 January 2014, p. 2 (in French).

According to an investigation by the International Consortium of Investigative Journalists, three of the world's largest banks play the biggest roles in Chinese tax evasion and money laundering: Credit Suisse, UBS and JPMorgan Chase. With €24 billion, Credit Suisse is the Western bank with the biggest Chinese wealth management portfolio.

According to Gabriel Zucman, assistant professor at the London School of Economics, the rich have transferred $5.8 trillion to tax havens.[68] The favourite destinations are Switzerland, which receives about one third of off-shore deposits, and Luxembourg.[69] Gabriel Zucman also says that the volume of the fortunes managed off-shore increased by 25% between 2009 and 2012. *The Economist*, which found concordant figures, says that Switzerland takes in a little more than $2 trillion of foreign origin; the UK, the Channel Islands and Ireland receive almost that much, while the Caribbean and Panama receive half that amount and the US (particularly the state of Delaware) and Luxembourg each receive half again.

Certain tax havens have more registered companies than they have inhabitants, a clear indication that they are only a letterbox: the British Virgin Islands have 1,995 registered companies for every 100 inhabitants; the Cayman Islands (also British) count 161 company registrations per 100 inhabitants; the state of Delaware has 104 per 100 inhabitants.[70]

Micro-states that belong to the chain of tax havens are widely used by the major multinational companies, including banks. Gérard Gourguechon underscores this:

> Very many off-shore jurisdictions are the creations of the main financial centres. Half of them were born under the impulse of their consultant lawyers in the City of London. Wall Street has its network of

---

68   Gabriel Zucman, 'The Missing Wealth of Nations: Are Europe and the U.S. Net Debtors or Net Creditors?', *The Quarterly Journal of Economics* (2013), pp. 1321–1364 http://gabriel-zucman.eu/files/Zucman2013QJE.pdf, p. 1345. This figure only includes household portfolios, not the investments made by financial corporations and industrial and commercial companies.
69   Ibid., p. 1341.
70   'Storm survivors', Special report on Offshore Finance, *The Economist*, 14 February 2013.

tax havens. Toronto has several islands in the Caribbean that have been groomed to adopt arrangements favourable to the extractive industries, making Toronto a place of expertise in the locating and listing of such companies. Frankfurt's banks are involved in the transformation of the Grand Duchy of Luxembourg into a tax haven. The Paris financial centre also has its tax-exempt territories in Europe, in the Atlantic, the Caribbean, and the Pacific and Indian Oceans. Off-shore territories apply banking regulations, business and tax laws, etc. that are often custom-written by resident lawyers and tax consultants linked to banks and multinational corporations. This partly explains the specialisation of tax havens and how they now complement each other, to the greater benefit of the largest multinationals. [71]

In the wake of an in-depth investigation by the US justice system in December 2012, the largest British bank, HSBC, admitted to assisting Mexican drug cartels, along with other criminal organisations, in money-laundering operations to the tune of $880 million. HSBC principally used the Cayman Islands. This matter will be dealt with in more detail in Chapter 22.

It is easy to see that while banks' off-shore subsidiaries are able to make copious profits, they also risk copious losses that can take their parent company to the brink of failure, requiring the authorities to bail them out.

---

71   Gérard Gourguechon, 'Reading Notes on Gabriel Zucman', CADTM, 21 December 2013, www.cadtm.org/La-richesse-cachee-des-nations (in French).

Since 2009, there has been very little real change, despite numerous announcements by the G20 leaders.[72] Under these conditions, it is clear that the scope of any action taken by national and international public institutions charged with encouraging finance to behave more responsibly is very limited. Regulators have not appropriated the means to uncover the true nature and extent of the activities of the banks they are supposed to control. As a result, a large percentage of financial transactions totally escape official control.

---

72 See, for instance, the Istanbul communiqué in 2012, http://www.bloomberg.com/news/articles/2015-02-10/g-20-communique-following-feb-9-10-meetings-in-istanbul-text-

5.
The quest for maximum Return on Equity

What is Return on Equity or ROE?

To understand private banks, their behaviour as capitalist corporations and what motivates their major shareholders and CEOs, we need further insight into their obsession with Return on Equity, sometimes also called ROE. ROE is a key to understanding why and how banks do what they do. ROE is the relationship, expressed as a percentage, between the net profit (or loss) of a bank and the shareholders' equity. This ratio measures the capacity of a corporation to generate profits from its equity alone (its 'return on net worth'). In other words, it expresses the profit that may potentially be paid to shareholders. The higher the ROE, the more attractive the bank is to its shareholders. ROE can thus be defined as net income (or net profit) / shareholders' equity.

From the 1990s to the beginning of the crisis in 2007-2008, there was a mad race for maximum ROE: 15% was common, but some banks were getting from 25% to 30%. In 2007, ROE stood at 15% in the Eurozone, 17% in the United Kingdom, and 19% in the US.[73]

For example, the two major US banks, Goldman Sachs and Morgan Stanley (the fifth- and sixth-largest banks in the country) both posted an ROE of 30% in 1999-2000, until the Internet bubble burst and Enron went bankrupt in 2001. From 2001 to 2004, the shareholders of these two banks had to settle for an ROE of between 12% and 16%.[74]

---

73   Patrick Artus and Marie-Paule Virard, *La liquidité incontrôlable* (Uncontrollable liquidity), Montreuil: Pearson France, 2010 (in French).
74   ROE must not be confused with dividends. The first is the rate of return on shareholders' equity, which is calculated as net profit / shareholders' equity, while the second is the portion of profits actually transferred to the

Thanks to the policy of all-out support for banks and big businesses pushed by the Fed and the Bush Administration (with Henry Paulson, the former CEO of Goldman Sachs, working as the Secretary of the Treasury), Goldman Sachs's ROE again reached 30% in 2006-2007, while Morgan Stanley's shot back up to nearly 25% in 2006, before falling again in 2007. Goldman Sachs advised its clients to purchase structured subprime products (the famous CDO – Collateral Debt Obligations), while at the same time speculating that they would fall in 2007. That is why it could post an ROE of 30% at the height of the banking crisis, while its chief competitors Bear Stearns, Merrill Lynch, and Lehman Brothers were beginning their descent into hell.[75] Then in 2008, Goldman Sachs's ROE fell to 10% and Morgan Stanley's to 2%. In 2009, Goldman's ROE went up to 20%, and Morgan Stanley's was 10% in 2010 and -0.3% in 2012.[76] In 2013, Goldman Sachs's ROE reached 12% and Morgan Stanley's was 5%.[77]

Generally speaking, a bank's equity is made up of the capital put up by its shareholders. Twenty-five years ago, this shareholders' equity was equal to 8% of a bank's assets (more specific information will be given in the chapter dealing with the Basel agreements). Regulatory authorities adopted this 8% ratio because it corresponded to the ratio reported, at that time, by the big US banks.[78] For example, for a bank that had assets worth €100 billion (in household and corporate loans, government bonds, corporate bonds, derivatives and other financial products), its minimum equity capital would have been €8 billion.

---

shareholders.

75   This policy conducted by Goldman Sachs was investigated by the SEC (Securities and Exchange Commission, the agency that regulates financial markets in the US) and resulted in payment of a $550-million fine for fraud.

76   The data on the Goldman Sachs and Morgan Stanley ROE are from Tom Braithwaite, 'Leaner and meaner', *Financial Times*, 30 September 2012, p. 9. These data are also available on http://www.thebankerdatabase. com (a *Financial Times* website), consulted on 17 October 2013.

77   Tom Braithwaite, 'Banking rivalries: Risk on, risk off', *Financial Times*, 10 January 2014.

78   Andrew G Haldane, 'Control rights (and wrongs)', speech given at the Wincott Annual Memorial Lecture, London, 24 October 2011, p. 14, http:// www.bankofengland.co.uk/publications/Pages/speeches/2011/525.aspx. According to Haldane, the choice of this 8% ratio has no objective foundation. It was chosen because it was the condition of the big US banks at the time of the first Basel agreements.

To achieve an ROE of 15%, net profit must be €1.2 billion (15% of €8 billion). It seems easy to obtain such net profit with assets that amount to €100 billion, as it represents only 1.2% of that amount.

If a bank, using leverage, then borrows €200 billion on the financial markets to purchase further assets, the volume in assets becomes €300 billion, the equity has remained the same at €8 billion, while the liabilities have also risen by €200 billion. If the bank continues to make a net profit of 1.2%, that becomes €3.6 billion. With equity still at €8 billion, that means an ROE of 45%. This is the fundamental reason for increasing leverage through borrowing: with the same equity capital, the greater the volume of the balance-sheet, the greater the potential to generate income, and the greater the net profit will be on each invested euro.

IMF bank profitability figures

The IMF has published the average difference between profits on assets and profits on equity in several countries in 2012. This difference is very small, and in some cases is negative.

Greece	-0.4%
Ireland	-0.8%
Italy	0.4%
Portugal	0.3%
Spain	0.2%
Austria	0.4%
France	0.2%
Germany	0.2%
Netherlands	0.4%
United Kingdom	0.0%
Denmark	0.1%
Switzerland	0.2%

Sweden	0.6%
United States	0.8%

Source: IMF, 2012.

This table seems to indicate that shareholders of European banks are not getting very good returns. However, from the ROE point of view we get a very different picture. According to the *Liikanen Report*[79], Deutsche Bank controlled €2,164 billion in assets, and we will suppose its profits corresponded to the rate the IMF declared for Germany (0.2% or a net profit of €4.33 billion). However, Deutsche Bank's asset/equity ratio was 2%,[80] which corresponds to €43.3 billion in shareholders' equity. In this case, its ROE would be 10%,[81] which shows what banking reality is in these times of crisis.

---

79 Most of the information here comes from Erkki Liikanen (Chairman), *High-level Expert Group on reforming the structure of the EU banking sector*, 2 October 2012, Brussels - in particular Table 3.4.1: 'Large EU banks (2011)', p. 39. The report was named after Liikanen, Governor of the Bank of Finland, who in 2011-2012 chaired a task-force of eleven experts appointed by European Commissioner Michel Barnier to make a diagnosis of the situation of European banks and propose reforms for the European banking sector. Hereinafter, it will be called the *Liikanen Report*. One of the interests of the report is that it officially confirms the manipulative behaviour of banks and the astounding risks they have taken to maximise their profits. As we will discover below, bankers were not pleased with this report. See the complete *Liikanen Report* at: http://ec.europa.eu/internal_market/bank/docs/high-level_expert_group/report_en.pdf.
80 Deutsche Bank, along with 26 other big European Banks, was supposed to achieve a higher asset/equity ratio (4.5%) before June 2012, but as the method proposed to calculate this Tier One ratio is dubious, we will not discuss it here. The figure included here is just to give an overall idea of the situation. To calculate Deutsche Bank's actual ROE, we would need the exact amount of its net profit and its shareholders' equity.
81 The *Financial Times*' specialised site *The Banker Database* reports the ROE of Deutsche Bank in 2011 as 10.99%: http://www.thebankerdatabase.com (consulted on 17 October 2013).

6.
Banks expand
their assets

A wide range of structured financial products and derivatives developed very rapidly from the mid-1990s. The big banks wanted a share of this buoyant and expanding market, fearing that if they were not well positioned, they would be overtaken and eventually eliminated by their competitors. The profits on these products are relatively small – usually around 1% –, and so profits are made by expanding volume. If the shareholders are pushing for a higher ROE, the directors are under pressure to greatly inflate their bank's assets, and thus its income base. In the example given above, the assets tripled in ten years to €300 billion, while the capital remained the same at €8 billion, or 2.66% of the assets. This growth in bank assets is funded by borrowing.

The bank concerned would use leverage, which consists of increasing its borrowing to increase the profitability of its equity capital (see Chapter 4). In our example, the leverage is 37.5:1, meaning that its liabilities are 37.5 times its equity capital. As competition between the big banks on the derivatives markets has increased over the years, the profitability of these products has decreased – in some cases it was no more than 0.1%. To maintain their ROE at 30% when interest-rates and the profitability of derivatives started decreasing from 2001, banks chose to increase the volume of their assets by purchasing more and more high-yield financial products, of which those derived from subprime loans are the most striking example.

The remarkable increase in the volume of bank assets

The IMF reports that global bank assets increased by about 140% from 2002 to 2007, rising from $40 trillion to $97 trillion.[82]

The assets of Société Générale (the eighth-largest European and third-largest French bank) increased from €410 billion in 1999, when the euro was launched, to nearly €1.2 trillion in 2008 (an increase of close to 300% over a decade). In 2010, its assets were still close to €1.2 trillion.[83] In Germany, the assets of Commerzbank (the fifteenth-largest European and second-largest German bank) went from €380 to €850 billion between 1999 and 2009.

If we consider the entire European banking sector, assets went from €25 trillion in 2001 to €43 trillion in 2008 (3.5 times the EU's GDP).[84] Bank debt followed the same trend. In terms of liabilities, inflated bank balance-sheets relied on more borrowing to finance banking activities. In terms in assets, there was a combination of real-estate loans, and for most major banks the development of trading activities (in particular high-frequency trading), which included derivatives trading. In the middle of the 1990s, the issuing of asset-backed securities (ABS) was completely monopolised by US banks,[85] but European banks also wanted their piece of the pie. They bought those asset based securities using short-term loans, while the purchased products matured much later, which increased their leverage. To cover the risks, banks would buy credit and other kinds of derivatives to protect themselves against currency-exchange and interest-rate fluctuations. In September 2008, the bankruptcy of Lehman Brothers and the bail-out of AIG (the biggest insurance company in the world) showed that those who issued derivatives like CDS (see box below) could not cope with the risks they were meant to cover. The total volume of derivatives literally exploded,

---

82 *Global Financial Stability Report: Restoring Confidence and Progressing on Reforms*, Washington, DC: International Monetary Fund, October 2012, http://www.imf.org/External/Pubs/FT/GFSR/2012/02/index.htm, p. 82.
83 *Liikanen Report*, p. 41.
84 These figures are taken from the *Liikanen Report*. See also: Damien Millet, Daniel Munevar and Éric Toussaint, *2012 World Debt Figures*, CADTM, 2012, Table 30, p. 23, which gives figures that concur with other sources: http://cadtm.org/2012-World-debt-figures
85 *Liikanen Report*, Chart 2.3.4.

from $100 trillion in 1998 to $750 trillion in 2007.[86]

What is a CDS?

A CDS or Credit Default Swap is a financial product that is not usually controlled by any government regulatory body. It was created by the JPMorgan Chase bank in the early 1990s, when deregulation was in full swing. It should normally permit the holder of a debt to be reimbursed by the seller of the CDS if the issuer of a bond (the borrower) defaults on repayment, whether the borrower is a public institution or a private corporation.

We say 'should' for two main reasons. First, buyers can use a CDS to cover the risk of non-repayment of a debt that they do not own. That would be like insuring your neighbour's house against fire hoping it will go up in flames in order to cash in the insurance premium. The second risk is that CDS sellers lacked the financial means necessary to indemnify all the big CDS holders. Should there be a series of bankruptcies of private companies that had issued bonds, or a default by a major bond-issuing country, it is quite probable that the CDS sellers would be unable to cover their promises.

The disaster that hit AIG in August 2008[87] and the collapse of Lehman Brothers in September 2008 are directly linked to the CDS markets, where both companies were very active.

CDS give banks that purchase them the illusion that they are covered against risks, thus encouraging them to be even more adventurous. In addition,

---

86 *Liikanen Report*, Chart 2.3.5. In 2012, the volume of OTC transactions was again $750 trillion.
87 AIG, the biggest North American international insurance company, was nationalised by President George W. Bush to avoid its total collapse.

a CDS is a speculative instrument. For example, in 2010-2011 banks and other financial corporations purchased CDS to hedge against the eventuality of a Greek sovereign-debt default. They hoped that Greece would ultimately default so that they would be indemnified. Therefore, whether or not they held Greek bonds, banks and financial corporations holding CDS on Greek debt had an interest in seeing the crisis get worse.

The principal holders of Greek debt in 2010-2011, the French and German banks, sold Greek bonds. This fuelled doubts as to Greece's capacity to repay while at the same time the banks were buying CDS so as to be indemnified if Greece defaulted on its debt.[88]

On 1 November 2012, the European authorities finally prohibited the purchase or sale of CDS associated with EU states where the potential purchaser does not hold the corresponding sovereign debt.[89] However, since this restriction only concerns sovereign debt, it only covers about 5 to 7% of the CDS market.

---

88 CDS also play another very important role for banks. They may also be used to reduce the weight of bank assets. We shall see below how banks are continually seeking to convince regulatory bodies that their asset/equity ratio complies with the regulations.

89 See EU Regulation No. 236/2012 of the European Parliament and Council dated 14 March 2012 on short selling and some aspects of credit risk on exchange contracts: http://eur-lex.europa.eu/LexUriServ/LexUriServ. do?uri=OJ:L:2012:086:0001:0024:en:PDF. This concerns restrictions on short selling, that is, selling securities one does not (or does not yet) own in the hope of buying them back later at a lower price. There are many exceptions to the rules and ways around them. See also Mathilde Damgé, 'L'Europe a une arme contre la spéculation sur la dette des Etats' (Europe has a weapon against sovereign-debt speculation), *Le Monde*, 19 July 2013, http://www.lemonde.fr/Économie/article/2012/11/01/l-europe-a-une-arme-contre-la-speculation-sur-la-dette-des-États_1783992_3234.html (in French). As if there were not enough exceptions, in September 2013 a counsellor for the prosecution at the European Court of Justice questioned the right of the European Union to prohibit short selling, even when there is a crisis.

It is worth noting that this important but limited measure (the only serious measure to be implemented since the crisis began) was followed by a significant reduction in CDS market activity, thus demonstrating its speculative nature.

Finally, we observe that the CDS market is dominated by a dozen or so big international banks, while hedge funds and other financial actors are only marginally present. In July 2013, the European Commission also threatened to prosecute thirteen big banks for conspiring to maintain their domination on the CDS Over-the-Counter (OTC) market.[90]

The growth of European banks did not rely on customer deposits, which increased only modestly, but on their own debts on the interbank market (the loans banks make between themselves), with central banks such as the ECB, the Fed and the Bank of England, or with Money Market Funds (MMF).[91]

What are Money Market Funds?

MMF are financial corporations in the United States and Europe, rarely supervised and subject to few regulations because they do not require a banking licence. The specialised press considers them to belong to the shadow banking world. In theory, MMF act with prudence, but the reality is very different. The Obama Administration is considering regulating them as in the event of an MMF going

---

90   See Alex Barker, Philip Stafford and Tracy Alloway, 'Europe steps up regulatory assault on CDS', *Financial Times*, 1 July 2013.
91   *Liikanen Report*, Chart 2.3.6.

bankrupt, the risk of having to bail it out with public money is very high. This is a worrying prospect, given the sharp drop in their profitability since 2008 and the vast quantities of money they handle. In the United States, they held $2.7 trillion in 2012, significantly less than the $3.8 trillion they held in 2008.

As investment funds, MMF collect capital from investors (banks, pension funds, etc.) and lend it for very short terms, often from day to day, to banks, businesses, and governments. During the 2000s, MMF financing has become an essential short-term financing source for banks. Among the biggest MMF in 2012 is the Prime Money Market Fund, created by JPMorgan Chase (the biggest bank in the United States), which handled $115 billion in 2012. Wells Fargo, the fourth-largest bank in the United States, has an MMF managing $24 billion. Goldman Sachs, the fifth-largest bank, controls an MMF worth $25 billion. US banks also operate MMF in Europe; JPMorgan Chase (€18 billion), BlackRock (€11.5 billion), Goldman Sachs (€10 billion), alongside European banks such as BNP Paribas (€7.4 billion), and Deutsche Bank (€11.3 billion). Some MMF also operate in British pounds. Michel Barnier, the European Commissioner for Internal Market and Services, has also announced that he would like this activity to be regulated, but that is most likely to remain wishful thinking.[92]

Moody's rating agency has worked out that during the period 2007-2009, many MMF had to be bailed out by the banks and pension funds that had created them: 36 in the US and 26 in Europe for a total cost of $12.1 billion. Between 1980 and 2007, 146 MMF had to be rescued by their financial backers.

---

92   Steve Johnson, 'EU "shadow banking plan" rapped', *Financial Times*, 25 March 2012; Eric Uhlfelder, 'Money Market Funds lose worth in low interest-rate world', *Financial Times*, 9 September 2012; Steve Johnson, 'EU abandons reform of Money Market Funds', *Financial Times*, 9 March 2014.

Again according to Moody's, 20 MMF were bailed out in 2010-2011.[93] These examples show how much of a menace they are to the stability of the financial system.

---

93   Ellen Kelleher, 'Almost 20 Money Market Funds bailed out', *Financial Times*, 20 October 2013.

7.
The banking collapse of 2008

After the derivatives and subprime markets crashed in 2007-2008, the banks and their specialised offshoots suffered losses, sometimes greater than their capitalisation. To illustrate this, let us return to our previous example (in Chapters 5 and 6) in which the bank had a leverage ratio of 37.5:1 (€8 billion in equity capital and total liabilities of €300 billion). If it were to record a loss resulting in a 3% decrease in the value of its assets, its equity capital would be swallowed up. Faced with this situation, a bank has four options:

1. To declare bankruptcy;
2. To be taken over by another bank or by the state;
3. To call on the state or private investors for a recapitalisation;[94]
4. Or to try to cover up its losses by 'cooking the books' while awaiting better times and the return of profits and/or recapitalisation when the storm has blown over (see Box below on Deutsche Bank).

These different cases actually occurred in 2008. In the US, when Lehman Brothers (the fourth-largest investment bank)[95] and Washington Mutual failed in 2007, they carried 400 other small and medium-sized banks with them into the void. Another US bank, Merrill Lynch, was taken over by Bank of America, and JPMorgan Chase bought Bear Stearns. In Belgium, the three principal banks (Fortis,

---

94 See below regarding the trick used by Barclays to get recapitalised.
95 Lehman Brothers was made up of 2,985 interconnected companies, with offices in 50 countries.

Dexia and KBC) were saved in extremis by state intervention. Fortis, the country's largest bank, was ultimately taken over by BNP Paribas in 2008. In Germany, the state has come to the assistance of several big banks such as Hypo Real Estate, to the tune of €50 billion, and Commerzbank, Germany's second-biggest bank, in which it has taken over 25%.

In Ireland, all the big banks (Anglo-Irish, Bank of Ireland and Allied Irish Bank) collapsed, and the state had to intervene. In the Netherlands in 2008, the government nationalised ABN AMRO and Fortis NL, and saved ING. In February 2013, the Dutch government nationalised SNS REAAL, a bank specialising in real-estate, at a cost of €3.7 billion (this bank had already been rescued once in 2008).[96] In Iceland, the authorities had to face the collapse of all the big banks, just a few years after they had been privatised. In the UK the government nationalised Northern Rock, one of the country's major banks, and Royal Bank of Scotland (taking control of 84% of its shares), and it saved Lloyds Bank by taking over 43% of its capital. The Portuguese state saved BPN (Banco Português de Negócios). In Spain, the state was obliged, with EU 'aid', to recapitalise its banks to the tune of €59 billion[97] and is certainly not yet out of the woods. In Italy, the bank Monte dei Paschi di Siena was recapitalised for €3.9 billion by issues of 'Monti Bonds' – named after Mario Monti, the former Prime Minister. The Italian state took on guarantees up to €13 billion and implemented a restructuring plan demanded by the European Commission, which included the closing of 5,000 branch offices. Laiki Bank in Cyprus failed in 2013, and had to be taken over by the Bank of Cyprus. The Greek government provided more than €50 billion to recapitalise Greek banks, while in Switzerland, the public treasury was forced to increase the capital of UBS, Switzerland's biggest bank.

In France, a special entity focusing on saving the banks, the Société de Prise de Participation de l'État (state holding company) was created in 2008 and agreed to assist the five biggest French banks (BNP Paribas, Société Générale, Crédit Agricole, Crédit Mutuel and BPCE) by purchasing their super-preferential securities and preferential shares for a total value of €19.75 billion and for an unlimited duration. An-

---

96   Patrick Jenkins, Matt Steinglass and James Boxell, 'Netherlands rescues SNS in €3.7bn bail-out', *Financial Times*, 1 February 2013.
97   In November 2013.

other structure, the Société de Financement de l'Economie Française (Company for Financing the French Economy), of which the French government owns a 34% minority share and the private banks hold the remaining 66%, has borrowed and lent the equivalent of €77 billion under state guarantee. The outstanding balance, at the end of 2012, was €24.2 billion. To this amount, we must of course add the Dexia slate,[98] which has so far cost French taxpayers €6.6 billion, and the €90-billion guarantee provided by the French, Belgian and Luxembourg governments.

The case of Northern Rock

In 2007, as seen across TV channels and newspapers, queues of customers formed in front of branches of the British bank Northern Rock, rushing to withdraw their deposits before it was too late. For European public opinion, Northern Rock became a symbol of the contagion of the subprime crisis across the continent. It was originally a building society, then changed its legal status in 1997 and took on an aggressive real-estate strategy. Between 1997 and its downfall in 2007, it grew by 23% a year to become the fifth-largest British mortgage bank, with 90% of its loans in real-estate. In order to finance its growth, Northern Rock isolated its deposits and became dependent on short-term borrowing. Leverage was used to excess, reaching over 90:1.

In June 2007, the UK banking regulator, the Financial Services Authority (FSA), authorised Northern Rock to use its own model of risk assessment.[99] On 13 September 2007, Northern Rock appealed to the

---

98 Dexia Bank came into existence in the 1990s through the privatisation of public funding structures in Belgium and France. Since the onset of the crisis, it has been one of the principal actors in a local administration financing scandal in France, where it proposed over a hundred often faulty and/or toxic financial products to local administrations. It has been renationalised as a rescue package under guarantee by the Belgian, French, and Luxembourg governments, and has twice been propped up with public money. Several associations such as ATTAC Belgium and CADTM had instigated legal actions against this guarantee.
99 Berenberg, 'European Banks. Capital: misunderstood, misused and misplaced', 2013, http://www.berenberg.de/fileadmin/user_upload/berenberg2013/02_Investment_Banking/Equity_Research/2013_06_13_european_banks.pdf.

Bank of England, depositors panicked, and a bank-run on Northern Rock took place. However, it was not the bank-run that caused the bank's downfall; rather it was the decision some months earlier, by major private lenders, to cut off the funds overnight that chimed the death knell for Northern Rock. The bank was nationalised in February 2008.[100]

Deutsche Bank concealed $12 billion in losses

A lesser-known case is that of Deutsche Bank, the world's biggest bank in terms of its balance-sheet.[101] This illustrates the practice of hiding losses to avoid scaring away investors, and even more importantly, to prevent an intervention by the regulatory authorities, which would trigger a sharp fall in share prices. This all happened in 2009[102] according to three ex-employees, who in 2010-2011 blew the whistle to the Securities and Exchange Commission (SEC), the United States' financial-markets regulatory authority. Deutsche Bank covered up a loss of $12 billion incurred on the US derivatives market. If the bank had entered this into its 2009 balance-sheet, its capital would have been reduced by 25%, and it would have been obliged to call for a bail-out from the German authorities, because banks in Germany must have capital equal to 8% of their assets. Rather than acknowledge the loss, Deutsche Bank ran a big communication campaign to increase the price of its shares. It announced a

---

100 See *Liikanen Report*, p. 59.
101 For a critical and interesting summary of the current and recent history of Deutsche Bank, see 'Deutsche Bank', *Wikipedia*, http://en.Wikipedia. org/wiki/Deutsche_Bank (consulted on 8 July 2015). What is described in this box is also mentioned in the *Wikipedia* article; see the section on 'Leveraged super-senior trades', in which there is a presentation of the collusion between Deutsche Bank and the Nazi regime.
102 *Financial Times* enquired into this scandal and published several well-documented articles such as Tom Braithwaite, Kara Scannell and Michael Mackenzie, 'Deutsche Bank hid up to $12bn losses, say staff', *Financial Times*, 5 December 2012. See also the issues of 7, 8 and 9 December 2012.

pre-tax profit of €1.8 billion in the first half-yearly report of 2009. Between January and April 2009, Deutsche Bank shares went up from €16 to €39.

Three employees had blown the whistle independently. Éric Ben-Artzi, a risk manager, was sacked three days after his testimony to the SEC and is suing Deutsche Bank for unfair dismissal;[103] the second whistleblower, Matthew Simpson, left the bank of his own accord with a severance package of $900,000; while the last one wishes to remain anonymous. This affair was an embarrassment for the SEC, because Robert Khuzami, one of its principal directors, was also director of legal affairs for Deutsche Bank in the US from 2004 to 2009. As for Dick Walker, Deutsche Bank's legal affairs director in the US in 2012, he was one of the principal SEC governors at the time. These events show that collusion and complicity between governments, regulatory bodies and big banks are not the monopoly of Goldman Sachs, however emblematic, but are practised by many big banks, including Deutsche Bank. In 2014, the affair was still under investigation in the US[104] and in Germany.[105] On 26th May 2015, the SEC said that Deutsche Bank made material misstatements about a giant derivatives portfolio, inflating its value at the height of the financial crisis. 'At the height of the financial crisis, Deutsche Bank's financial statements did not reflect the significant risk in these large, complex illiquid positions,' said Andrew Ceresney, director of the SEC's Enforcement Division. 'Deutsche Bank failed to make reasonable judgments when valuing its positions and lacked robust internal controls over financial reporting.'

---

103   Éric Ben-Artzi had worked at Goldman Sachs and Citigroup before joining Deutsche Bank.

104   William D. Cohan, 'Is the SEC's New Enforcement Zeal for Real?', *BloombergView*, 25 November 2013, http://www.bloomberg.com/news/2013-11-25/is-the-sec-s-new-enforcement-zeal-for-real-.html.

105   Frédéric Therin, 'Enquête sur des "oublis" de la Deutsche Bank' (Enquiry into Deutsche Bank's 'forgetfulness'), *L'Écho*, 5 April 2013 (in French).

Deutsche agreed to pay $55 million to resolve the allegations. Deutsche said: 'The SEC acknowledged the bank's co-operation throughout the investigation, and did not bring any charges against individuals in this matter. The bank does not admit or deny the charges outlined in the order.'[106]

Barclays let off scot-free in 2008

Barclays is facing a thorough investigation by the UK government's Financial Services Authority (FSA) and Serious Fraud Office (SFO) into the legality of the bank's manner of increasing its capital. In the depths of the banking crisis, when the FSA was bailing out Lloyds and the Royal Bank of Scotland, Barclays' management wanted to avoid intervention by the public authorities. Between June and October 2008,[107] they obtained €8.4 billion from a Qatari investment fund. According to several sources, in return, Barclays paid high commissions to members of the Qatari family[108] who invested perhaps $400 million. Moreover, it seems that the bank lent vast sums of money to the same investors so that they could then inject it back into the bank's equity.[109]

---

106   Tom Braithwaite and Kara Scannell, 'Deutsche Bank fined for misstating value of derivatives', *Financial Times* May 26, 2015 http://www.ft.com/intl/cms/s/0/f9d4d8e8-03b2-11e5-b55e-00144feabdc0.html#axzz3jNPzLHid See also: Yves Smith, 'SEC Vindicates Deutsche Bank Derivatives Whistleblowers Éric Ben-Artzi and Matthew Simpson', http://www.nakedcapitalism.com/2015/05/sec-vindicates-deutsche-bank-derivatives-whistleblowers-Éric-ben-artzi-and-matthew-simpson.html
107   Reuters, 'UK authorities probe Barclays over Qatar loan: FT', 1 February 2013, http://www.reuters.com/article/2013/02/01/us-barclays-probe-idUSBRE9100E420130201. See also 'Barclays', *Wikipedia*, http://en.Wikipedia.org/wiki/Barclays#Qatari_capital_raising_regulatory_investigations.
108   Caroline Binham and Patrick Jenkins, 'UK fraud office steps up probe into Barclay's dealings with Qatar', *Financial Times*, 11 May 2014; and 'Serious Fraud Office mulls Barclays bribery charges as investigation into Qatar fundraising is drawing to a close', *This is Money*, 15 August 2014.
109   Mark Kleinman, 'Barclays Battles Watchdog Over £50m Deal Fine', *SkyNews*, 17 September 2013; Daniel Schäfer, Caroline Binham and Simeon Kerr, 'Barclays in Qatar loan probe', *Financial Times,* 1 February 2013; Ca-

If one were to make a complete list of the ploys, legal or otherwise, used by large private banks to get through the crisis of 2008 and its aftermath, it would be very long. Many of the banks that gave the impression they were doing without state help were in fact close to failure. As we shall see later, they got huge windfalls of money from governments without having to open their books, without states obtaining a seat on their boards of directors to monitor the proper use of public funds, and without drastically altering their adventurous and, indeed, unethical behaviour.

---

roline Binham, Daniel Schäfer and Patrick Jenkins, 'Qatar connection adds to Barclays' woes', *Financial Times*, 1 February 2013. The Icelandic bank Kaupthing engaged in the same kind of operation as Barclays, at the same time and with the same Qatari partners. See Richard Milne, 'Icelandic bank pair jailed for five years', *Financial Times*, 12 December 2013.

8.
Permission to reduce equity/asset ratios

Markets have become too huge, complex and fast-moving to be subject to twentieth-century supervision and regulation. No wonder this globalised financial behemoth stretches beyond the full comprehension of even the most sophisticated market participants. Financial regulators are required to oversee a system far more complex than what existed when the regulations still governing financial markets were originally written.[110]

All the leaders of the highly industrialised countries have repeated this remark by Alan Greenspan, chairman of the US Federal Reserve from 1987 to 2006. They had imagined that banks and financial corporations would regulate themselves whilst satisfying their own interests. Alan Greenspan adds:

Today, supervision of these transactions is essentially by means of individual-market-participant counterparty surveillance. Each lender, to protect its shareholders, keeps a tab on its customers' investment positions. Regulators can still pretend to provide supervision, but their capabilities are much diminished and declining.[111]

---

110   Alan Greenspan, *The Age of Turbulence*, London: Penguin Books, 2007, p. 529.
111   Ibid.

The supposed willingness of banks and other financial-market actors to regulate themselves is a smokescreen allowing them to do whatever they like.

Thus Alan Greenspan, the leaders of the industrialised countries and an army of experts and financial pundits have repeated endlessly, *ad nauseam*, the old fable of self-regulating markets:

> Since markets have become too complex for effective human intervention, the most promising anti-crisis policies are those that maintain maximum market flexibility – freedom of action for key market participants such as hedge funds, private equity funds and investment banks.[112]

Under these assumptions, national and international regulatory authorities of the banking institutions have systematically reduced the constraints banks are subject to, and the banks quite naturally push their advantage as far as they can!

As we have seen, from 1988 onward, the Basel I Accords stipulated that banks must hold equity amounting to 8% of their total assets. This means that if they have 1 euro in equity (generally shareholders' money), they are allowed to lend 12.5 euros. This also means that in order to lend 12.5 when they only have 1 in equity, they can borrow 11.5. Compared with the regulations that had been in force since the 1930s, this measure was already a significant encouragement for banks to borrow more in order to increase their business activities.

The Basel Committee on Banking Supervision and the Bank for International Settlements

The Basel Accords were drawn up by the Basel Committee on Banking Supervision. This committee, whose membership has evolved since the

---

112   Ibid., p. 530.

1980s, brings together the principal bankers of the G20 countries under the aegis of the Bank for International Settlements (BIS). It is entrusted with four principal missions:

1. To improve the security and stability of the financial system;
2. To establish minimum banking control standards;
3. To spread best practice in banking;
4. To exchange experience and know-how between banks from different countries.

The BIS is an international organisation founded in 1930, charged with promoting worldwide monetary and financial cooperation. It also acts as a bank for central banks. The Bank is a forum for discussion and analysis of the central banks' financial and monetary policies; a centre for economic and monetary research; and the prime counterparty and financial agent of central banks in their international transactions. Fifty-six central banks, including those of the G10,[113] are members. Within it are several committees and organisations concerned with financial and monetary stability in the international financial system, such as the Basel Committee and the Committee on the Global Financial System (CGFS).[114]

---

113 The Group of Ten (G10), despite its name, is an informal group of eleven countries (Belgium, Canada, France, Germany, Italy, Japan, the Netherlands, the United Kingdom, the United States, Sweden and Switzerland). This group was formed in the 1960s with the original mission of supplying additional resources (the 'General Agreements to Borrow', then the 'New Arrangements to Borrow') to the IMF. Its range of activities has gradually increased. The G10 currently meets under two configurations – the G10 Ministers and Governors (annual meeting, in the framework of the IMF and World Bank meetings), and the G10 Governors (every two months, at the same time as BIS board meetings).
114 Source: Banque de France, *Documents et débats*, No. 4, May 2012, 'Glossaire' (Glossary) https://www.banque-france.fr/fileadmin/user_upload/banque_de_france/publications/Documents_Economiques/documents-et-debats-numero-4-glossaire.pdf (in French)

What has been described above, however, needs considerable qualification. In reality, the amount banks can lend (on the basis of one euro in equity) is not 12.5, but 25 (as is the case for BNP Paribas), or even 50 (as is the case for Deutsche Bank and Barclays), while still adhering to the Basel I recommendations (and indeed to those of Basel II, currently in force). How can this be? Because they can adjust the denominator of the equity-to-assets ratio,[115] since the ratio is not applied to all assets. In fact Basel I (and also Basel II and Basel III, discussed below) makes it possible for banks to reduce the value of their assets by assuming that most of them carry no risk. As such, the value in assets is calculated on the basis of the risk they are exposed to. Securities on sovereign debt from OECD members are supposedly not exposed to any risk at all. Loans to banks rated AAA and AA- are considered as entailing a 20% risk. Basel I set up five categories of risk depending on the debtor: 1) states or public authorities, 2) corporations outside the finance industry, 3) banks, 4) individuals and small retailers, and 5) others.

How a ratio of 4% can be turned into a ratio of 10%

If a fictitious bank that we will call Banxia has 4 in equity and 100 in assets that would represent a ratio of 4%, whereas it must attain a level of 8% under Basel I (and Basel III, which was to enter into force in 2013-2015, but has been postponed until 2018-2019). How can it attain that ratio without changing anything? The answer is: by weighting its assets as a function of the risk taken.

A theoretical case will help us understand this situation: for a total of 30 out of that 100, the Banxia bank holds government bonds from countries whose rating is between AAA and AA-. It can then subtract those 30 from its total assets. Why? Because the legislation in force considers that loans to countries rated between AAA and AA- do not require any capital to offset possible losses. That leaves 70 in assets for which the bank must hold a sufficient amount of capital. Its capital / assets ratio of 4/70 is now 5.7%, which is still insufficient.

---

115   We will see below that they can also act on the numerator - that is, the equity.

Of the remaining 70, 30 consist of loans[116] to banks or companies rated between AAA and AA-. In this case, since Basel I (and Basel II) rules consider that these loans represent only a 20% risk, the bank can consider that the 30 owed only count for 6 (20% of 30). Therefore, Banxia no longer needs to come up with equity for assets equivalent to 70, but assets of 70 minus 24 – that is, 46. The equity / assets ratio therefore improves greatly, attaining 8.7% (4 in equity for 46 in risk-weighted assets).

Now let us assume that of the remaining 40 in assets, 2 are loans to companies or banks to which the rating agencies have assigned poor scores – that is, less than B-. In this case, the risk is 150%. These 2 debt assets then count for 3 (150% of 2). The equity required to counter this risk has to be calculated in terms of 3 and not 2.

Let us suppose that of the 38 in remaining assets, 10 represent loans to SME. In this case, 10 counts as 10 because banks' SME debts cannot be reduced: since the Basel authorities consider that they represent a high risk, their 'risk' is fixed at 100%.

The remaining 28 in assets consist of loans to individuals. The risk for loans to individuals is 75%, and therefore the 28 in assets counts for 21 (75% of 28).

In this theoretical case, the assets calculated in terms of risk end up representing 40 (0+6+3+10+21) for total assets of 100. The equity / assets ratio is 4/40, or 10%.

116　This can be loans or financial instruments. It can also be structured CDO products that were rated AAA to AA- prior to the crisis that erupted in 2007-2008.

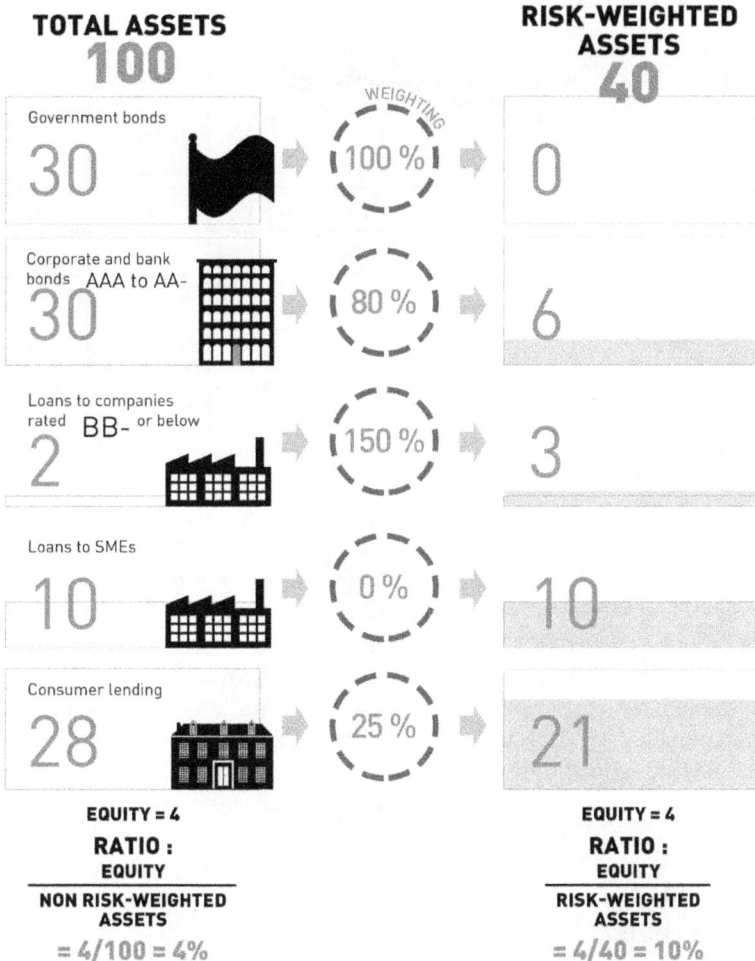

TOTAL ASSETS
100

RISK-WEIGHTED ASSETS
40

	WEIGHTING	
Government bonds 30	100 %	0
Corporate and bank bonds AAA to AA- 30	80 %	6
Loans to companies rated BB- or below 2	150 %	3
Loans to SMEs 10	0 %	10
Consumer lending 28	25 %	21

EQUITY = 4
RATIO :
EQUITY
────────────
NON RISK-WEIGHTED ASSETS
= 4/100 = 4%

EQUITY = 4
RATIO :
EQUITY
────────────
RISK-WEIGHTED ASSETS
= 4/40 = 10%

Bingo! A bank whose equity accounts for only 4% of its total assets can declare that its actual ratio is 10%, for which it will be congratulated by the regulatory authorities.

Perhaps you think this is all merely theoretical? Surely, banks and regulatory authorities would not really espouse and conduct the practices described? Think again. In the next section, there is a very convincing example; and many others are available. Meanwhile, below is a table that summarises the applicable rates for weighting risk, for both Basel I and Basel II.

Table of risk-weightings[117]

Rating / risk-weighting					
	AAA / AA+	A+ / A-	BBB+ / BBB-	BB+ / B-	Lower than B-	not rated
States	0%	20%	50%	100%	150%	100%
Banks	20%	50%	50%	100%	150%	50%
	AAA / AA+	A+ / A-	BBB+ / BB-		Lower than BB-	not rated
Companies	20%	50%	100%		150%	100%
Individuals						75%

Source: Basel Committee on Banking Supervision, 2004 & 2006.

As indicated above, the Basel Committee places a lot of faith in the credit rating agencies. Yet it is a well-established fact that these agencies have been wrong time and again. They assigned ratings of AAA to AA- to companies like Enron, Lehman Brothers, AIG, RBS and Northern Rock right up to the day they went under. Similarly, the rating agencies gave AAA ratings to toxic structured products like CDO until 2007-2008, before they collapsed. However, the Basel authorities have also adopted discriminatory measures regarding loans to SME – which of course are not rated by rating agencies and therefore represent a 100% risk according to the established standards – and to households (a 75% risk according to Basel), which has caused banks to reduce direct credit to these participants in the real economy.

A large share of loans to households have been securitised – that is, removed from banks' balance-sheets and sold to other financial institutions. In this way the banks no longer bear the risks of the loans

117 This table was compiled from documents adopted by the Basel Committee on Banking Supervision. See Basel II, version 2004: *International Convergence of Capital Measurement and Capital Standards*, Basel: BIS, June 2004, http://www.bis.org/publ/bcbs107.pdf; for version 2006, see Basel II: *International Convergence of Capital Measurement and Capital Standards*, Basel: BIS, November 2005, http://www.bis.org/publ/bcbs128.pdf. For risk weighting see the part that begins on page 19.

they grant, which is one of their traditional core activities. The reason for banks restricting credit to SME and households since 2008 is that such loans are too heavy in terms of asset weighting. Private banks have prevailed on the Basel authorities to encourage the development of securitised financial products rather than direct loans to people in the productive economy. ECB president Mario Draghi, working on the same assumptions, found no better way of helping small businesses find financing than by creating asset-backed securities (ABS) containing loans to small businesses.[118]

118   Ralph Atkins, 'Packaged loans to fill EU banking void', *Financial Times*, 19 February 2013; see also Christopher Thompson, 'Italian banks put packaged business loans back on the menu', *Financial Times*, 3 July 2013.

9.
Basel II:
neoliberal euphoria and
maximum permissiveness

The Basel II Accords were a product of the period of neoliberal euphoria during which bankers succeeded in having the few remaining prudential rules dating from the post-crisis period of the 1930s swept aside. As we saw then, Alan Greenspan, Chairman of the Fed – the US central bank – was pontificating about the ability of financial institutions to self-regulate and argued for the removal of all constraints on what he called bankers' 'creativity'. The Basel II Accords came into force in 2004-2005, just before the outbreak of the crisis in 2007. They are still in force in 2013-2014.

Basel II pushed the deregulation imposed by Basel I even further. Two important points in the accords should be underlined. First, the amount of hard capital required was lowered; secondly, banks were allowed to adopt their own method of calculating the assets that are taken into account in calculating the required equity-to-assets ratio.

Basel II and the reduction of the hard capital requirement

The required amount of hard (= Core Tier One) capital, that is, the capital provided by the shareholders and undistributed profits, was reduced at the request of the banks. It is now only 2% of the volume of risk-weighted assets.

Basel I had set a minimum ratio of 8% of equity against the total credit extended by banks. With Basel II, beyond the 2% of hard capital, banks can include various other elements, such as subordinated debt securities that are in fact not capital in the strict sense, in calculating their equity. The various national authorities are in charge of defining what can be taken into account by banks beyond the 2% of hard capital to reach 8%.

So while the reference to the 8% set by Basel I has been maintained, the method of calculation has been radically changed: on the numerator side (equity), the categories of debt that banks can include have been extended far beyond hard capital; on the denominator side, banks have been allowed to define the way they weight assets according to risk.

In Chapter 8 we saw how Banxia could manipulate its assets. Now Basel II makes it possible to also fiddle with the numerator, on the equity side, consisting of the bank's assets and what it can add to them to reach a ratio of 8%.

In the terminology of the Basel Accords we speak of Tier 1 and Tier 2.[119] Basel II considers that Tier 1 (i.e. 4% of risk-weighted assets) consists of two parts: 2% of hard capital and 2% in which the banks can count various elements that are not strictly speaking part of the company's equity. French and Belgian banks, for instance (with the blessing of their national regulators), have included hybrid securities (half-capital, half-bond). Tier 2 embraces elements even further removed from strict capital. Japanese banks in the 1990s, for instance, were allowed by their national authorities to include their latent stock-market capital gains in Tier 2. A few years later, when the Japanese housing bubble burst, they found themselves below the regulation ratios overnight. But that did not prompt the Basel Committee to draft a stricter definition of what could be included in Tier 2 or even in Tier 1. Not until 2010 did it announce more demanding standards, which may be implemented in 2018 or 2019 with the Basel III Accords.

To get an idea of what a bank is allowed to use to reach the 8% target, here is an excerpt from Dexia's 2008 Annual Report:

> BIS-eligible capital consists of two parts:
> Tier 1 capital which comprises: share capital, share premium, retained earnings in-

---

119   See the 2006 revision of *Basel II* (op. cit.), http://www.bis.org/publ/ bcbs118.htm pp. 12 to 19.

cluding current year profit, hybrid capital, foreign currency translation and minority interests from which are deducted intangible assets, accrued dividends, net long positions in own shares and goodwill;

Tier 2 capital which includes the eligible part of subordinated long-term debt from which are deducted subordinated debt from and equities in financial institutions. Tier 1 capital is required to be at least 4% and total eligible capital at least 8% of risk-weighted assets (RWA).[120]

We find similar statements in Dexia's 2012 Annual Report[121] (for more details on this point, see the Dexia box below).

Basel II: giving banks a free rein

Basel II is based on total trust in bankers. Each bank can decide on its own model of risk assessment, and indeed, practically all major banks do.

More specifically, Basel II gives banks a choice between two options. One is to use the method for calculating risk-weighted assets proposed by the Basel II Committee (the standardised approach); the other is to define their own method of evaluating assets in terms of the risks they represent. To adopt this system, they can set up an internal model and submit it for approval by the regulatory authorities – generally a complex process, but an exercise that is well within the means of a large bank with extensive resources and numerous experts.

The standardised approach calls upon standards devised by the Basel Committee that favour the influence of rating agencies. In our the-

---

120   See *Dexia Annual Report 2008*, Dexia, 2008, http://www.dexia.com/EN/shareholder_investor/individual_shareholders/publications/Documents/annual_report_2008_UK.pdf, p. 128.
121   See *Dexia Annual Report 2012*, Dexia, 2012, http://www.dexia.com/EN/shareholder_investor/individual_shareholders/publications/Documents/RA_2012_EN.pdf, p. 78.

oretical example of Banxia, we used the standardised approach. As we saw, bank claims on government or public-sector entities that are rated between AAA and AA- are weighted as a 0% risk. As a consequence, the corresponding assets should not be counted at all. This in turn means that banks do not require equity to write off possible losses on these claims. Claims on banks or corporations that are rated between AAA and AA- are weighted as 20% risk, so banks can deduct 80% in assets corresponding to such claims. Claims on banks and corporations rated between A+ and A- are weighted at 50%, and claims on banks and corporations rated between BB+ and B- at 100%. If their rating is below B-, claims are weighted at 150%. Claims on individuals are weighted at 75%, and on small and medium-sized enterprises (SME) at 100% since they are not rated by rating agencies.

Deregulation played a major role in the outbreak of the financial crisis, enabling banks as it did to pursue the goal of reaping maximum profits by taking ever-greater risks. After the crisis in 2007-2008, it seemed reasonable to expect regulators to have learned a lesson from the debacle and tighten the screws on finance. That did not happen. Instead, as we shall see, in the years immediately after the crisis, further measures were taken to serve the banks and their private interests.

Dexia: a telling illustration of regulatory soft options

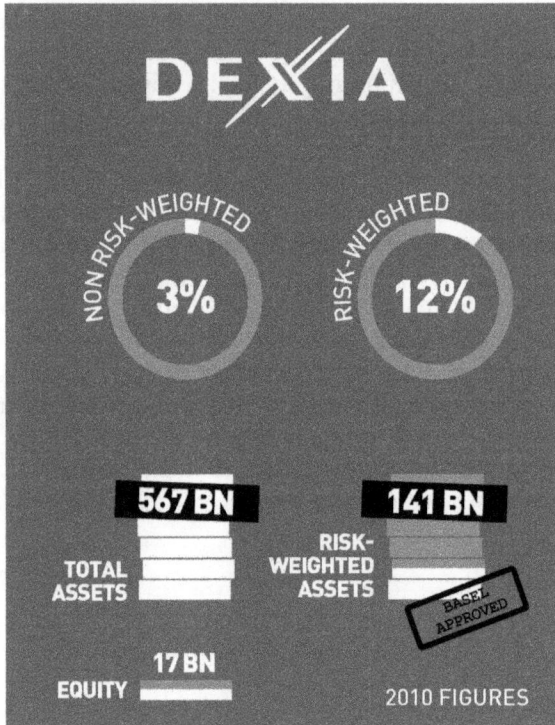

The case of Dexia is a telling illustration of how dangerous the system of risk-weighted assets is, whether using the standardised approach or the internal rating approach. In June 2011 Dexia passed the 'stress test', imposed by the European regulatory authority on 90 major European banks, with flying colours.[122] Four months later it had to be bailed

---

122   These 90 banks represented 65% of European bank assets. See 'Stress tests bancaires : un nouveau round en pleine crise de la dette' (New round of bank stress tests in midst of debt crisis), http://www.lesechos.fr/entreprises-secteurs/finance-marches/dossier/0201290575344-stress-tests-bancaires-un-nouveau-round-en-pleine-crise-de-la-dette-131527.php (in

out for the second time in three years. The report Dexia presented to pass this test is revealing.[123]

While the total amount of (non-weighted) assets reached €567 billion,[124] risk-weighted assets only amounted to €141 billion.[125] In the theoretical example, risk-weighting had made it possible for our fictitious bank, Banxia, to reduce its assets from 100 to 40. Dexia did much better than this in June 2011 when its assets shrank by 75%, from 100 to 25. Hats off to the Dexia conjurors! Truth is stranger than fiction!

In its report to the European authority Dexia claimed that its equity / risk-weighted assets ratio reached 12.01%. This was bound to impress the regulators! If non-weighted assets had been taken into account, the ratio would have been only 3%, which would have been closer to reality. That is what the example of Dexia shows.

Had the regulatory authorities allowed banks, including Dexia, to add financial products that are not capital (for example hybrid securities – see above) to their hard capital, their ratio would have been even more unbalanced. It should be emphasised that if the Basel III regulations (to be fully implemented in 2018-2019) had been in force regarding the equity / non-weighted assets ratio and the equity / weighted assets ratio, Dexia would still

French). The two Cypriot banks at the heart of the crisis in March 2013 had also passed the test without any problem. Of those 90 banks, 59 (the biggest ones) had used their own risk-rating model.

123   See Dexia report 'Composition of capital as of 30 September 2011 (CRD3 rules)', EBA, http://www.eba.europa.eu/documents/10180/26923/BE004.pdf.

124   See *Dexia Annual Report 2010*, Dexia, 2010: http://www.dexia.com/EN/shareholder_investor/individual_shareholders/publications/Documents/annual_report_2010_UK.pdf, p. 100.

125   See EBA report 'Results of the 2011 EBA EU-wide stress test', EBA, http://www.eba.europa.eu/documents/10180/15935/BE004.pdf, p. 2.

have passed the test – which shows that Basel III
will not provide any real solution.

Basel III: more of the same

The Basel III Accords were negotiated in 2010 under pressure from the
crisis, and revised in 2011[126]. They are still undergoing interpretation and
negotiation. And they are not due to enter into force until 2018-2019.

Most of the mainstream media and economic analysts are focusing
their attention – and that of the public – on Basel III, whereas today
and in the coming years, it is the Basel II Accords that are in force and
that have the most bearing on the current situation. Regulatory authorities, governments working hand in hand with major private banks and
the mass media would like the public to believe that serious constraints
have been imposed on the finance industry. This is a lie. As we shall see,
even the Basel III measures will not really change the slack regulations
that allow banks to act as they please. Indeed banks will still be able
to cook their books and fiddle their health reports thanks to a system
where their assets are weighted relative to the degree of risk. They will
also be allowed to trade off the balance-sheet and engage in shadow
banking quite legally, thus prompting them to take more risks. These
two facts alone are enough to undermine the array of small measures
that have been widely and loudly advertised. To show how harsh the
Basel III standards are, banks grumble and try to get the authorities to
soften the measures or delay their implementation. This is just taking
the public for a ride. Political leaders and regulatory authorities are in
total complicity with large private banks.

---

126   BIS, 'Basel III: A global regulatory framework for more resilient banks
and banking systems', December 2010 (revised June 2011), http://www.bis.
org/publ/bcbs189_dec2010.htm.

Why Basel III will not bring in real financial regulation

Basel III calls for a single major change: instead of the 2% hard capital required by Basel II, banks will have to show 4.5%.[127] The remaining 3.5% will be calculated in a more flexible way to reach the 8% already required by Basel I and II.

However, assets will continue to be calculated according to the risks they present and will be assessed by the banks themselves. This completely invalidates all claims about Basel III providing solutions to the banking crisis. Clearly, with so many possible loopholes in the regulations, the requirement of 4.5% hard capital in proportion to risk-weighted assets is a joke.

A study carried out by the Basel Committee in 2012-2013 concluded that the same type of assets might be risk-weighted within a range of 1 to 8, depending on the bank. Bank X may estimate that it needs only 1/8th of the capital that Bank Y considers necessary to cushion the risk on interest-rates in a given portfolio of derivatives. Out of fifteen major banks in nine different countries, the differences, all assets taken together, varies by a factor of 1 to 3.[128] A Barclays bank study

---

127   For a more favourable presentation of Basel III, see *Finance Watch*, 'Basel III in 5 questions', May 2012, http://www.finance-watch.org/ifile/Publications/Reports/Basel-3-in-5-questions.pdf. For the EU, certain elements of Basel III were to be implemented in 2014. The accords still have to be finalised, despite the fact that the European Parliament adopted the reform of banking prudential rules CRD IV/CRR on 16 April 2013. See 'Parliament votes reform package to strengthen EU banks', *European Parliament News*, 16 April 2013, http://www.europarl.europa.eu/news/en/pressroom/content/20130416IPR07333/html/Parliament-votes-reform-package-to-strengthen-EU-banks. In the meantime, the EU Regulation has been published in the Official Journal: http://eur-lex.europa.eu/JOHtml.do?uri=OJ:L:2013:176:SOM:EN:HTML. Note that the bank Natixis has published a synthesis of Basel III and the reform of banking prudential rules CRD IV/CRR: http://cib.natixis.com/flushdoc.aspx?id=70138. *Finance Watch* has also produced a position paper on the subject: http://www.finance-watch.org/press/press-releases/505.
128   See Brooke Masters and Patrick Jenkins, 'Risk models fuel fears for bank safety', *Financial Times*, 1 February 2013. See also a paper published by *Finance Watch* in the context of a hearing at the Bundestag, *Finance Watch statement and opinion on the CRD IV / CRR package* (chart, p. 5), http://www.finance-watch.org/ifile/Publications/Hearings,%20

shows that risk-weighting is used by banks to reduce required equity to a minimum. Barclays bank reports that 20 years ago banks considered that weighted assets represented on average 53% of their total assets, whereas in 2012, they represented only 32%.[129] The European Banking Authority (EBA) has published the results of a study showing that half of the risk-weightings calculated by banks are not based on any objective factors. The study was carried out using the accounts presented by 89 banks from 16 EU states. It shows differences of 70% in the evaluation of the same type of risk from one bank to another.[130]

The Basel Committee doggedly ignores the evidence and maintains the present system of risk-weighting, even though certain other official bodies, such as the OECD, have started producing documents in favour of abandoning risk-weighting in assets. In an OECD report of 2013, the authors propose counting assets without weighting them for risk, in order to obtain a reliable equity / assets ratio.[131] The study, based on an analysis of 94 banks between 2004 and 2011, also shows that the Core Tier One ratio gives no valid indication of a bank's risk of failure – demonstrating the innocuousness of the method of calculating the capital required by Basel principles.

Indeed, several regulators recognise this. Andrew Haldane, director of the Department of Financial Stability at the Bank of England, agrees that the increase in the ratio of equity to the banks' balance-sheets, which is to be generalised as of 2018-2019, is totally inadequate and unlikely to diminish the risks and effects of bankruptcy. Thomas Hoenig, of the US Federal Deposit Insurance Corporation (FDIC), an institution created during the Roosevelt presidency to regulate the banking system, also considers that the level of equity to be required from 2018-2019 needs to be multiplied by at least three.[132] Like the

speeches,%20presentations/20130507_Bundestag_StatementCRDIV.pdf.

129   See article already quoted, Caroline Binham, Daniel Schäfer and Patrick Jenkins, 'Qatar connection Adds to Barclay's Woes', *Financial Times*, 1 February 2013.

130   Brooke Masters, 'Bank risk weightings in spotlight after EBA uncovers discrepancies', *Financial Times*, 27 February 2013.

131   *OECD Journal: Financial Market Trends*, Vol. 2012/2, #103, 'Business models of banks, leverage and the distance-to-default', OECD, January 2013, http://www.oecd.org/finance/BanksBusinessModels.pdf.

132   The summary of remarks by Andrew Haldane and Thomas Hoenig is based on the *Financial Times* article, 'Warnings over steps to reform biggest

author of the OECD report cited above, Andrew Haldane and Thomas Hoenig are in favour of abandoning risk-weighting in the calculation in assets and wish to see an absolute ratio (i.e. with no weighting) between equity and assets. Dan Tarullo, one of the governors of the Federal Reserve, has declared that an equity / non-risk-weighted assets ratio, if fixed at 3% (as decided by the Basel Committee), is insufficient. The US authorities intend to impose a ratio of 5% on their biggest banks, which goes to show that the Basel Committee's decision, within the framework of Basel III, to fix a ratio of 3% really is minimalist. The Vickers Commission, tasked by the British Government in 2011 with making recommendations to answer the banking crisis, suggested a ratio of 4% in 2011, which the British Prime Minister found too restrictive. And in July 2013, the *Financial Times* produced an editorial on the subject, proposing a ratio of 6%.[133]

banks', 28-29 October 2012.
133   In the *Financial Times* editorial of 10 July 2013, 'In praise of bank leverage ratios', we read: '[...] there is a strong case for complementing the risk-weighted metric with a blunter tool: a leverage ratio, limiting how many assets can accumulate on given equity, regardless of the perceived risk. [...] the leverage ratio should be tough enough to bite. A threshold that is twice as high as the one agreed in Basel would not be a scandal.'

10.
Banking regulations: truth and lies

If Basel III does not bring change, what can we hope for from the other banking regulations that governments are so keen to pontificate about in the media? The financial cataclysm of 2007-2008 and its dramatic long-term effects have clearly demonstrated the inability of the financial markets to regulate themselves. They feel no compunction to do so, and this suits them very well. All the crises that have punctuated the history of capitalism clearly demonstrate that fact. After the present crisis broke, leaders had to change their tune: President Sarkozy of France announced that 'Self-regulation as the solution to all problems is finished. *Laissez-faire* is finished. "The market always knows best" is finished'.[134] Yet seven years after the onset of the crisis and six years after the promises of a return to stricter regulation, nothing serious has been done. The evidence is compelling. In collusion with the banks, political leaders and lawmakers have taken very few steps to restrain financial companies.

In the United States, new banking regulation legislation, the Dodd-Frank Act (which includes the Volcker Rule),[135] was adopted during President Obama's first term. Passed in 2010, this law is soft in com-

134   Speech by Nicolas Sarkozy, 25 September 2008 at Toulon (in Damien Millet and Éric Toussaint, *AAA. Audit Annulation Autre politique* (Audit, Abolition, Alternative Policies), Paris: Le Seuil, 2012, p. 34). See also the opinion piece by Didier Reynders, Belgian Minister of Finance between 1999 and 2011: 'Tirer les leçons de la crise financière' (Drawing lessons from the financial crisis), *Le Soir*, 24 April 2009, http://archives.lesoir.be/tirer-les-lecons-de-la-crise-financiere_t-20090424-00MQK2.html (in French).
135   See Daniel Munevar, 'Un pequeño recordatorio de parte de JP: La importancia de la Volcker Rule' (A little reminder from JPMorgan Chase: the importance of the Volcker Rule), CADTM, 25 May 2012, http://cadtm.org/Un-pequeno-recordatorio-de-parte (in Spanish only).

parison with the regulation imposed by President Roosevelt in 1933, but even so there are delays in its implementation. The banks and their lobbyists, together with the Republicans and Democrats over whom they exercise direct influence, have managed to limit its application.[136] The Volcker Rule prohibits banks from practising proprietary trading – that is, speculating with their own funds on their own account. It sets limits on the positions banks may hold in hedge funds or private equity funds that are not subject to serious regulations. Implementation of the rule was originally scheduled for July 2014, but it actually came into effect in July 2015.[137]

After the banks almost failed in 2008 in the United Kingdom, the government created the Vickers Commission, named after Lord John Vickers, a former chief economist at the Bank of England. This commission submitted its report in 2011, and in December 2013 a law reforming financial services was passed that included some of the recommendations made in the report.[138]

At the European level, a commission headed by Erkki Liikanen, Governor of the Bank of Finland, submitted the *Liikanen Report* (see footnote 99 above) in October 2012.[139] The recommendations in both the Vickers and *Liikanen reports* go further than the Dodd-Frank Act and the Volcker Rule and include the beginnings of ring-fencing the many and varied activities of banks. None, however, propose reviving the Glass-Steagall Act or the measures that were taken in Europe after the 1930s crisis.

---

136   See Matt Taibbi, 'How Wall Street Killed Financial Reform', *Rolling Stone*, 10 May 2012, http://www.rollingstone.com/politics/news/how-wall-street-killed-financial-reform-20120510. See also *Les Échos*, 'La réforme de Wall Street reste aux deux tiers inachevée' (The Wall Street reform remains two-thirds unfinished), 12 December 2012, p. 28;Gina Chon, 'Federal Reserve Considers Delay to Volcker Rule', *Financial Times*, 17 November 2013; Tom Braithwaite and Gina Chon, 'Volcker comes of age in spite of protests', 10 December 2013; Gina Chon, 'Banks hope for ballot blow to Dodd-Frank', *Financial Times*, 22 September 2014.
137 Daniel Roberts, 'The Volcker Rule takes effect today after years of delays', *Fortune*, 22 July 2015, http://fortune.com/2015/07/22/volcker-rule/
138   See UK Parliament, 'Financial Services (Banking Reform) Act 2013', http://services.parliament.uk/bills/2012-13/financialservicesbankingreform.html.
139   This was the High-level Expert Group on reforming the structure of the EU banking sector; (*Liikanen Report*), 2 October 2012, Brussels.

However, neither do any of their recommendations clearly propose the separation of commercial banks and investment banks, or dismantling what have come to be known as universal banks (see Chapter 2).[140] These reports and laws, along with the proposed banking reform law put by the French government to the National Assembly in December 2012[141] (adopted eight months later) and the measures taken by Germany, Belgium and others, only go halfway. They propose ring-fencing measures that will prove to be very limited if indeed they are ever implemented. The investment branches of banks will draw on customers' deposits and put them at great risk because no serious measures have been taken to prevent this.[142] As mentioned above, in the framework of a universal bank, the commercial banking section and the investment banking section are jointly liable; which implies that losses by the investment banking section will be borne by the commercial banking section. That is what happened in France, where the €8 billion – as estimated by its CEO, Laurent Mignon – lost by Natixis since its creation were covered by the 17 regional commercial banks of the Banque Populaire group and the 19 banks of the Caisse d'Epargne (savings bank) network, which became members of the same BPCE group after their merger in 2009.

140   As we saw in Chapter 2, the universal bank groups all the banking professions – commercial banking, finance and investment banking, asset management, insurance. Its danger is that losses due to high-risk activities jeopardise the assets of small savers.

141   Full text: *Projet de Loi de séparation et de régulation des activités bancaires, N° 566* (Proposed Law on the separation and regulation of banking activities), *Assemblée nationale* (the French Parliament), 19 December 2012, http://www.assemblee-nationale.fr/14/projets/pl0566.asp (in French). The Dutch and Danish authorities are also working on projects, but the result will probably be disappointing.

142   See the excellent review by Gaël Giraud concerning the French Bill and the measures known as Dodd-Frank, Vickers, and Liikanen: http://www.lavie.fr/www/files/medias/pdf/gael-giraud-note-separation-bancaire.pdf (in French). Gaël Giraud shows that this law is more favourable to the status quo, and so to the banks, than the Dodd-Frank law and the recommendations of the Vickers and Liikanen commissions. See also ATTAC, 'Les 20 propositions d'ATTAC pour une véritable réforme bancaire' (20 proposals by ATTAC for true banking reform), Paris: ATTAC France, 14 February 2013, http://www.france.attac.org/articles/les-20-propositions-dattac-pour-une-veritable-reforme-bancaire (in French).

With regulatory authorities making so many concessions to the banking lobbies, it is remarkable to hear John Reed, the retired director of Citigroup, declare that the abrogation of the Glass-Steagall Act was a serious 'error'. He was one of the most ardent proponents of the disastrous repeal of this law during the Clinton Administration. Yet in 2013, he declared that it was urgent to reinstate the Glass-Steagall Act, adding that the financial sector was very flexible and there would be no difficulty in separating commercial from investment banking activities. He argued that unlike industry, in reality banks do not have large, fixed capital bases.[143]

Although the Vickers and Liikanen recommendations for banks were very soft, the European banks (like their US counterparts) nevertheless organised an intensive lobbying campaign to avoid their implementation. *Challenges*, a French weekly, reported in 2012 what French bankers think of the *Liikanen Report*: 'Usually these reports end up in the wastepaper basket', said one. 'Liikanen hardly knows what a bank is', another sarcastically commented. 'Finland only has subsidiaries of foreign banks'. *Challenges* continued in a different tone, noting this comment from Martin Wolf, editorialist at the *Financial Times*: 'I fear that under pressure from the bankers too many market activities will be excluded from the ring-fencing. This report is a step forward; the next stage must not be a step backwards'.[144] It just so happens that the *Financial Times* has also probed into the banking world. It reports that Christian Clausen, CEO of the Swedish bank Nordea and director at the European Banking Federation, says that the *Liikanen Report* is mistaken concerning the ring-fencing of trading and retail banking activities.[145] Both European and US lawmakers, not to mention top civil servants, have been subjected to intense pressure. In Brussels, where 754 members sit in the European parliament, there are between 700 and 1,000 representatives of the banks, with a budget of €300 million.[146] In 2014 the Corporate Europe Ob-

143   John Authers, 'Culture clash means banks must split, says former Citi chief', *Financial Times*, 9 September 2013.

144   'La cloison bancaire est bien fragile' (The banks' ring-fencing is very fragile), *Challenges*, 11 October 2012, p. 28.

145   Richard Milne and Patrick Jenkins, 'Nordea chief takes a swipe at Liikanen', *Financial Times*, 30 October 2012.

146   'Finance Watch, Le poil à gratter des lobbies bancaires' (The thorn in the side of banking lobbies), *Les Échos*, 23 January 2013, http://www.lesechos.fr/23/01/2013/lesechos.fr/0202521376170_finance-watch--le-

servatory estimated that the number of financial lobbyists in Brussels had increased to a staggering 1,700.[147] The banks can also count on reliable and highly placed allies, like Mario Draghi, President of the ECB and former director of Goldman Sachs. Some voices are being raised among the regulatory authorities criticising the absence of serious banking regulations. Andrew Haldane (mentioned previously in relation to the Basel III project), Chief Economist at the Bank of England, spoke at a meeting of financial directors in London in 2012 to criticise the way the 29 systemically important banks take advantage of the danger they represent to obtain favourable conditions to access money from the ECB, the Fed, the Bank of England and other financial institutions. He considers that the loans these institutions have made to the banks are equivalent to subsidies amounting to $700 billion.[148] Since then, the ECB has lowered its interest-rates, thus generously increasing the value of its aid to the banks.

The G20's Systemically Important Financial Institutions

In November 2011 the G20 established a list of Systemically Important Financial Institutions (SIFIs). Like Lehman Brothers, these banks are considered to be too important for their governments to let them go bankrupt; they are 'Too Big to Fail'. Due to their size and the dangerous consequences if one of them failed, they have become preponderant in the international financial system. In 2011, among the 29 banks listed, eight were of US origin (JPMorgan Chase, Bank of America, Morgan Stanley, Goldman Sachs, Citigroup, Bank of New York Mellon, Wells

poil-a-gratter-des-lobbies-bancaires.htm (in French).
147 Corporate Europe Observatory, 'The fire power of the financial lobby', April 9th 2014, http://corporateeurope.org/financial-lobby/2014/04/fire-power-financial-lobby
148 See the report published by Green MEP Philippe Lamberts, *Implicit subsidies in the EU banking sector*, The Greens/EFA, December 2013, http://www.philippelamberts.eu/wp-content/uploads/2014/01/Implicit-Subsidy-of-Banking-sector_Greens-in-the-EP-study_January-2014.pdf.

Fargo, State Street), four British (HSBC, Lloyds, Barclays and Royal Bank of Scotland), four French (Société Générale, Crédit Agricole, BNP Paribas and BPCE), three were Japanese (Sumitomo, Mitsubishi UFJ FG, Mizuho FG), two were German (Deutsche Bank and Commerzbank), two Swiss (UBS, Credit Suisse), one each from Italy (UniCredit), Spain (Santander), the Netherlands (ING), Sweden (Nordea), and China (Bank of China), and one Franco-Belgian (Dexia). In 2012, the G20 withdrew three banks from the list (Dexia, Commerzbank and Lloyds), and added two (Spain's BBVA and Britain's Standard Chartered).

Andrew Haldane recommended a dramatic reduction in the size of the banks. Thomas Hoenig of the US Federal Deposit Insurance Corporation (FDIC) said that the ring-fences put into place to separate different banking activities are easily breached. He pleaded for the adoption of a Glass-Steagall type law in order to strictly separate commercial banks from investment banks.[149]

In January 2013, the Basel Committee stepped back from enforcing one of the flagship rules it had promoted for banks. They would no longer be required to maintain a safety net of permanent reserves (liquidity coverage ratio – LCR) sufficient to endure a thirty-day period of crisis. This rule would have come into effect in 2015; it has now been postponed until 2019! The financial press announced this victory of the banks over the authorities on its front pages. On 8 January 2013, headlines in the *Financial Times* announced the victory of European banks after the relaxation of the Basel rules,[150] and on 12 January *The Economist* headlined: 'Bank liquidity. Go with the Flow. Global regu-

---

149   The summary of what Andrew Haldane and Thomas Hoenig said is drawn from: *Financial Times*, 'Warnings over steps to reform biggest banks', 28-29 October 2012, p. 3.
150   Brooke Masters, 'Banks Win More Flexible Basel Rules', *Financial Times*, 8 January 2013.

lators soften their stance on liquidity.'[151] Not only is implementation of these measures postponed until 2019, which considering the urgency of the situation is tantamount to indefinite postponement, but the banks can use structured and/or toxic products such as Mortgage Backed Securities (MBS) as guarantee capital.

So banking folly has a great future – especially as there is more to come. At the end of January 2013, to the bankers' delight, Michel Barnier, the European Commissioner in charge of financial markets, announced that he would not follow the *Liikanen Report*'s main recommendation to ring-fence investment banking activities from commercial banking activities. On 30 January 2013, the *Financial Times* headline was 'Brussels retreat on key bank reform'[152] and explained in its columns that the European Commission had retreated on the requirement that could be imposed on banks to force them to separate their highly speculative market activities from their core activities.

In January 2014 Michel Barnier announced a proposal concerning the thirty biggest European banks.[153] This excludes the British banks, which are regulated by the Financial Services (Banking Reform) Act of 2013, following the recommendations of the Vickers report. The bankers responded with cries of horror, because the Commission wanted to force them to separate their potentially riskiest operations and transfer them to *ad hoc* subsidiary companies.[154] *The Economist*,

151   'Bank liquidity. Go with the Flow. Global regulators soften their stance on liquidity', *The Economist*, 12 January 2013, p. 60.

152   'Brussels retreat on key bank reform', *Financial Times*, 30 January 2013.

153   For an idea of who is on this list, see European Commission, Impact Assessment, 29 January 2014, p. 9, http://eur-lex.europa.eu/resource.html?uri=cellar:e186ddob-89b3-11e3-87da-01aa75ed71a1.0001.01/DOC_1&format=PDF.

154   The complete text of the proposal is available on the European Commission Website: *Proposal on banking structural reform*, 29 January 2014, http://ec.europa.eu/internal_market/bank/structural-reform/index_en.htm#140129. For an official summary, see the press release: http://europa.eu/rapid/press-release_IP-14-85_fr.htm. For a favourable review, see *Le Monde*, 'L'ambitieuse réforme des grandes banques européennes de Michel Barnier' (Michel Barnier's ambitious reform of major European banks), 29 January 2014, (in French) http://www.lemonde.fr/Économie/article/2014/01/29/michel-barnier-propose-une-reforme-ambitieuse-des-grandes-banques-europeennes_4356337_3234.html. See also this positive reaction, with qualifications, by the European Green

which rejects the proposal, was quite clear and frankly cynical:

> Happily, Mr Barnier does not have the final
> word. His proposal must now be approved
> both by European governments and by the
> European Parliament. There is still time for
> the elaborate to-ing and fro-ing of Europe-
> an law-making to improve his proposal – or
> to bury it.[155]

Due to the European elections in May 2014, the proposal could not be adopted before the end of 2015, giving the banks ample time to put pressure on the European authorities. In fact, as the *Financial Times* forecast in January 2013, Michel Barnier and the European Commission are not proposing to split up banking activities at all, but only to shift risky assets to an *ad hoc* subsidiary. And the decision to actually require banks to create a subsidiary will emanate from the regulatory authorities in the bank's country. In the Eurozone, that is the ECB, which has little inclination to impose any strict regulation on the banking sector.

Under the evocative title 'La réforme bancaire en Europe sera (aussi) une coquille vide' (Banking reform in Europe will (also) be an empty shell), the French financial daily *La Tribune* aptly sums up the situation:

> This is not really a surprise. The proposed
> European reform that aims to separate re-
> tail banking activities from investment on
> the financial markets will prove to be little
> more than hot air. According to a source

Party: 'Séparation des métiers bancaires. Les Verts au PE appellent à des mesures plus ambitieuses' (Separation of banking activities. Green MEPs call for more ambitious measures), http://www.philippelamberts.eu/sep-aration-des-activites-bancaires-reaction-a-la-proposition-de-la-commis-sion-europeenne/ (in French). *Finance Watch* was also favourable: http://www.finance-watch.org/press/press-releases/828-eu-bank-structure-pro-posal-jan-2014.

155 'Safeguarding European banks. Volcker plus. The European Union proposes a radical overhaul of its banks', *The Economist*, 1 February 2014, http://www.economist.com/news/finance-and-economics/21595469-euro-pean-union-proposes-radical-overhaul-its-banks-volcker-plus.

at the Banque de France, the most recent version of the proposed law will be very similar to the 'German and Belgian laws' already adopted in 2013 and 2014 – in other words, it will not separate much of anything. And yet a real separation of banking activities would seem to be indispensable in order to avoid a repeat of the spread of a financial catastrophe into the real economy by contagion, as unfortunately happened in 2008-2009. Then, a law requiring large banking groups to separate deposit banking activities from trading or investment banking would have prevented taxpayers' implicit guarantee of retail banks – which is legitimate as long as such banks play a vital role in the real economy – from being applied to the riskiest forms of speculation engaged in by those same groups. [...]

Initially, the proposed European law separating banking activities, called the 'Barnier Proposal' – filed before the renewal of the European Parliament last May –, went farther than the French and German banking laws, for example, where separation is concerned. But, after nearly being abandoned under pressure from the banks, it will probably be presented to the MEPs in a heavily modified form. (...) In other words, the publication of the *Liikanen Report* will not have produced any changes as far as Europe is concerned. Yet more dashed hopes which, this time, may very well signal the end of legislative debate about the structure of banks in Europe.[156]

---

156   Mathias Thépot, 'La réforme bancaire en Europe sera (aussi) une coquille vide' (Banking reform in Europe will (also) be an empty shell), *La Tribune,* 29 April 2015 http://www.latribune.fr/entreprises-finance/banques-finance/la-reforme-bancaire-en-europe-sera-aussi-une-coquille-vide-472289.html

Iain Hardie and Huw Macartney do a good job of showing how the German and French governments came to the defence of the interests of the big private banks in their countries and prevented the adoption of measures separating certain banking activities:

> [...]Both French and German governments have sought to undermine the EU-level constraints on their large banks. They have done so by introducing their own national-level ring-fencing regulations, which, while claimed to be in line with the EU proposals, actually undermine them.

> In the final analysis, the *purpose* of the EU and French and German national reforms are at odds: the EU seeks to promote more substantive change in banking structures, but national authorities are using their reforms to protect the status quo. The initial political rhetoric in both countries (largely in the context of elections) called for substantial reform in response to the perceived failures of the respective banking systems. However, the *need* for a national political response to the banking crisis did not determine the *strength* of that response. As the ring-fence debate unfolded, weak French and German reforms emerged, and the *timing* of these national laws – as part of a coordinated response by the two governments – sought to forestall emerging EU legislation. While claiming to separate 'speculative' activities from those central to the financing of the real economy, national authorities are using the national laws to protect structural aspects of their domestic banking systems.[157]

---

157 Iain Hardie and Huw Macartney, 'Too Big to Separate? A French and German defence of their biggest banks', 26 March 2015, http://www. finance-watch.org/hot-topics/blog/1067-bsr-blog-hardie-macartney

A large number of proposals in the long-term financing initiative have now been rebranded Capital Markets Union. The European Commission published a preliminary report highlighting its early priorities for Capital Markets Union in February 2015.

These 'new' proposals by the EU Commission are nothing short of disastrous: Capital Markets Union is nothing more or less than a promotion of shadow banking and a vast operation in support of the universal bank model.[158] As Aline Fares of Finance Watch wrote: 'Whereas the Banking Union aims to make the European banking system safer and to protect public money, the Capital Markets Union aims to increase the competitiveness and profitability of the EU finance industry (hence the support from the financial industry) by developing non-bank lending, or "shadow banking", in Europe.'[159]

And lastly, the negotiations between the USA and the EU on the Transatlantic Free Trade Area (TAFTA) include a chapter that seeks to increase financial deregulation.[160]

The repeated U-turns, compromises and half-measures that we have seen over a long period of time are clear proof that the current governments and authorities cannot be trusted to really put order into the murky world of finance. Banks have contributed to the worst economic and social crisis since the 1930s through the decisions they made. The decisions of the central banks to give them unlimited access to credit, without imposing any changes in the rules of the game, have aggravated its effects.

---

158 For a soft critique of this new European Commission proposal, see: *Finance Watch*, 'Capital Markets Union in 5 questions', 23 March 2015, http://www.finance-watch.org/our-work/publications/1061-cmu-in-5-questions-en

159 Aline Fares, 'Broad support for CMU… from the financial industry', 10 June 2015, http://www.finance-watch.org/hot-topics/blog/1107-cmu-financial-industry See also from the same author: http://www.etui.org/content/download/20408/167398/file/Présentation+d%27Aline+Fares+-+Seven+-years+on+from+the+crisis.pdf

160 Lori Wallach, 'The corporation invasion', *Le Monde diplomatique*, December 2013, http://mondediplo.com/2013/12/02tafta. See also another agreement in negotiation: 'Public Citizen, TISA Leak Reveals 10 KeyThreats to Commonsense Financial Regulations', 2 July 2015, https://wikileaks.org/tisa/financial/04-2015/analysis/Analysis-TiSA-Financial-Services-Annex.pdf

The real crux of the problem is that, because of the size of banks and the devastating effects their mismanagement has on the economy, banking is much too important an activity to be left in private hands. The banking sector uses public money, has a state guarantee and provides an essential and fundamental service to society. Banking should therefore be considered a public service.

Governments must take back their power to manage and direct the country's economic and financial activities. They must also have methods for investing and for reducing public borrowing from private institutions to a minimum. This requires that private banks be expropriated without compensation, transferred to the public sector and placed under citizen control. Such radical action will make it possible to protect savings and financial activities for the common good and to guarantee the jobs and working conditions of bank employees. For this it is essential to create, under citizen control, one public system for savings, credit and investment.[161] The necessary choices involve the elimination of the capitalist banking sector, both for credit and savings (commercial banks) and in the field of investment banking. In fact there should only be two types of banks: public banks with public service status (under citizen control) and moderate-sized co-operative banks. This will be discussed further on.

161   See Patrick Saurin, 'Socialiser le système bancaire' (Socialisation of the banking system), 2 February 2013, http://cadtm.org/Socialiser-le-sys-teme-bancaire.

11.
The nature of the major European banks

In 2011, the ten biggest European banks each controlled more than €1 trillion in assets:

Country	Bank	Assets (in € Bn)	Assets in % of the bank's home country GDP	Number of employees
Germany	Deutsche Bank	2,164	84%	101,000
United Kingdom	HSBC	1,968	120%	288,000
	Barclays	1,871	114%	141,000
	Royal Bank of Scotland (RBS)	1,804	110%	147,000
	LLOYDS Banking Group	1,162	70.7%	99,000
France	BNP Paribas	1,965	99.8%	198,000
	Crédit Agricole	1,880	95.4%	162,000
	Société Générale	1,181	60%	160,000
	BPCE	1,138	58%	117,000
Spain	Santander	1,275	118%	193,000

Source: Author's calculations from *Liikanen Report*.

THE 15 LARGEST BANKS OF THE EU

HOLD
€20,000 BILLION
IN ASSETS

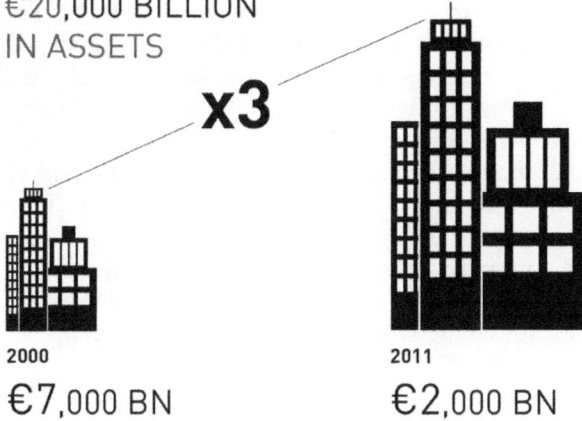

x3

2000
€7,000 BN

2011
€2,000 BN

Ten years ago, none of the big banks had a volume of assets that was greater than the GDP of their country of origin. In most EU countries, banking concentration has increased. In Belgium, between 1997 and 2010 the five biggest banks increased their market share from 52% to 75%, in France from 50.9% to 86%, in Greece from 55% to 70%, in Ireland from 40% to 57%, and in Germany from 17% to 33%.

There are 8,000 banks in the EU. They fall into three categories:
1. 4,000 small co-operative banks with less than €1 billion in assets;
2. Those with between one and €100 billion in assets;
3. Major banks that have more than €100 billion and up to €2.2 trillion in assets.

The twenty biggest banks, that is 0.25% of the total number, own 50% of the total assets – more than €23 trillion (figures for 2011). The small banks are generally more solid and do proportionally more domestic and industrially productive lending than the big banks. Because of their smaller size they are also less risky. Numerous studies show that small co-operative or savings banks are more efficient, reliable and useful than the big banks.[162] They are more helpful to their clients and are more involved in useful local investments, especially when local institutions are involved.[163] According to the *Liikanen Report*, Austria, Finland, Germany and the Netherlands are the European countries where co-operative and savings banks are most effective. In recent years, one of the strategies of the big banks, with the collusion of governments and states, has been to undermine the specific characteristics of co-operative and mutual banks. In France, since 2009, this is illustrated by two telling developments. The 'A' savings accounts (*Livret A*), previously the exclusive domain of the Caisse d'Epargne, the Banque Postale and the Crédit Mutuel, can now be commercialised by any bank; and the centralisation of these savings at the Caisse des Dépôts et Consignations (CDC), to be used as funds for council housing, has been challenged.

---

162   See *Liikanen Report*, p. 58.
163   There are of course many exceptions. Very often public management has abandoned the original purpose of public banking. This is the case of most of the Spanish *Cajas* that took part in the real-estate bubble, or of different *Landesbanken* in Germany.

Deutsche Bank

Deutsche Bank

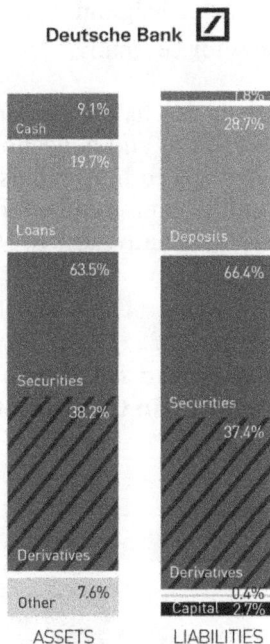

Source: Author's calculations from Deutsche Bank Annual Report, 2012, Available at
https://www.db.com/ir/en/download/Deutsche_Bank_Annual_Report_2012_entire.pdf

As we have seen, the dominant banking model has become the 'universal bank', which groups together big financial groups, which provide the complete range of banking and financial services. Clearly this endangers small savers and public finances. Over the last two decades and more, these institutions have taken greater and greater risks. The share of their revenue that comes from traditional banking activities, such as lending to households and businesses and holding public debt securities, has decreased significantly in contrast to revenue from speculative activities.

The Deutsche Bank balance-sheet is an example of the way the big banks allocate a smaller amount of their assets to traditional lending than the deposits that are put into their care.

This can be seen in the following figures for the amounts households and non-financial companies contributed to the financing of banks (i.e. their debt) in 2011: 41% for Belgium, 23% for France, 28% for the United Kingdom, and 36% for Germany.[164]

In comparison, among their assets, the percentage of loans given to non-financial companies (NFCs) and households was very small: for Belgium, 10% to NFCs and 9% to households; for the United Kingdom, 5% to NFCs and 15% to households; for France, 10% to NFCs and 12% to households; for Germany, 10% to NFCs and 17% to households.[165]

Percentages for deposits and for loans to households and non-financial corporations, in total assets of banks (in 2011)

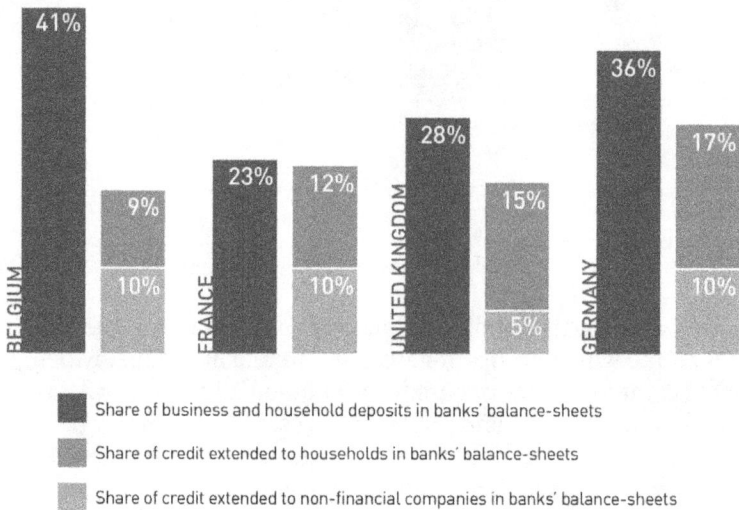

Share of business and household deposits in banks' balance-sheets

Share of credit extended to households in banks' balance-sheets

Share of credit extended to non-financial companies in banks' balance-sheets

Source: *Liikanen Report.*

---

164   *Liikanen Report*, Table 2.3.8, figures for year 2011.
165   *Liikanen Report*, Table 2.3.9.

By prioritising speculation over traditional banking activities, the big banks ran up considerable losses in 2008-2009, which led to the need for massive public bail-outs. Between 2008 and 2011, the ten biggest European banks received more than half of the €1.62 trillion (13% of the EU's total GDP) of public aid disbursed in the form of recapitalisations and guarantees.

As is the case on other continents, the major European banks make their business activities as opaque as possible by setting up a large number of companies. In a significant number of cases, there are more than one thousand different legal entities for a single bank (see Chapter 4, on tax havens). In addition to making the work of auditors very difficult, most of these entities are based in tax havens with a view to paying the least possible tax for themselves and their wealthy clients, and to laundering money.[166] At the same time they continue to create ways and means of increasing their speculative activities and growing ever bigger.

---

166 *Liikanen Report*, p. 52.

The equity gap

According to the *Liikanen Report*,[167] in 2011 equity capital represented only 2 to 8% of the total assets of the major banks. For Deutsche Bank, it barely exceeded 2%. For ING and Nordea (Sweden), it was a little below 4%, while for BNP Paribas, Crédit Agricole, BPCE, Société Générale, and Barclays, it represented about 4%. For the Spanish banks Santander and BBVA, the Italian banks Intesa Sanpaolo and UniCredit, and also for the Belgian bank KBC, it was around 6%.[168]

As we have seen, the regulatory authorities have allowed these ratios to be so low and the leverage effects so high. They created the conditions where Deutsche Bank has 'loaned' 50 times its capital, meaning that a 2% loss in its assets could lead to its collapse. The same regulatory authorities have permitted BNP Paribas to reach a leverage level of 25. There too, the loss of 4% of its assets could signal imminent collapse. Such excessive tolerance makes serial banking crises inevitable.

The size of the big US and European banks

If the declared assets of US banks are considered according to US accounting standards, six European banks are bigger than JPMorgan Chase, the biggest US bank. However, US accounting standards are more liberal than European standards (IFRS standard). The US authorities permit their banks to grossly underestimate their assets, particularly the value of their derivatives (a method called 'netting'). According to Olivier Berruyer,[169] the value of derivatives in JPMorgan Chase's accounts, by US standards, was $75 billion in 2012, whereas before applying netting methods[170] the derivatives would be estimat-

---

167 *Liikanen Report*, p. 47, Table 3.4.13.
168 This paragraph presents the ratio between equity capital and assets. If we compare equity capital to liabilities, we get about the same result. For Barclays and Deutsche Bank see the *Liikanen Report*, Charts 3.4.18 and 3.4.19.
169 Olivier Berruyer is a French economist and actuary. He is a member of the board of the French Actuaries Association, founder of the Diacrisis association, and a regular commentator on economic issues in French-speaking media.
170 For an explanation of netting, see Olivier Berruyer's remarkable and highly recommended article: 'Solvabilité réelle des banques systémiques mondiales'

ed at \$1.662 trillion – 22 times more! Bloomberg says the same: if JPMorgan Chase's accounts were drawn up applying European standards, its assets would total \$4.5 trillion instead of the \$2.3 trillion it declared. Bloomberg goes on to say that if European standards were applied to US banks, JPMorgan Chase, Bank of America and Citigroup would be, by the weight of their assets, the world's three biggest banks.[171] The conclusions of Olivier Berruyer and Bloomberg concur, even though the figures they present differ.[172]

Nevertheless, European banks remain relatively larger than their US counterparts. When compared with the GDP of the country where they are based, their assets are often the equivalent to 50% or more of the country's GDP. The size of JPMorgan Chase, the biggest US bank, is a little less than one-third the size of the US GDP.[173] In 2011 the Swedish bank Nordea represented 197% of Swedish GDP, and Denmark's Danske Bank represented 194% of Danish GDP. As for Belgian banks, by 2007 Fortis was already worth 260% of Belgian GDP, while Dexia was worth 180%.[174]

(The real credit ratings of the world's systemically important banks), http://www.les-crises.fr/solvabilite-banques-systemiques/, 4 June 2013, accessed 12 December 2013. It provides a serious estimation of the true size of US banks and of the real leverage effects of systemically important banks (in French).

171   Yalman Onaran, 'US Banks Bigger than GDP as Accounting Rift Masks Risk', *Bloomberg*, 19 February 2013, http://www.bloomberg.com/news/2013-02-20/u-s-banks-bigger-than-gdp-as-accounting-rift-masks-risk.html.

172   The difference between Berruyer's and Bloomberg's estimates is mainly due to the fact that the latter includes another way of accounting for mortgage loans in the calculation in assets. US standards allow US banks to reduce the weight of these loans in their assets.

173   This is in applying European standards to JPMorgan Chase, that is, in recording the assets as \$2.3 trillion instead of \$4.5 trillion.

174   See Philippe Lamberts, www.pechesbancaires.eu.

Total assets of main European banks (in 2012, €bn and as % of GDP)

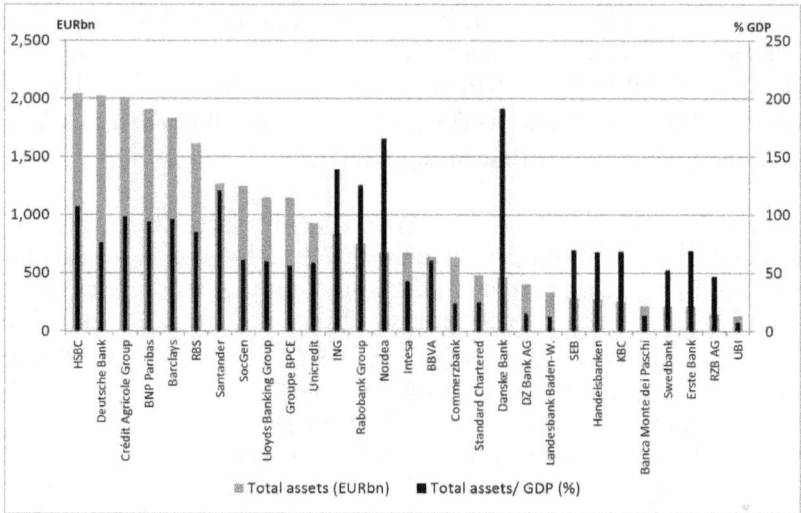

Source: European Commission

There are also four European banks that are particularly active on Wall Street and in the United States in general: HSBC, Deutsche Bank, Credit Suisse and Barclays, who in 2011 held 23% of the US debt market. In the take-overs / mergers market, Credit Suisse, Deutsche Bank and Barclays are respectively in fourth, fifth and sixth positions, just after Goldman Sachs, JPMorgan Chase and Morgan Stanley.

A common characteristic shared by US and European banks is to have made use of the crisis to increase their strength and dominate the market even more. This is particularly true in the United States and the European Union, where the authorities are supposed to promote competition and prevent monopolies or oligopolies. In 2012, the top five US banks accounted for 43.7% of deposits compared to 37.1% in 2007. The assets of the four major banks (JPMorgan Chase, Bank of America, Citigroup and Wells Fargo) have increased by 56% since 2007, reaching $7.7 trillion.[175]

---

175 *The Wall Street Journal,* 12 December 2012.

12.
The art of deception

The big banks camouflaged their real equity / non-weighted assets ratio to pass the June 2011 stress test by showing an equity / risk-weighted assets ratio of more than 10%. Regulatory authorities not only had created the conditions that made manipulations possible but deliberately failed to seriously control the banks.

The CADTM, in its 2012 annual report published in 2013, calculated the equity / risk-weighted assets ratio and the equity / non-weighted assets ratio (leverage ratio) for two major European banks with a reputation for stability: BNP Paribas and Deutsche Bank. As the following illustration shows, the results should worry even the most trusting among us.

Both banks have used risk-weighting in assets to make a good impression. In the case of BNP Paribas, risk-weighted assets represent 'only' €552 billion while their total assets, including the non-weighted assets, are three and a half times that amount and reach €1.907 trillion. As a result, the equity / assets ratio is skewed: officially it was reported as 11.7%, while in reality it is less than 3.5%. Deutsche Bank has camouflaged its accounts even more effectively than BNP Paribas.

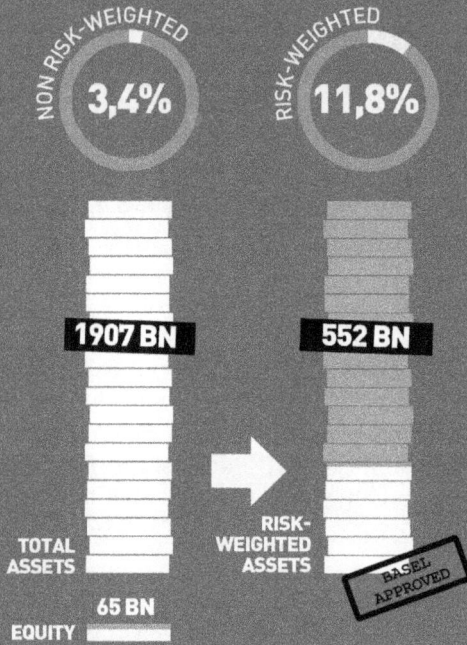

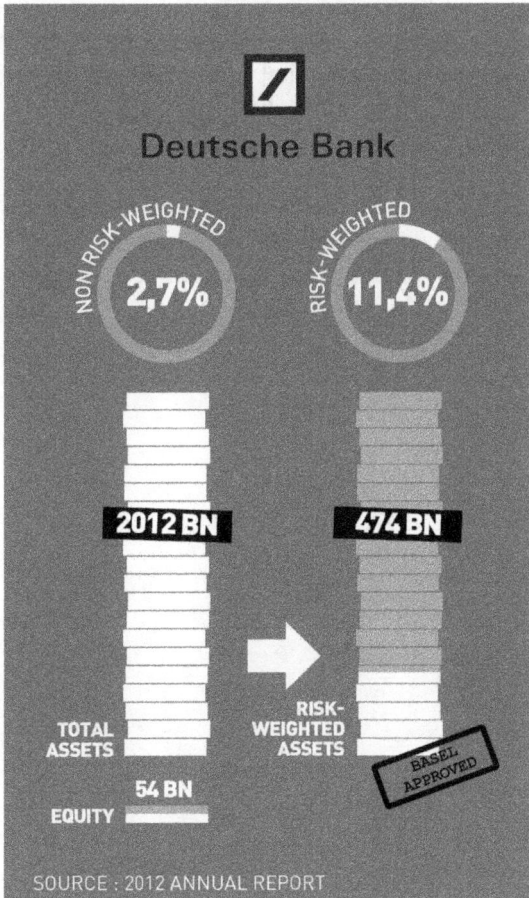

Deutsche Bank

NON RISK-WEIGHTED **2,7%**

RISK-WEIGHTED **11,4%**

2012 BN

474 BN

TOTAL ASSETS

RISK-WEIGHTED ASSETS

BASEL APPROVED

54 BN

EQUITY

SOURCE : 2012 ANNUAL REPORT

If the *Financial Times* is to be trusted – and it is certainly not in its interests to create panic in the markets – Deutsche Bank's situation is even more worrying and scandalous than the above diagram suggests. The leverage ratio of Europe's biggest bank, which appears as 2.7% (or 1/37), is really only 1.6% (1/62)![176] This implies that if Deutsche Bank were to register a 'minor' loss of €10 billion out of its €2 trillion in assets, it would be on the verge of bankruptcy; if the loss was

---

176   See Patrick Jenkins, 'Banks feeling bruised by new capital ratios', *Financial Times*, 5 July 2013, p. 15. The *Financial Times* calculation refers to the 4th quarter of 2012. This is the 'ratio of adjusted tangible equity to adjusted tangible assets'.

of €32.2 billion, all its capital would be swallowed up! In the same article, the *Financial Times* claims that UBS's (the major Swiss bank's) ratio amounts to 2.5%, that of the Société Générale (France) 2.8%, and that of Barclays (United Kingdom) 2.5%.[177] In the US, according to *Bloomberg*:

> If the banks used international standards for derivatives and consolidated mortgage securitisations, the ratio for JPMorgan Chase and Bank of America, the two largest US lenders, would fall below 4%. It would be just above 4% for Citigroup and Wells Fargo.[178]

177   In 'Solvabilité réelle des banques systémiques mondiales' (The real credit ratings of the world's systemically important banks), Olivier Berruyer provides a useful diagram on the leverage of the 29 banks considered to be systemic by the G20; see http://www.les-crises.fr/solvabilite-banques-systemiques/.
178   Yalman Onaran, http://www.bloomberg.com/news/2013-02-20/u-s-banks-bigger-than-gdp-as-accounting-rift-masks-risk.html.

13.
High leverage
is maintained

Bankers and governments claim that the banks have cleaned up and reduced their assets, but the reality is very different. Between 2007 and 2011 the volume of banks' assets increased again to $105 trillion.[179] They did not start to diminish until relatively recently, and then only marginally. According to the IMF, between the third quarter of 2011 and the second quarter of 2012, European banks reduced their assets by only 2%.[180]

The authors of the *Liikanen Report* expected that, because of the severity of the crisis, the banking sector would be restructured, bank balance-sheets reduced, and the weaker firms closed down. This did not happen. The volume in assets has not shrunk since the crisis struck in 2008.[181] It was then €43 trillion and grew to €45 trillion in 2011. Given that European GDP has decreased slightly, in 2011 the assets (including the debts) of the European banks were equivalent to 370% of European GDP!

Between 2007 and 2011 Deutsche Bank's assets increased by 12.4%, and those of HSBC by 22.2%; BNP Paribas by 16%; Crédit Agricole by 22%; Barclays by 12%; Santander by 37.1%; Nordea, the main Swedish Bank, by 84.1%; Commerzbank by 7.3%; Intesa by 11.6%, and BBVA by 19.1%. Of the eighteen top-ranking European banks, only three have

179 More than half of the world's assets are held by EU banks. This proportion of the assets held by European banks increases if Swiss banks are included.
180 IMF, *Global Financial Stability Report: Restoring Confidence and Progressing on Reforms*, Washington: IMF, October 2012, http://www.imf.org/External/Pubs/FT/GFSR/2012/02/index.htm , p. 29.
181 The situation varies from one country to another. Some have seen a reduction in their banks' assets, while others have seen an increase.

seen their assets decrease: Royal Bank of Scotland -28%, the main Dutch bank ING -3.33%, and the main Italian bank UniCredit -9.3%.[182]

However, European banks are trying to dispose of some of their assets (this can concern certain subsidiaries and departments of the banks). What they have liquidated so far is very little compared to their total balance-sheet (with the exception of Dexia and KBC, who have sold many assets). In practice, banks are reluctant to sell some of their dubious products because the value is very low. They prefer to wait for better selling conditions, which may never occur. In the end, when the contracts reach maturity they may have to be written down, with considerable losses.

In collusion with US banks, the Fed has bought a significant amount of US toxic assets (see glossary) – approximately $40 billion per month in 2012 and 2013. Mortgage Backed Securities (MBS) in the Fed's balance-sheet at the end of 2013 totalled more than $1.5 trillion! Since late 2011 the ECB has been accepting deposits of high-risk, toxic assets from Eurozone banks[183] as collateral against the loans it grants them. The ECB decided in early December 2011 to relax the eligibility criteria of certain assets accepted as collateral, such as Asset Backed Securities (ABS) and bank credit claims. The ECB, like the Fed, has also taken onto its balance-sheets some of the bad assets that private banks find it hard to dispose of.[184]

---

182 *Liikanen Report*, Chart 3.4.1., p. 39.

183 This is what the Banque de France says about the decisions taken by the ECB in December 2011: 'The range in assets accepted as collateral has again widened, creating a parallel increase in discounts. The minimum rating for Asset-Backed Securities (ABS) was lowered, adding to the ABS already eligible for Eurosystem operations. ABS, the underlying assets of which include mortgages and loans to small and medium enterprises, will be eligible if they have two single A minimum notations when they are issued, and for their full life. Then the national central banks will have temporary authorisation to accept as collateral additional private collateral claims (i.e. bank loans) that satisfy specific eligibility criteria.' (Trans. CADTM). See: http://www.banque-france.fr/fileadmin/user_upload/banque_de_france/publications/Documents_Economiques/documents-et-debats-nume-ro-4-integral.pdf, p. 68 (in French).

184 According to the *Financial Times*, the list of products accepted by the ECB in 2012 as collateral included 40,000 different financial products. See Ralph Atkins, Phillip Strafford and Brooke Masters, 'Regulation: collateral damage', *Financial Times*, 24 October 2012.

14.
Structured products – time-bombs ticking

In Europe, 70% of the structured financial products backed by commercial mortgages (CMBS – Commercial Mortgage-Backed Securities) that matured in 2012 were not paid in full.[185] In 2013 this rate reached 80%![186] These products were sold between 2004 and 2006, just before the subprime bubble burst, reaching maturity from 2012 to 2014. According to the rating agency Fitch, only 24 of the 122 CMBS that matured in the first eleven months of 2012 were paid (less than 20%). In 2013-2014, the contracts that reached their term amount to €31.9 billion. In 2012 JPMorgan Chase hit the headlines when it lost $5.8 billion on the European CMBS market through its London office because of bad management by one of its agents nicknamed 'the Whale'.[187] This did not stop Deutsche Bank or the Royal Bank of Scotland from creating new CMBS for the European market! Why do these banks get involved in these operations? It is because the high level of risk is compensated by the expectation of higher returns than on other products. Whether they win the gamble remains to be seen.

European and US banks still have several trillion dollars of residential Mortgage Backed Securities (MBS) on their balance-sheets, notably subprime MBS and other categories of Asset Backed Securities (ABS). It is hard for banks to unload these securities without accepting big losses. At the end of December 2011, MBS were selling for 43% of

---

185   Mary Watkins, 'Europe's property loans go unpaid', *Financial Times*, 3 December 2012.
186   Christopher Thompson, 'Bundled mortgage defaults hit two-year high', *Financial Times*, 20 January 2014.
187   Mary Watkins and Daniel Shäfer, 'Mortgage-backed securities make a comeback', *Financial Times*, 15 October 2012.

their nominal value, but there were very few buyers.[188] In the United States, banks and other institutional investors will only buy MBS that have a guarantee.[189] Banks are very discreet about the exact volumes of MBS they hold on their balance-sheets, and even more so concerning their off-balance-sheet holdings.

CLO (Collateral Loan Obligations), another structured product invented during the period preceding the subprime crisis, gives cause for concern while at the same time attracting the most aggressive European banks, such as Royal Bank of Scotland, into the zone of high yields associated with high risk. Used to procure the sums needed by investors for company take-overs through Leveraged Buy-Outs (LBO), as they come to maturity the holders wonder if they are going to be paid in full, and if so, how. The European CLO market is lethargic, but US sales reached $39 billion in 2012, so the European banks purchase US CLO products expecting a good return.[190]

JPMorgan Chase and other major banks propose to create structured products comparable to the subprime mortgage Collateral Debt Obligations (CDO) for credit linked to international trade. CDO were created out of different types of mortgage, which the banks wanted to unload by securitising them (that is, by transforming mortgages into a more easily tradable security).[191] JPMorgan Chase wants to do this all over again using export credits instead of mortgages. This is the same bank that in 1994 created the ancestor of CDO.[192] The export credit market is $10 trillion per year. JPMorgan Chase is trying to persuade banks that are active in this market to structure the credits into CDO so as to render them more liquid. The spin is that this approach will reduce assets, thereby reducing the leverage effect, in accordance with the new Basel III regulations on the need to increase capital ratios. In fact, for JPMorgan Chase and the other big banks that are always seeking profitable financial innovation, this is a new mine to open and

188   *Financial Times*, 21 December 2011, p. 24.
189   Tracy Alloway and Mike Mackenzie, 'Mortgage bankers face the fear in Las Vegas', 23 January 2014.
190   Stephen Foley, 'Investors eye sting in the tail of CLOs', *Financial Times*, 14 November 2012, p. 24.
191   Another objective was to reduce the amount of certain products in the total volume in assets, and replace them with more profitable ones.
192   See Gillian Tett, *Fool's Gold*, New York: Free Press, 2009.

exploit on a major market.[193] And JPMorgan Chase's strategy works well: there are high prospects of further damage from a new bubble.

In 2013, Citigroup decided to put new synthetic CDO on the market. This is the riskiest and most toxic category of all, whose origin goes back to the beginning of the 2000s. Over the period 2005-2007 the big banks put $30-$60 billion of them a year on the market. The crisis put a stop to the issue of synthetic CDO. At the beginning of 2013, JP-Morgan Chase and Morgan Stanley tried, unsuccessfully, to put new life into demand for this category of CDO.[194] A few months later, Citigroup tried to put them back into 'production' and distribution, selling about $1 billion's worth. This action produced an outcry from the specialist press who feared Citigroup was opening a Pandora's box.[195]

A few examples illustrate the magnitude of the risks that banks continue to take. There was the blow to Société Générale in France (€4.9 billion) resulting from the continual mishaps of its trader Jérôme Kerviel. This affair goes back to January 2008 and one might imagine that the banks would have since learned their lesson. Not at all! In September 2011, the Swiss bank UBS announced losses of $2.3 billion through unauthorised transactions by Kweku Adoboli, a manager at Global Synthetic Equities Trading in London. And it was in London that, as mentioned above, JPMorgan Chase's 'Whale' lost $5.5 billion for 'his' bank. These affairs are only the tip of the iceberg.

Speculative bubble on corporate bonds

Many financial-market observers and fund managers consider that a speculative bubble has developed in the sector of corporate bonds, issued by big companies to seek stable financing. So this new bubble is forming on the debt of major corporations. How can an $11-tril-

193   Joris Luyendijk, 'Former head of structured credit: "We saw numbers behave in ways barely conceived possible"', *The Guardian*, 5 April 2012.
194   Tracy Alloway, Tom Braithwaite and Dan McCrum, 'Bid to relaunch synthetic CDO unravels', *Financial Times*, 15 June 2013.
195   Tracy Alloway and Michael Mackenzie, 'Boom-era credit deals poised for comeback', *Financial Times*, 3 December 2013. See also, Matt Levine, 'Welcome Back, Leveraged Super Senior Synthetic CDO', *Bloomberg*, 27 November 2013, http://www.bloomberg.com/news/print/2013-11-27/welcome-back-leveraged-super-senior-synthetic-CDO.html.

lion-a-year market create a bubble? The returns that banks and other institutional investors get from the United States Treasury and the sovereign bonds of the main EU powers are at a historic low. Investors searching for a better sector with no apparent risk find that the corporate bonds of non-financial companies offer a more attractive return of about 4.5%.

Another reason that banks prefer to purchase obligations rather than to take on loans is that obligations can easily be converted into cash on the secondary market if need be.[196] This rush on bonds has caused a serious drop in their yield, which fell from 4.5% at the beginning of 2012 to 2.7% in September of that same year. A major corporation like Nestlé was able to issue €500 million in 4-year obligations offering no more than 0.75% p.a. This case is exceptional, but it shows that the rush on corporate bonds does exist. According to JPMorgan Chase, demand for these bonds is such that the yield on junk bonds was in free fall during the summer of 2012, dropping from 6.9% to 5.4%. If the trend continues, institutional investors may look elsewhere for better returns.[197] Such a consequence would severely destabilise private companies' access to finance.

Pay-in-Kind bonds

The craving for profit is such that companies manage to issue PIK (Pay-in-Kind) bonds, which were in vogue before 2006-2007 then found no new buyers until 2012. These bonds receive no interest until the capital is fully paid off. Of course, the promised final repayment is high, but there is a great risk that the company borrowing will not be in a position to pay back either interest or capital when the loan matures! It would in fact be prudent for a lender to ask how a company

196   In addition, consumer or business loans are reducing or rising only marginally. This trend is the result of the banks applying stricter conditions to making loans. They prefer to buy securities (even high risk ones). Medium and small companies cannot float bonds on the financial markets, and so encounter difficulties in obtaining financing.
197   See Michael Stothard and Michael Mackenzie, 'Fears grow of price rout after the bond rush', *Financial Times*, 21 November 2012; Michael Stothard and Alexandra Stevenson, 'Fund managers warn on corporate bonds', *Financial Times*, 16 October 2012.

that is unable to pay regular interest over the duration of the loan will be able to repay the full amount at the end.[198] Once again, the craving for profit and the availability of liquidity (because of central bank loans) has led to a keen interest in these high-risk products. In 2013 the appetite for PIKs was greater than in 2012, which was already a good year. Behind this market we find Goldman Sachs.[199]

A shortage of good collateral

Up to 2007-2008, the financial markets experienced a period of growth and exuberance. Banks and other institutional investors lent capital and structured products to each other in a joyful merry-go-round of assets without any verification as to the credit-worthiness or the capacity of those signing a contract to assume their responsibilities when it came to maturity. For example, bankers paid insurance premiums to Lehman Brothers and AIG to provide cover against the risk of payment defaults without first verifying whether they had the means to pay the indemnity if required.

In most transactions, the borrower must put up an asset as a guarantee. This is called collateral. The way it has always worked, and often still does, is that the same collateral is used to guarantee several different transactions. A borrows from B and puts up collateral as a guarantee. B borrows from C and uses the same collateral as a guarantee, and so on. If the chain is broken anywhere, there is the risk of not finding the collateral. As long as the markets were euphoric and nobody asked embarrassing questions about collateral, business went on as usual. Since 2008, things have not quite been the same and the co-contractor who wants collateral may insist on having assurances that it is really available if required, that its value is authentic and on knowing what its grade is. Collateral circulates less and doubtful collateral is refused.[200]

198 James Mackintosh, 'Change would pop the corporate bond bubble', *Financial Times*, 25 November 2012. See also the article mentioned above.
199 Tracy Alloway and Vivianne Rodrigues, 'Boom-era credit deals raise fears of overheating', *Financial Times*, 22 October 2013.
200 See Manmohan Singh, 'Beware effects of weakening collateral chains', *Financial Times*, 28 June 2012. See also, Manmohan Singh and Peter Stella, 'The (other) deleveraging: what economists need to know about the modern money creation process', *Vox*, 2 July 2012, http://www.voxeu.org/article/

It is not unreasonable to refuse toxic assets, such as subprime CDO, as collateral. This has led to the beginning of a shortage of collateral. In 2011 and 2012, the Franco-Belgian financial company Dexia suffered from insufficiently high-grade collateral, and was unable to cover its financial needs. In 2012, Dexia borrowed nearly €35 billion from the ECB at 1% within the Long Term Refinancing Operation (LTRO) framework. The enormous loans from the ECB were still not enough, so in October-November 2012, Dexia turned once again to the French and Belgian states for a €5 billion recapitalisation. The end of the programme is in sight but its cost to the public purse will have been colossal.

According to the *Financial Times*, Spanish banks have become experts in the creation of collateral. They created structured ABS products from dubious mortgage credits and other equally dubious products, and pushed them on the ECB as collateral for treasury needs.[201] The ECB accepts low-grade collateral that has been custom-made for it. This example offers more evidence of how the ECB bows down to the bankers.

---

other-deleveraging-what-economists-need-know-about-modern-money-creation-process.
201   See Ralph Atkins, Phillip Strafford and Brooke Masters, 'Regulation: collateral damage', *Financial Times*, 24 October 2012.

15.
New crises ahead

Trading and short selling

High-frequency trading places orders on the market in 0.1 millisecond, i.e. the ten-thousandth part of a second. In the time it takes to read this sentence (about 5 seconds), 50,000 orders can be placed. The bill on banking regulation and the separation of banking activities that was introduced at the French *Assemblée Nationale* (parliament) by Pierre Moscovici, the French Minister for Economy and Finance, on 19 December 2012, describes high-frequency trading as follows:

> High-frequency trading (HFT) is a market activity that relies on computers using algorithms that simultaneously extract and analyse information, and place orders at an ever higher frequency. They can send up to several thousand orders a second to trading platforms, which has occasionally led to saturation. The risks are high, for a coding mistake can result in an anomalous financial move (like the one that almost led Knight Capital Group to bankruptcy in August 2012, for instance). In 2011, 60% of orders on shares at the Paris stock exchange were placed by HFT with about 33% of them resulting in an actual transaction.[202]
> (Translation CADTM.)

---

[202] See texts (in French) at http://www.gouvernement.fr/gouvernement/separation-et-regulation-des-activites-bancaires and http://www.Économie.gouv.fr/files/projet-loi-reforme-bancaire.pdf. In October 2012, the French Senate was pressured by the banking lobby into not taxing HFT, even though it amounts to 40% of transactions on the Paris stock exchange. See *L'Écho*, 24 October 2013.

HFT is speculative and destabilising: it manipulates financial markets to influence prices and so make greater profits. Among the best-known manipulative techniques is 'quote stuffing', which is 'a tactic of quickly entering and withdrawing large orders in an attempt to flood the market with quotes that competitors have to process, thus causing them to lose their competitive edge in high-frequency trading'.[203] The vast majority of these orders will not be carried out, since they fall outside the Best Bid/Offer, but are a powerful weapon when each millisecond counts.[204] To sell a block of shares at the highest possible price, high-frequency traders can also use 'layering', which consists of placing a number of bids up to a ceiling price, so creating layers of orders; once the ceiling is reached, they sell massively before the price has time to fall, and at the same time cancel all the invalid orders. This process fills their competitors' sales ledgers with offers to buy, and then surprises the market by reversing the trend.

On 6 May 2010, the New York Stock Exchange experienced a 'Flash Crash'[205] resulting from HFT, including quote stuffing. On that day between 14:42 and 14:52 the Dow Jones index lost 998.52 points (before recovering some 600 points). A 9.2% drop within 10 minutes was an unprecedented event in the history of the stock market. The incident exposed the involvement of HFT in crashes, representing as it does two thirds of Wall Street stock transactions.

Such accidents are sure to recur. Big banks, all of which use HFT, refuse to have it monitored on the pretext that this would hinder the liquidity of the financial markets.

Proprietary trading – that is, when banks trade for themselves – is a major banking activity which produces significant amounts of revenue and profit, but carries very heavy risks. Banks use their own resources (equity, customer deposits, loans) to buy or sell positions on the different financial markets: stocks and shares, interest-rates,

---

203 *Investopedia*, 'Quote Stuffing', http://www.investopedia.com/terms/q/quote-stuffing.asp.
204 Nanex, 'Analysis of the 'Flash Crash', 6 May 2010, http://www.nanex.net/20100506/FlashCrashAnalysis_Part4-1.html.
205 The FDIC and the SEC published a detailed report on the Flash Crash that occurred on 6 May 2010: *Findings Regarding the Market Events of May 6, 2010*, September 2010, http://www.sec.gov/news/studies/2010/marketevents-report.pdf.

foreign currency, raw materials, derivatives, futures, forwards, commodities (including foods) and their futures, and real-estate.

Trading is definitely a speculative venture, because it is based on short-term price movements that are largely influenced by their own actions. One illustration of the speculative nature of trading is Société Générale's €4.9 billion loss in 2008 because of the positions taken by one of its traders, Jérôme Kerviel, which engaged close to €50 billion. JPMorgan Chase allowed $100 billion to be engaged by a person in its London proprietary trading department staff known as 'the Whale'. The sums involved by the banks in proprietary trading action are so huge that the losses can threaten the survival of the bank itself.

Short selling is the sale of stock that the seller does not hold at the moment, but intends to buy later so as to provide it to the buyer. There are two basic types of short selling. The first is covered short selling: in this case, the seller has borrowed (or made a borrowing agreement for) the stock that must eventually be sold at the end of the operation. In fact, the stock that this person borrows will be sold, and he or she promises to return the same kind of stock to the lender. The second type is naked or uncovered short selling: in this case, there is no borrowed stock or borrowing agreement before the sale of the stock. The seller must then buy identical stock to be able to pass it on to the buyer.[206]

Yet according to the Fédération Bancaire Française (French Banking Federation), 'short selling is a useful device for the proper functioning of markets. (...) It increases the liquidity of the market'.[207] Who are they fooling?

Short selling is done by a large number of market participants, such as banks, hedge funds and financial institutions, including pension funds and insurance companies. It is a purely speculative activity. A speculator gambles that the price of the share concerned will fall and, if the guess is right, it is purchased at a lower price than sold, thus making a profit. This kind of practice undermines market stability.

206   Quoted from Hedge Funds Consistency Index, 'Definitions', http://www.hedgefund-index.com/d_shortselling.asp.
207   Fédération bancaire française (FBF), *Rapport d'activités 2010* (2010 Annual Report), Paris, 2011.

Short selling aggravated the sharp fall in the price of bank shares during summer 2011. It is easy to understand why this kind of activity should simply be prohibited.[208]

Big banks still play with fire because they are convinced that whenever they need it, the government will bail them out. This encourages them to take greater risks without ever having to face the consequences; state guarantees play a key role in bank bail-outs. Thus banks have no serious obstacles in their path; they are continually flirting with catastrophe. In spite of showy campaigns to rebuild their customers' confidence they have no intention whatsoever of doing anything other than seeking maximum profits and influencing governments' decisions in their own best interests – against the interests of the population. Their strength lies in governments' current *laissez-faire* attitudes.

208   The issue of Credit Default Swaps (CDS) is discussed in Chapter 6 Box 3. It was examined in some detail in Éric Toussaint's article, 'CDS and rating agencies: factor(ie)s of risk and destabilisation', CADTM, 23 September 2011, http://cadtm.org/CDS-and-rating-agencies-factor-ie.

16.
Sovereign debt
is not to blame

Mainstream mass media continually espouse the discourse of bankers and political leaders who claim that the reason for the banks' current fragility is the burden of public debt. This amounts to systematic disinformation of the public. The same lie is constantly repeated, so some trace of it is bound to stay in people's minds. The idea that public debt threatens bank stability has become both a smokescreen to conceal the banks' responsibilities and a pretext to justify antisocial policies to clean up public finances. It is thus essential to shed light on the issue and propose some counter-arguments.

Since 2007-2008, major central banks (the ECB, the Bank of England, the Fed and the Bank of Switzerland) have given absolute priority to preventing the collapse of the private banking system. Contrary to the dominant discourse, the main risk that threatens banks is not a government deciding to suspend payment of its sovereign debt. None of the bank bankruptcies that have come about since 2007 was because of such a default. None of the governments' bail-outs was needed because an over-indebted state had defaulted. The real threat for banks is the private debt they have schemed to build up since deregulation started at the end of the 1970s. Since the crisis broke out in 2007-8, beyond empty promises and grand declarations, governments have not taken any measures to end laissez-faire. Private banks' balance-sheets and off-balance-sheet valuations are still loaded with bad assets. As we have seen, they range from toxic assets that are like time-bombs, to non-liquid assets (i.e. assets that cannot be sold on the financial markets), including assets of overestimated value. Selling and depreciating assets in order to defuse their explosive potential is not sufficient. A significant number of them depend on short-term financing (provided or guaranteed by public bodies with taxpayers' money).[209]

his is how Dexia, a French-Belgian bank that behaves like a large hedge fund, found itself on the verge of bankruptcy three times within four years: in October 2008, October 2011[210] and October 2012[211] before its final demise in that year. The Belgian daily *Le Soir* observed that the equity of Dexia's parent company fell from €19.2 billion to €2.7 billion between late 2010 and late 2011. In the consolidated accounts, equity had become negative (-€2.3 billion on 30 June 2012).[212] At the end of 2011, Dexia SA's immediately payable debts amounted to €413 billion and debts on derivatives to €461 billion. Taken together, these amounts are equivalent to over 2.5 times Belgium's GDP. Yet Dexia's executive officers, the Belgian Deputy Prime Minister Didier Reynders and major

---

209 Many banks depend on short-term financing because they encounter huge difficulties in borrowing from the private sector at a sustainable rate (i.e. as low as possible), for instance through issuing debt securities. The ECB's decision to give a loan of over €1 trillion at a 1% interest rate over three years to more than 800 European banks from the end of 2011 to early 2012 in the context of LTRO (Long-Term Refinancing Operations) was a life-jacket that saved many of them. Subsequently, the ECB has repeatedly lowered its reference rate, down to 0.05% in September 2014. It has even announced that the LTRO will continue.

210 On the October 2011 episode, see Éric Toussaint, 'Dexia Krach: The start of a domino effect in the EU?', CADTM, 4 October 2011, http://cadtm. org/Dexia-Krach-The-start-of-a-domino.

211 On the October 2012 episode that resulted in a new bail-out in the guise of recapitalisation, see Éric Toussaint's independent opinion piece in *Le Soir*, 2 November 2012, 'Fallait-il à nouveau injecter de l'argent dans Dexia?' (Did more money need to be injected into Dexia?), http://cadtm. org/Fallait-il-a-nouveau-injecter-de-l; see also 'Pour sortir du piège des recapitalisations à répétition, le CADTM demande l'annulation des garanties de l'État belge aux créanciers du groupe Dexia' (To get out of the serial recapitalisation trap, the CADTM demands cancellation of Belgium's guarantees to Dexia creditors), CADTM, 31 October 2012, http://cadtm.org/Pour-sortir-du-piege-des; CADTM, 'Pourquoi le CADTM introduit avec ATTAC un recours en annulation de l'arrêté royal octroyant une garantie de €54 milliards (avec en sus les intérêts et accessoires) à Dexia SA et Dexia Crédit Local SA' (Why the CADTM and ATTAC are suing to cancel the royal decree guaranteeing 54 billion to Dexia), CADTM, 22 December 2011, http:// cadtm.org/Pourquoi-le-CADTM-introduit-avec.

212 Pierre-Henri Thomas, Bernard Demonty, 'Dexia sera recapitalisé pour le 7 Novembre' (Dexia to be recapitalised by 7 November), *Le Soir*, 31 October 2012, p. 19 (in French), http://tinyurl.com/omkq5mz.

media still claimed that Dexia's financial difficulties resulted from the crisis of sovereign debt in the south of the Eurozone. As a matter of fact, Greece's debt to Dexia was under €2 billion in October 2011 – that is, 1/200th of the bank's immediately payable debts. By October 2012 Dexia's shares were worth about €0.18, or 1% of their value in September 2008. However, the French and Belgian governments decided yet again to bail out the bad bank created for Dexia's toxic assets, thus increasing their countries' public debt. In Spain, BFA (Banco Financiero y de Ahorros, Bankia's parent company) almost went bankrupt, again because of dubious financial dealings and not at all because of a government or central bank defaulting. Since 2008 the same pattern has been played out again about thirty times in Europe and the US. Public bodies have rushed to bail out private banks with public loans. Sovereign debt has increased as a consequence. The main reason for the steep increase of the public debt since 2008 can be traced to private banks.

In a recent survey that was not reported in the media and which did not produce flowery statements from bankers or political leaders, the IMF (for once) confirmed our analysis. The survey shows that a high level of private debt is less favourable to growth than a high level of public debt. The British conservative weekly *The Economist* states in its 26 October 2013 edition:

> High private debt is more detrimental to growth than high public debt, according to recent research by the IMF. Indeed the IMF study finds that excessive sovereign debt reduces growth only when household and corporate sectors are heavily indebted too.[213]

Finally, while sovereign debt has not so far resulted in any disaster for the banking sector, it is clear that in countries such as Spain and Italy, banks have greatly increased their purchases of debt securities issued by their governments. They have two good reasons for doing this: on the one hand they can rely on the ECB's generous loans at very low interest-rates (between 0.05% and 1%), and on the other, those securities have a high return rate (between 4 and 7% over 10

---

213 'Debtor's prison. The Eurozone is blighted by private debt even more than by government debt', *The Economist*, 26 October 2013, pp. 69-70.

years depending on when they were issued). But austerity measures are so extreme that it is by no means certain that the Spanish and Italian governments will be in a position to pay. The problem is not imminent, but there may be difficulties in the future.[214]

Ultimately, these difficulties will affect states and their populations if radical measures are not taken – starting with the cancellation of state guarantees to certain banks, such as Dexia. To achieve fundamental change in the banking system, it is necessary to expose collusion between political leaders and bank executives and put an end to their impunity when they commit crimes.

---

214   The inevitable recurrence of these problems is why this book's central thesis is that we must both cancel illegitimate public debt and socialise the banking sector. If we take these two measures (with a number of additional ones), it is quite possible to find a positive way out of the crisis.

17.
Speculation on raw materials and food

Banks, through their trading activities, have become the principal speculators on the over-the-counter (OTC) markets and ultimately on the commodity market, as they possess far greater financial means than other protagonists in the field. A quick glance at the Commodity Business Awards[215] website reveals a list of banks and brokers playing a major role both on the commodity markets (the markets where raw materials are bought and sold) and on the commodity-backed derivatives market. The most frequent players among these banks are BNP Paribas, Morgan Stanley, Credit Suisse, Deutsche Bank and Société Générale. Some banks go even further by developing instruments that enable them to directly influence the stocks of raw materials. Such is the case for Credit Suisse, in partnership with Glencore-Xstrata, the biggest international trading/brokerage company dealing in raw materials.[216]

---

215   Commodity Business Awards 2013, http://www.commoditybusinessawards.com/winners/winners-2013.html.
216   Glencore-Xstrata is a trading and brokerage company for raw materials founded by trader Marc Rich. They are based in Baar, in the canton of Zug in Switzerland, known to be a tax-haven favoured by high-flying tax evaders. Marc Rich, who died in 2013, was repeatedly charged with corruption and tax evasion. US President Bill Clinton gave him amnesty on the last day of his presidential term, which caused quite a scandal. Glencore-Xstrata owns part or all of 150 mines and metallurgy sites. According to available data, before its 2013 merger with Xstrata, Glencore controlled about 60% of global zinc stocks, 50% of copper, 30% of aluminium, 25% of coal, 10% of cereals and 3% of oil. In 2008, this highly controversial company won the Public Eye Award for Most Irresponsible Multinational. Present in 50 countries, Glencore-Xstrata has 190,000 employees (see: http://www.glencorexstrata.com/about-us/at-a-glance/ and http://www.glencorexstrata.com/assets/Uploads/20130711-GlencoreXstrata-Factsheet.pdf). It is headed by its main shareholder, with 16% of the shares, Ivan Glasenberg, who is said to have

Among European banks, BNP Paribas, along with Deutsche Bank, is one of the most influential banks in the commodity market, playing a key role in the raw-materials derivatives sector.[217] In 2013, BNP Paribas created and marketed a new product containing various credits for raw materials traders that they could use to buy oil, minerals and agricultural produce. The issue of these credits in the form of bonds has two objectives: first, to remove them from the banks' books (as they are heavily weighted in terms of risk); second, to earn revenue on the sale of these structured products. Before launching this new product on the markets, BNP Paribas managed to get the Fitch Agency to attribute a Triple A rating to the higher tranches of this potentially high-risk product.[218] The other big banks are keeping an eye on the outcome with a view to creating their own, should BNP Paribas succeed in winning over pension funds and other institutional investors to their commodity-backed securities.

Several US banks have gone further in the strategy for control in a share of the commodity market, specifically JPMorgan Chase, Morgan Stanley and Goldman Sachs. For example, in the first four months of 2013, JPMorgan Chase imported 31 million barrels of oil to the United States! The US banks own oil refineries, power stations, power grids, metals, companies stocking metals, agricultural produce, shale-gas exploitation companies, and more. How did this come about? In 2003, the Fed authorised the universal bank Citigroup to

been paid around $60 million in 2013; see 'Les rémunérations des patrons de Glencore Xstrata et Credit Suisse épinglées' ('Shamefully high pay for Glencore and Credit Suisse CEOs'), *L'Express*, 25 August 2013, http://lexpansion.lexpress.fr/economie/les-remunerations-des-patrons-de-glencore-xstrata-et-credit-suisse-epinglees_399326.html) (in French). Credit Suisse and Glencore-Xstrata are close collaborators on the Chinese market. Other big companies specialised in commodities trading (other than the banks, which are very active) are Vitol (the Netherlands), Cargill (US), Trafigura (the Netherlands), Noble Group (Hong Kong/Singapore), Wilmar (Singapore), Louis Dreyfus Commodities (France), Mitsui (Japan), Mitsubishi (Japan) and ADM (US). In 2012, the combined income of Glencore and these 9 companies amounted to a colossal $1.2 trillion. See Javier Blas, 'Commodities: tougher times for the trading titans', *Financial Times*, 14 April 2013.
217 See the dedicated BNP Paribas site: http://cib.bnpparibas.com/Products-services/Managing-your-risks-and-assets/Commodity-Derivatives/page.aspx/100.
218 Alaj Makan, 'BNP Paribas in commodity securitisation first', *Financial Times*, 22 August 2013.

buy the trading company Phibro, on the grounds that it was normal to complement banking activity on the derivatives market in commodity futures by holding stocks of raw materials (oil, cereals, gas, minerals, etc.). As for Morgan Stanley and Goldman Sachs – who until 2008[219] had the status of investment bankers – after the 1999 law on banking reform that accompanied the abrogation of the Glass-Steagall Act they were able to buy power stations, oil tankers and other infrastructures. This is how Morgan Stanley came to own barges, tankers, pipelines and oil and gas terminals. JPMorgan Chase, for their part, bought up the Royal Bank of Scotland's commodities division in 2010 for $1.7 billion, enabling them to acquire 74 metal storage warehouses in the UK and the USA, while Goldman Sachs hold 112. Thus these two banks together hold more metal storage warehouses than Glencore, who has 179. Storage warehouses are crucial, especially if a company or a cartel of companies (for example banks) wants to speculate on prices by maximum stockpiling in order to force prices up or by destocking to bring them down. This is exactly what has been happening in, for example, the aluminium market, since 2008. According to an investigation conducted by the *New York Times*, since 2010 when Goldman Sachs bought up the aluminium warehouses of Detroit, delivery time for aluminium bars has gone from 6 weeks to 16 months. Prices have risen sharply despite the fact that the amount of aluminium stocks on the global market has increased. As a result, there have been strong reactions from companies which consume large quantities of aluminium in the manufacture of cans, such as Coca-Cola and the brewer Miller. Goldman has amassed $220 million in revenue from aluminium stockpiling in Detroit alone.[220]

After making juicy profits by manipulating stock prices, the most active banks in the actual commodity markets have adopted an exit strategy. This is for the following reasons: first, the regulatory authorities have become aware of the manipulations practised by several banks. JPMorgan Chase, Barclays and Deutsche Bank have been

219   Morgan Stanley and Goldman Sachs obtained a universal banking licence in the middle of the crisis to obtain stronger support from the state and avoid the same fate as Lehman Brothers.
220   'Des banques Americaines accusées de manipuler les matières premières' (US banks accused of manipulating raw materials), *L'Écho*, 24 July 2013, http://www.lecho.be/actualite/entreprises_finance/Des_banques_Americaines_accusees_de_manipuler_les_matieres_premieres.9379357-3027.art (in French).

fined over several incidents, including the manipulation of California's electricity market. JPMorgan Chase has agreed to pay a fine of $410 million in this affair.[221] The American authorities, under pressure from companies competing with banks and faced with popular discontent with the banking industry as a whole, are seriously considering putting a curb on banks' activities on the markets of actual commodities. Second, the hard capital (Core Tier 1) required for investments in trading companies is greater than for other types of investment (such as sovereign debt, for example). Consequently, as the banks have to increase their own equity/risk-weighted-assets ratio, they reckon that they are better off getting rid of all or part of their investments in the physical commodity market.[222] Nevertheless, the banks will maintain high activity in the commodity-based derivatives market and in all areas of the financial markets relating to raw materials. The damage that they can do will remain considerable unless radical measures are taken.

These banks are the prime movers and shakers in the development of the speculative bubble, which has grown out of the commodity markets. When it finally bursts, the fallout will hit the banks, which will mean further damage. Even more serious are the disastrous repercussions for the populations of countries in the South, which export raw materials. People all over the planet stand to be affected in one way or another.

Food and oil price inflation in 2007-2008 due to speculation

Speculation on the main US exchanges where world prices of commodities (farm products and raw materials) are negotiated played a fundamental role in the food price increases in 2007–2008. This price explosion caused a dramatic increase of 140 million in the numbers suffering from malnutrition, bringing the total to one billion (one person in seven). The principal players in this speculation were not

---

221   Gregory Meyer and Camilla Hall, 'JPMorgan Chase nears commodities sale', *Financial Times,* 5 February 2014. As for Barclays, they paid a fine of $470 million in the same case.
222   In early 2014, JPMorgan Chase announced their intention to sell off their actual commodities activities, quickly followed by Deutsche Bank. Morgan Stanley made an agreement with the Russian oil company Rosneft, handing over part of their business.

isolated cowboys, but institutional investors: investment banks,[223] pension funds, mutual funds, insurance companies, commercial banks and the big brokerage companies such as Cargill. Hedge funds and sovereign wealth funds[224] were also involved, though to a lesser extent.[225]

Michael W. Masters, who directed a Wall Street hedge fund for twelve years, testified about the harmful effect that institutional investors have on commodity price increases before a Congressional Committee held to examine this in Washington on 20 May 2008 [226] He declared: 'You have asked the question "Are institutional investors contributing to food and energy price inflation?" And my unequivocal answer is "Yes."' In his testimony, he explained that food and energy price inflation is not the result of insufficient supply but rather a sudden increase in demand from new players in the commodity 'futures' market. In the futures market, investors purchase the upcoming production – the next wheat harvest or oil production three or six years down the line. Theoretically, the principal investors in these markets are companies wishing to guarantee their supplies of commodities essential to their operations, for example airline companies that ensure their future supplies of fuel, or agro-industrial firms that purchase specific cereals. Masters demonstrated that in the US, assets allocated by institutional investors to commodity index trading rose from $13 billion at the end of 2003 to $260 billion by March 2008.[227] The

---

223   Goldman Sachs, Morgan Stanley and, until their dissolution or takeover, Bear Stearns, Lehman Brothers and Merrill Lynch.
224   Sovereign wealth funds are public institutions, which, apart from a few exceptions, belong either to emerging countries like China or to oil-exporting countries. The first sovereign wealth funds were created during the second half of the twentieth century by those governments that wanted to put aside a portion of their earnings from oil and manufactured products.
225   Globally, at the beginning of 2008, institutional investors represented $70 trillion, sovereign wealth funds $3 trillion, and hedge funds $1 trillion.
226   Testimony of Michael W. Masters, Managing Member / Portfolio Manager, Masters Capital Management, LLC, before the Committee on Homeland Security and Governmental Affairs of the United States Senate, 20 May 2008, http://hsgac.senate.gov/public/_files/052008Masters.pdf.
227   Testimony of Michael W. Masters, 'Assets allocated to commodity index trading strategies have risen from $13 billion at the end of 2003 to $260 billion as of March 2008', ibid., p. 3.

prices of the 25 commodities listed on these markets climbed 183% during the same period. He explained that the commodity market is a narrow market.[228] Institutional investors such as pension funds need only allocate 2% of their assets to overwhelm the system. In 2004, the total value of contracts on this market was about $180 million whereas the total value worldwide traded on shares was $44 trillion, about 240 times more. Masters stated that during the same year, institutional investors had placed $25 billion in the futures market, about 14% of the market, and then, during only the first quarter of 2008, they dropped $55 billion into the futures market. It is not surprising that prices skyrocketed.[229]

The price of commodities on the futures market has an immediate impact on the current price of these goods. When institutional investors purchased enormous quantities of grain between 2007 and 2008, this resulted in immediate massive price inflation.

In 2008 the Commodity Futures Trading Commission (CFTC) ruled that institutional investors could not be considered as speculators; these destructive players are legitimate 'commercial market participants'. This allows the CFTC to assert that speculation does not influence the commodity market's prices. Michael W. Masters criticises the CFTC severely, but not as severely as Michael Greenberger, lecturer in law at the University of Maryland and ex- Director of the Division of Trading and Markets at the CFTC from 1997 to 1999. Before a Senate Committee[230] held on 3 June 2008, he criticised the laxity of CFTC directors who bury their heads when faced with energy-price manipulations by the institutional investors, and quoted a number of their declarations that would make up an anthology of human hypocrisy and idiocy. According to Michael Greenberger, an acknowledged expert, 80% to 90% of energy transactions on US stock markets are speculative.

---

228 Testimony of Michael W. Masters, ibid., p. 5.
229 A critique of the CFTC can be found in Michael W. Masters' Testimony: The CFTC Has Invited Increased Speculation', p. 7.
230 Testimony of Michael Greenberger, Law School Professor at the University of Maryland, before the US Senate Committee regarding 'Energy Market Manipulation and Federal Enforcement Regimes', 3 June 2008, http://www.michaelgreenberger.com/files/June_3_2008_testimony.pdf, June 3, 2008, p. 22.

On 22 September 2008, in the heart of the United States' financial crisis, when President Bush announced a bail-out plan of $700 billion (not to mention the massive liquidities also made available), the price of soybeans jumped 61.5% because of speculation.

Jacques Berthelot, who devotes six pages of his study[231] to the effects of speculation, also shows the crucial role that it plays in price rises. He gives the example of the Belgian bank KBC, which ran an advertising campaign in order to sell a new commercial product to savers called 'KBC-Life MI Security Food Prices 3' that proposed to invest in six agricultural raw materials. The KBC advertising spin was: 'Take advantage of the rising prices of food commodities!' The sales pitch presented the 'shortage of water and farmland' as an 'opportunity' since it means a 'shortage of food products that has led to rising prices of food commodities'.[232]

With regard to the American justice system, speculators are within their rights. Paul Jorion, in an 'op-ed' published in the newspaper *Le Monde*, queries the decision of a Washington tribunal on 29 September 2012 which invalidated measures taken by the CFTC 'intended to fix a maximum limit to the volume of positions that one operator can take on the commodity futures market in order to ensure that the operator alone is not able to destabilise it'.[233]

Jean Ziegler, formerly United Nations Special Rapporteur on the Right to Food, does not mince his words:

> The 2007-2008 financial crisis, caused by banksterism, has had two notable consequences. Firstly, the hedge funds and major banks reoriented their activity after 2008, dropping certain segments of the financial markets and turning towards the

231 Jacques Berthelot, 'Démêler le vrai du faux dans la flambée des prix agricoles mondiaux' (Telling truth from falsehood in the skyrocketing of world crop prices), CADTM, http://cadtm.org/Demeler-le-vrai-du-faux-dans-la, pp. 51 to 56 (in French).
232 Jacques Berthelot, ibid., p. 54.
233 Paul Jorion, 'Le suicide de la finance' (The suicide of finance), *Le Monde*, 9 October 2012 (in French).

commodity markets, particularly in agricultural produce. If we examine the three main staple crops (maize, rice and wheat), which account for 75% of world food consumption, their prices have skyrocketed. In 18 months the price of maize has increased by 93%, the ton of rice has risen from $105 to $1,010 and the price of a ton of milling wheat has doubled since September 2010 to reach €271. This price explosion procures astronomical profits for the speculators but kills hundreds of thousands of women, men and children in the shantytowns. A second consequence is the rush on the part of the hedge funds and other speculators to buy arable land in the southern hemisphere. In 2011, according to the World Bank, 41 million hectares (over 101 million acres) of arable land were taken over by investment funds and multinationals in Africa alone. The result has been the expulsion of small-scale farmers.[234]

In February 2013, in a report entitled 'Réforme bancaire: ces banques françaises qui spéculent sur la faim' (Banking Reform: the French banks that speculate on hunger), the NGO Oxfam France indicates that in November 2012, the four main French banks – BNP Paribas, Société Générale, Crédit Agricole and Natixis (BPCE) – managed at least eighteen funds for their clients that speculate on the commodity markets. Clara Jamart, head of Food Security at Oxfam France, explains:

There are two ways of speculating: by taking positions on markets of agricultural

---

234   Jean Ziegler, 'Hunger is man-made and man can unmake it', interview given to Éric Toussaint, published 11 February 2012, http://cadtm.org/Hunger-is-man-made-and-man-can. Jean Ziegler is the author of *Destruction massive, géopolitique de la faim*, Paris: Le Seuil, 2012 translated into English as *Betting on Famine. Why the World still goes Hungry*, New York: The New Press, 2013.

commodity derivatives. Or by these index
funds, which monitor the prices of agricultural commodities and push them up.[235]

Most of these funds were created after the start of the food crisis in
2008, with the specific purpose of making profits by speculating on
food and other commodities.
Similarly, in 2013 the Alternative Financing Network (*Réseau
Financement Alternatif*) in Brussels denounced the involvement of
six banks working in Belgium in speculating on famine in the world.
Some €950 million belonging to clients of Belgian banks are used to
speculate on food commodities.[236]

Alternative proposals[237]

To bring an end to this state of affairs, what follows are eighteen proposals for an alternative to the food crisis:

1. Ban speculation on food: it is a crime to speculate
   on people's lives. For this reason governments and
   international institutions must stop speculative investments on agricultural produce;
2. Prohibit commodity-backed derivatives;

235   See (in French) 'Quatre banques françaises accusées de "spéculer sur
la faim"' (Four French banks accused of 'speculating on famine'), *Le Monde*,
11 February 2013, http://www.lemonde.fr/economie/article/2013/02/11/
quatre-banques-francaises-accusees-de-speculer-sur-la-faim_1829956_3234.
html. For Oxfam's international campaign, see Ellen Kelleher, 'Food price
speculation taken off the menu', *Financial Times*, 3 March 2013. See also
the Oxfam website for 'EU deal on curbing food speculation comes none too
soon', 15 January 2014, http://www.oxfam.org/en/eu/pressroom/reactions/
eu-deal-curbing-food-speculation-comes-none-too-soon
236   See 'Des centaines de millions d'euros belges pour spéculer sur la
faim' (Hundreds of millions of Belgian euros to speculate on hunger),
L'Écho, 18 June 2013, http://blogs.lecho.be/argentcontent/2013/06/des-
centaines-de-millions-deuros-belges-pour-sp%C3%A9culer-sur-la-faim.
html (in French).
237   The section entitled 'Alternative proposals' is derived from La Via
Campesina, 'Position on Agricultural Prices and Speculation', *La Via
Campesina Policy Documents, 5th Conference*, Mozambique, October 2008,
p. 152. http://viacampesina.org/downloads/pdf/policydocuments/POLICY-
DOCUMENTS-EN-FINAL.pdf

3. Prohibit banks and other private finance companies from 'participating' in the commodity market;
4. Socialise the banks, under popular control, with a mission to finance food sovereignty projects giving priority to smallholdings, co-operatives and the public agricultural sector;
5. Establish or re-establish international organisations to regulate the markets for and the production of the main export products (coalitions of countries that produce tea, coffee, cocoa beans, bananas, etc.) so that stable prices are ensured on an international level;
6. End Structural Adjustment Programmes (SAP) that force countries to give up their food sovereignty;
7. End land-grabbing;
8. Set up global land reforms (for farmland, but also for water and seeds) to ensure that the farmers who produce food for local populations have access to resources, rather than favouring large corporations that produce for export purposes;
9. Create an international legal framework on food sovereignty that formally recognises (particularly in the International Covenant on Economic, Social and Cultural Rights) and protects every country's right to develop its own policies in order to protect its agriculture, without harming other countries;
10. End the thrall of exploitation caused by the mechanisms of external or internal public debt, mainly led by private banks, and put an end to the slave-like subjugation of smallholders to private lenders;
11. Put a moratorium on industrial bio-fuels and ban genetically modified organisms;
12. Reform the EU's Agricultural Policy and the United States' Farm Bill, both of which have disastrous effects on the agricultural markets;
13. Refuse to sign, and if need be end, multilateral (WTO) or bilateral (FTA and EPA) free-trade agreements that conflict with food sovereignty;
14. Establish or re-establish agricultural import restrictions;

15. Restore public food reserves in every country;
16. Re-establish mechanisms that will guarantee stable prices for foodstuffs;
17. Develop production control policies in order to stabilise agricultural prices;
18. Control the profit margins of intermediaries.

Food security for all starts with stable food prices that cover the cost of production and ensure producers a fair income. The model of low prices, promoted by Western governments to increase the mass consumption of manufactured products and services (tourism, entertainment, telecommunications, etc.), is neither socially nor environmentally sustainable. This model mainly benefits large agribusiness companies and private banks, and also – by diverting the population's attention away from democratic ideas towards mass consumption – helps the political and economic elite of those countries to grab power.

Faced with the current food and environmental crises, radical changes must be made quickly. The proposals listed below are practical ideas for agricultural and business policies based on food sovereignty. They would stabilise food prices at levels capable of assuring sustainable food production in the great majority of countries.

At the local level:

1. Support local agricultural production, in particular by supporting farming and by facilitating small producers' access to credit, whether they be men or women;
2. Support and develop short/direct-marketing channels between producers and consumers in order to ensure that prices are profitable to farmers and affordable for consumers;
3. Encourage the consumption of local produce;
4. Support more autonomous forms of production that are less subject to price fluctuations than production that uses chemical fertilisers (grass-grazing instead of being fed corn or soya bean meal, for example).

18.
Currency speculation and exchange-rate manipulation

Banks are major actors on the currency market. They foster constant instability in exchange rates. Over 95% of currency transactions are speculative. Only a tiny portion of currency transactions involves investment, trading in goods or services related to the real economy or migrants' remittances. In 2013 the daily volume of transactions on the currency market was around $5.3 trillion. Banks, like mutual funds, can call upon significant liquidities and push currencies up or down in order to profit from exchange-rate fluctuations. They also play on exchange derivatives, which can lead to considerable losses, not to mention the detrimental effect of currency instability for society as a whole. From May 2013 onward, the currencies of large emergent countries (for example India, Brazil, South Africa, Russia, Turkey and Argentina) have been the targets of speculative attacks and lost up to 20% of their value.[238] The exchange rate between the dollar and the euro has also been the target of speculation.

In 2013 four banks controlled 50% of the *foreign-exchange* market (Deutsche Bank, 15.2%; Citigroup, 14.9%; Barclays, 10.2%; and UBS, 10.1%). If we add six more banks (HSBC, JPMorgan Chase, Royal Bank of Scotland, Credit Suisse, Morgan Stanley, and Bank of America), these ten banks cover 80% of the market.[239] Half of these trans-

---

238 Such speculative attacks are related to the massive withdrawal of capital by institutional investors (banks, mutual funds, private pension funds, hedge funds, insurance companies).
239 See Daniel Schäfer, Alice Ross and Delphine Strauss, '*Foreign-exchange*: the big fix', *Financial Times*, 12 November 2013; see also Georges Ugeux, 'Après le LIBOR, le marché des changes risque-t-il d'imploser ?'

actions occur on the London exchange.

The scandal of exchange-rate manipulation

While the LIBOR[240] scandal was considered by the regulatory authorities to be almost over,[241] a new scandal broke out at the end of 2013
over manipulations on the *foreign-exchange* markets.[242] Regulatory
authorities for the financial markets in the US, the UK, the EU, Hong
Kong and Switzerland suspected at least fifteen major banks of col-
luding to manipulate exchange rates, including the rate of exchange
between euros and dollars which alone accounts for a daily volume of
$1,300 billion. Among the suspected banks are Barclays, Citigroup,
Deutsche Bank, Goldman Sachs, HSBC, JPMorgan Chase, Morgan
Stanley, Royal Bank of Scotland, Standard Chartered and UBS. Eighteen traders are said to have been suspended or sacked in relation to
this scandalous affair. The British regulatory authorities stated that
the extent of damage was at least equal to the manipulation of the
LIBOR that led to $6 billion in fines.[243]

To top it all, it seems that executives of the Bank of England have been
implicated in both of these affairs. In April 2012 traders specialising
in the exchange market told senior executives at the Bank of England
about what they were doing, and the Bank of England took no action.[244] Laxity, if not outright collusion, between bank executives and

---

(After the LIBOR scandal, could the foreign-exchange market implode?),
Le Monde, 1 December 2013, http://finance.blog.lemonde.fr/2013/12/01/
apres-le-LIBOR-le-marche-des-changes-risque-t-il-dimploser/ (in French).
240   London InterBank Offered Rate, the average interest rate for interbank borrowing (see Chapter 18).
241   The LIBOR scandal resurfaced in March 2014 when the US Federal
Deposit Insurance Corporation (FDIC) sued some sixteen major banks:
http://www.businessweek.com/news/2014-03-14/bofa-citigroup-credit-
suisse-sued-by-fdic-over-LIBOR-rigging.
242   Daniel Schäfer and Caroline Binham, 'Biggest banks face Forex questions', *Financial Times*, 12 November 2013.
243   Delphine Strauss and Daniel Schäfer, 'Forex claims "as bad as LIBOR"
– says FCA' *Financial Times*, 4 February 2014.
244   Caroline Binham and Daniel Schäfer, 'Bank of England faces scrutiny
over Forex', *Financial Times*, 7 February 2014; Sam Fleming, Daniel Schäfer
and Caroline Binham, 'Bank of England calls for Forex rigging review',
Financial Times, 11 February 2014.

regulatory authorities has been brought to light little by little, though information is difficult to get and is rarely relayed in the mainstream media.

In 2013-2014 several US pension funds sued seven banks (Barclays, Citigroup, Deutsche Bank, HSBC, JPMorgan Chase, Royal Bank of Scotland, and UBS) for losses faced as a consequence of this manipulation of exchange rates. They claim they are owed $10 billion in compensation. Pension funds in the Netherlands (including the largest one, PGGM) and in other European countries are also considering taking legal action.[245]

Financial transaction taxes in limbo

Over forty years ago, in 1972, James Tobin, who had been a member of John F. Kennedy's Council of Economic Advisors, proposed to 'throw some sand in the wheels of our excessively efficient international money markets'.[246] Notwithstanding some political leaders' fine speeches, the plague of speculation on *foreign-exchange* markets has increased. The lobby of bankers and other financial institutions actually received a guarantee that there would be no obstacle to their profit making. Yet since Tobin's proposal, the daily volume of transactions on the currency market has multiplied by over 500.

The European Council Directive proposed by eleven governments of the Eurozone[247] in January 2013 calling for a tax of 1/1000th to be levied on financial transactions, excluding transactions on currencies, [248] is completely insufficient, and may never be implemented.

245 Madison Marriage, 'Banks face Forex legal battle', *Financial Times*, 9 February 2014; Daniel Schäfer and Madison Marriage, 'Seven banks face new Forex market-rigging claims', *Financial Times*, 12 February 2014.
246 James Tobin (July–October 1978). 'A Proposal for International Monetary Reform', *Eastern Economic Journal*, Eastern Economic Association, 1978, pp. 153–159, http://www.stampoutpoverty.org/wp-content/uploads/2012/12/A-Proposal-for-International-Monetary-Reform.pdf.
247 The eleven countries involved are Austria, Belgium, Estonia, France, Germany, Greece, Italy, Portugal, Slovakia, Slovenia, and Spain.
248 European Commission, *Proposal for a Council Directive implementing enhanced cooperation in the area of financial transaction tax*, 14 February 203, http://ec.europa.eu/taxation_customs/resources/documents/

Moreover, it does not cover *foreign-exchange* transactions at all. Banks lobbied hard to avoid its implementation and to further restrict its scope.[249] The French government has very close relations to the banks and actively intervenes to support the demands of their lobbying efforts.[250] As expected, the French-German summit on 19 February 2014 did not result in a clear position.[251] Not only are *foreign-exchange* operations not targeted, but also the matter of exactly which derivative products are to be taxed is still being negotiated. There can be no fair solution in such a biased context.

This is why it is high time to stop the spiral of speculation by enforcing a genuine Tobin-like taxation system bearing on *foreign-exchange* markets and on all financial transactions on more than a given amount. This would be the first step towards complete prohibition of speculation on currencies, commodities and food[252] along with the prohibition of high-frequency trading, structured financial products, credit default swaps, operations on derivatives, and transactions that pass through tax havens.

---

taxation/com_2013_71_en.pdf.

249   Philip Stafford and Alex Barker, 'European financial transactions tax suffers backlash', *Financial Times*, 11 December 2013.

250   See 'Lettre ouverte européenne à François Hollande: ne cédez pas au lobby des banques !' (European open letter to François Hollande: don't cave in to the banking lobby!), published by ATTAC France on 12 February 2014, https://france.attac.org/actus-et-medias/salle-de-presse/article/lettre-ouverte-europeenne-a (in French).

251   'Germany and France move closer to deal on diluted transaction tax', *EurActiv*, 19 February 2014, http://www.euractiv.com/euro-finance/germany-france-move-closer-deal-news-533615; also 'Taxe sur les transactions financières : une faute politique majeure du gouvernement français' (The tax on financial transactions: A major political error by the French government), ATTAC France, 19 February 2014, http://france.attac.org/actus-et-medias/salle-de-presse/article/taxe-sur-les-transactions-2907?id_rub=?id_mo (in French).

252   Éric Toussaint, 'Banks speculate on raw materials and food', 10 February 2014, http://cadtm.org/Banks-speculate-on-raw-materials

19.
Giants with
feet of clay

Alan Greenspan, former director of the Fed, wrote in 2007:

> In order to facilitate the financing, insuring,
> and timeliness of all that trade, the volume
> of cross-border transactions in financial in-
> struments has had to rise even faster than
> the trade itself. Wholly new forms of finance
> had to be invented or developed; credit de-
> rivatives, asset-backed securities, oil futures
> and the like all make the world's trading sys-
> tem function far more efficiently.
>
> In many respects, the apparent stability of
> our global trade and financial system is a
> reaffirmation of the simple, time-tested
> principle promulgated by Adam Smith in
> 1776: individuals trading freely with one
> another, following their own self-interest,
> leads to a growing, stable economy.[253]

The financial innovations presented as a panacea by Alan Greenspan
have been a big flop and caused the most serious banking, economic
and social crisis since the 1930s. The banks have not cleaned up their
accounts since 2007-2008. Worse still, they have actively created
new bubbles and new structured financial products.

Institutional investors (insurance companies, pension funds, other
banks and sovereign wealth funds among others) no longer have con-

---

253 Alan Greenspan, *The Age of Turbulence*, New York: Penguin Books,
2007, p. 368.

fidence in banks, and hesitate to buy their covered bonds or contingent convertible bonds (CoCo)[254] issued in the hope of finding stable long-term financing. Fund managers consider these investments to be risky and want 7% or 8% in return.

In 2013 Barclays had to promise a return of 7.65% to potential buyers of its CoCo. The Belgian bank KBC proposed a return of 8%, Crédit Agricole 7.8% and the Bank of Ireland 10%. The total amount of issues in 2012 was the lowest since 2002.[255] The market had a small upward turn in 2013 but remains very depressed. As demanded by regulatory authorities, the banks have to sell their bonds in order to improve their equity / assets ratio.

As they cannot find sufficient long-term funds on the markets, the banks are dependent on the €1 trillion's worth of three-year loans granted by the ECB, which have seen a progressive cut in interest-rates from 1% to 0.05%, and more generally on the liquidity facilities made available to them by the central banks of the most industrialised countries (led by the Fed, the Bank of England, the Swiss National Bank and the Bank of Japan).

Other than funds in deposit and savings accounts which show barely any growth because of the crisis, much of their financing must be found on the short-term market. According to the *Liikanen Report*, the big European banks need €7 trillion for their day-to-day functioning. The volume of banks' short-term debt increased significantly between 1998 and 2007 from €1.5 to €6 trillion, while from 2010 to 2012 it remained at €7 trillion.[256] Where do banks find this short-term money? They are dependent on Money Market Funds (MMF) which have up to $2.7 trillion available for day-to-day trading depending on how the winds of crisis are blowing in Europe. MMF shut off the flow in June 2011, and reopened it when the ECB lent €1 trillion.[257]At any moment, they may close

254 These bonds, which can be converted into shares, may also be simply incorporated into the capital of a bank in trouble. A hybrid product, they replace more traditional types of financing such as emissions of subordinated debt, considered less as capital of the second category (Tier 2).
255 *Financial Times*, 27-28 October 2012. See also'Contingent Convertible Bonds (Cocos) Issued by European Banks (2014)', http://static.norges-bank.no/pages/102086/Staff_Memo_19_2014.pdf.
256 *Liikanen Report*, Table 2.5.1., p. 27.
257 'The ECB and the Fed at the service of the major private banks',

or restrict the flow again. The surest supply of funding is once again the central banks. Since December 2013, the ECB has made massive loans at rates starting at 0.25% and later cut to 0.15% and then 0.05%.

The conclusion is clear. Without the ECB's €1 trillion in loans over three years, its day-to-day loans and the support of the national central banks linked into the Eurosystem (within the framework of the Emergency Liquidity Assistance scheme), to which must be added the Bank of England and the National Bank of Switzerland, many big European banks would be threatened with suffocation and bankruptcy. This is more evidence that the banks have not cleaned up their accounts. They must find massive short-term funding, whereas they hold long-term assets of doubtful value. In many cases, the value of the assets on their balance-sheets will not be realised when they come to maturity, and the losses suffered may absorb their whole capital.

Funding from the stock exchanges is also blocked. The price of bank shares has dropped, on average, to a fifth of their 2007 level.[258] Almost all the capitalised values of stock-exchange-quoted companies were reduced, and the banks were the worst hit. As we shall see later, after the chaos of 2007-2008, the banks' situation worsened again in 2008. The institutional investors unloaded many of their shares in the banks, convinced that keeping them would lead to further losses. Due to interventions by the ECB, the Bank of England, the Fed and the Swiss National Bank amounting to €1 trillion starting at the end of 2011, the drop in bank share prices stopped and banks started to look a little better, encouraging institutional investors to hold on to the bank shares they still had. Massive buying of Asset Backed Securities (ABS) by the Fed also helped US banks to stay afloat. Throughout 2012 the central banks continued to pour liquidities into the financial markets through the banks. The stock markets in the industrialised countries showed improvements from January 2013.

In 2014 and until these lines were written on 26 August 2015, share prices have continued to rise but another speculative bubble is just around the corner. In fact, in 2013, while real economic activity in the Eurozone was down 0.4% and up in the US by 1.9%, in the UK by 1.8% and in Japan by 1.7%, the stock markets were up 18% in the Eurozone,

CADTM, 29 December 2012, http://cadtm.org/The-ECB-and-the-Fed-at-the-service
258 *Liikanen Report*, Table 2.4.1., p. 20.

22% in the US, 13% in the UK and 42% in Japan.[259] Bank shares followed this tendency, which has improved their financial situation.

This is not the only advantage banks get from the stock-exchange bubble. The banks are intermediaries in stock-exchange transactions, for which they are paid commissions – this is a trading activity. In 2013, the big banks such as Morgan Stanley, Goldman Sachs, Deutsche Bank, Credit Suisse, UBS, Citigroup, Bank of America and JPMorgan Chase[260] made 50% of their Banking and Investment department revenues from this activity. As reported in the *Financial Times* in January 2014, 'Banks are becoming increasingly dependent on surging equity markets, generating nearly half of total investment-banking revenues from equity trading and underwriting in the fourth quarter of 2013.'[261]

Any textbook on practical economics will tell you that shares should be considered long-term investments, to be retained, on average, for about eight years. In theory, the stock exchange is supposed to help listed companies gain access to long-term investment capital. However, this scenario just does not work, because the stock exchange is no longer a place where companies can find long-term funding, but a place of sheer speculation and hostile take-over bids. In practice, stock-exchange investments can be very short-term and highly speculative, and these phenomena are amplified by today's high-frequency trading.

Banks are giants with feet of clay, requiring proper recapitalisation, and here again they depend heavily on government funding. According to a

259   In 2013, Italy's GDP was down 1.8% and its stock market rose 23.8%; in Spain, GDP was down 1.2% and the stock market rose 24.8%; in Greece, GDP was down 3.6% , the stock market up 40.8 %; in Germany, GDP was up by 0.5% and the stock market by 25.3 %; in Belgium, GDP was up 0.4% and the stock market by 19.5%; in France, GDP was up by 0.2 and the stock market by 18.2%; in the Netherlands, GDP was down 1% and the stock market rose 16%. These rises are clearly artificial and bear no relationship to the real economy.
260   Camilla Hall and Daniel Schäfer, 'Big banks lean on equities businesses', *Financial Times*, 12 January 2014. See also Daniel Schäfer, Martin Arnold and Alice Ross, 'Deutsche Bank's results cast a shadow over rivals', *Financial Times*, 20 January 2014.
261   Ibid.

study published in June 2013 by Berenberg,[262] a major consultancy that advises institutional investors on stock investment, European banks must be recapitalised at a cost of between €350 and €400 billion (of which two thirds would be for banks in the Eurozone), while European authorities generally mention a far lower amount. Berenberg considers the requirements of the Basel Committee to be totally inadequate to guarantee the financial standing of the largest private banks. A bank-by-bank analysis led Berenberg to recommend that investors should offload their shares in Credit Suisse, Crédit Agricole, Deutsche Bank, Santander, Société Générale and Commerzbank. Berenberg finds the real hard-capital ratio relative to total assets to be below 2% for the first four of those banks. This confirms what we have highlighted in this book, bringing fresh evidence of the abysmal distance between the theory of capitalism as its promoters would have it, and reality.

262   Berenberg Equity Research, *European Banks. Capital: misunderstood, misused and misplaced*, Berenberg, Gossler & Co. KG, June 2013, http://www.berenberg.de/fileadmin/user_upload/berenberg2013/02_Investment_Banking/Equity_Research/2013_06_13_european_banks.pdf.

20.
The 'Too Big to Jail' doctrine

We all know the saying, 'Too Big to Fail'.

The way governments have managed the crisis caused by the banks has now given rise to the equally laconic 'Too Big to Jail'! [263] [264]

Although the US government let Lehman Bros. go to the wall in September 2008, no other bank has been closed or broken up, and no director has been given a custodial sentence.[265] The only exception in the Western world is Iceland, where the courts have imprisoned three bank directors. In December 2012, Larus Welding, the CEO of Glitnir, Iceland's third-biggest bank at the time it went bankrupt in 2008, was sentenced to nine months in prison. Sigurdur Einarsson and Hreidar Mar Sigurdsson, the two principal directors of Kaupthing,[266] were

263   The author thanks Daniel Munevar, a CADTM economist who made his useful and concise preliminary study on the subject available to me. I have built on his research. See the original article by Daniel Munevar, 'La doctrine « trop grandes pour être condamnées » ou comment les banques sont au-dessus des lois' (The 'Too Big to Jail' doctrine, or how banks are above the law), 20 September 2013, www.cadtm.org/La-doctrine-trop-grandes-pour-etre (in French or Spanish).
264   The English-speaking media have been using this phrase for about two years - see for example: ABC News, 'Once Again, Is JPMorgan Chase Too Big to Jail?', 7 January 2014, http://abcnews.go.com/Blotter/madoff-ponzi-scheme-prosecutors-find-J.P. Morgan-chase-big/story?id=21448264 or Forbes, 'Why DOJ Deemed Bank Execs Too Big to Jail', 29 July 2013, http://www.forbes.com/sites/tedkaufman/2013/07/29/why-doj-deemed-bank-execs-too-big-to-jail/.
265   In other words, no bank has had its obligatory licence for banking activities revoked.
266   The failure of the bank's Icesave subsidiary in the UK and the Netherlands caused a diplomatic crisis between those two countries and Iceland.

sentenced to five years and five and a half years in December 2013.[267]

Yet the US and European justice systems are faced with serious wrong-doing by the biggest banks – organised fraud against their customers, small shareholders and public shareholders, laundering money from organised crime, high-level tax evasion, plotting to manipulate in-terest-rates (Euribor, LIBOR), exchange rates and financial markets (CDS and Commodities), fraud and forgery, insider trading, destruc-tion of evidence, embezzlement, complicity in war crimes ... the list goes on. But no-one has faced prison sentences for any of this.

Eric Holder, Attorney General of the United States, when interrogat-ed by a Senate Committee, clearly defined the foundations of the 'Too Big to Jail' doctrine:

> 'I am concerned that the size of some of these institutions becomes so large that it does become difficult for us to prosecute them when we are hit with indications that if you do prosecute, if you do bring a crim-inal charge, it will have a negative impact on the national economy, perhaps even the world economy.'[268]

The implications are clear. The fact that speculation and financial crime have caused the worst economic crisis for nearly a century weighs little in the scales of justice. Even if such excesses are closely

---

The crisis is not over, since the two countries are attempting to bring the case before Icelandic courts despite the judgement without possible appeal by the EFTA court that ruled in favour of Iceland in January 2013. See Richard Milne, 'Iceland premier repels Icesave lawsuit', *Financial Times*, 12 February 2014.

267   'Iceland, almost uniquely in the Western world, has launched criminal cases against the men who used to lead its three main banks that collapsed after the global financial crisis in 2008 after collectively becoming 10 times the size of the island's economy.' See Richard Milne, 'Icelandic bank pair jailed for five years', *Financial Times*, 12 December 2013.

268   Mark Gongloff, 'Holder admits some Banks too big to jail', Huffing-tonPost, 6 March 2013, http://www.huffingtonpost.com/2013/03/06/Eric-holder-banks-too-big_n_2821741.html. The page includes a link to video of Eric Holder making his statement.

associated with large-scale fraud at all levels of US banking,[269] these institutions have *de facto* authorisation to continue their operations and settle their infringements 'out of court'.

Imagine if, after a long investigation, the police arrested a criminal who had stolen €1 million. Then during the preliminary proceedings the criminal says, 'Now listen, here's what we'll do; I'll pay a €2,000 fine, then you let me go and we'll say no more about it! What do you say?' The judge replies, 'No problem! Sorry for the bother. Please try not to get caught again. It would be such a shame.' This imaginary conversation corresponds to the special treatment the banks get. Berthold Brecht hit the nail on the head when he asked, 'What's breaking into a bank compared with founding a bank?'[270]

The direct consequences of the banks' damaging activities are extremely serious: 14 million families in the US were evicted from their homes between 2007 and 2013 (see chart below). This includes nearly half a million illegal expulsions.[271] Millions lost their jobs, forcing their family's income below the poverty line. There has been an increase in suicides among those affected, public debt has exploded and pension funds in the developed countries have lost $4.5 trillion.[272]

269   A recent study of banking practices in the US showed that, notwithstanding their heterogeneity, irregularities and fraud are common at many levels of activity in all the institutions studied. See 'Asset Quality Misrepresentation by Financial Intermediaries: Evidence from RMBS Market', SSRN, 12 February 2013, http://papers.ssrn.com/sol3/papers.cfm?abstract_id=2215422.
270   Berthold Brecht, The Threepenny Opera (in German: Die Dreigroschenoper). [Berlin 1928], trans. Ralph Manheim and John Willett, London: Penguin Classics, 2007.
271   'Banks to pay $8.5 billion to speed up housing relief', New York Times, 7 January 2013, http://dealbook.nytimes.com/2013/01/07/banks-to-pay-8-5-billion-to-speed-up-housing-relief/?_php=true&_type=blogs&_php=-true&_type=blogs&_r=1.
272   OECD, 'The Impact of the Financial Crisis on Defined Benefit Plans and the Need for Counter-Cyclical Funding Regulations', OECD, 2010, http://www.oecd.org/pensions/private-pensions/45694491.pdf.

Home repossessions in the US and Spain[273]

	United States	Spain
2005	532,833	
2006	717,522	
2007	1,285,873	
2008	2,330,483	49,848
2009	2,824,674	59,632
2010	2,871,891	81,747
2011	1,887,777	94,825
2012	1,836,634	76,724
Total	14,287,687	362,776

When the justice system shies away from the crimes committed by banks and their directors to avoid them spending even a single day behind bars, the private banking system is clearly playing such an important role in the capitalist system that it transcends the legal and constitutional frameworks of modern societies. When all is said and done, the directors of banking institutions can hardly be prosecuted for 'doing God's work',[274] as Lloyd Blankfein, the CEO of Goldman Sachs, put it.

Such a statement would be laughable if the relations between banks and legal or regulatory authorities did not so often confirm the practice of the 'Too Big to Jail' principle on both sides of the Atlantic. The

---

273 Sources (for United States): '1.8 Million U.S. Properties With Foreclosure Filings in 2012', *RealtyTrac*, http://www.realtytrac.com/content/foreclosure-market-report/2012-year-end-foreclosure-market-report-7547; (for Spain): '2007–2012 : Restrospectiva sobre desahucios y ejecuciones hipotecarias en españa, estadísticas oficiales e indicadores' (2007–2012: retrospective on evictions and foreclosures in Spain, official statistics and indicators), Plataforma de Afectados por la Ipoteca, http://afectadosporlahipoteca.com/wp-content/uploads/2013/02/RETROSPECTIVA-SOBRE-DESAHUCIOS-Y-EJECUCIONES-HIPOTECARIAS-EN-ES-PAÑA-COLAUALEMANY1.pdf.

274 'Goldman Sachs' Blankfein on Banking: "Doing God's Work" ', *The Wall Street Journal*, 9 November 2009, http://blogs.wsj.com/marketbeat/2009/11/09/goldman-sachs-blankfein-on-banking-doing-gods-work/.

law imposes small fines that are only fractions of the profits reaped from illegal activities, and then it is 'business as usual', and the culprits are troubled no further. Some scapegoats, like Jérôme Kerviel, do get sentenced, but never the bosses who pushed them to maximise company profits using all the slyest tricks in the game.

In the chapters that follow, four examples will suffice to describe the current situation. First, there are the agreements between US banks and various authorities to avoid prosecution in affairs concerning subprime mortgages, foreclosures, and illegal expulsions. Then there is the case of HSBC (the biggest British bank), fined in the US for laundering money for Mexican and Colombian drug cartels. Next we have manipulation of the interbank markets and derivatives rates, as happened in the LIBOR affair. And finally, there is the international tax evasion network organised by the major Swiss bank UBS.

21.
Abusive foreclosures in the United States

The US authorities made agreements with the banks not to prosecute them in the home-mortgage and illegal-repossessions scandal; they were merely asked to pay a small fine. As seen in the previous chapter, since the outbreak of the crisis in 2006-2008, more than 14 million families have been evicted from their homes – at least 500,000 illegally. One of the allegations made against banks is based on their failure to provide documents justifying the eviction of homeowners who are behind with their mortgages. The dearth of regulations and the high volume of subprime loans granted just before the crisis led the banks to take on staff just to 'robo-sign' dozens, or even hundreds, of documents every day, approving foreclosures without following the correct legal procedure. The banks repossessed some 500,000 homes with no economic or legal justification. (Our figure only covers finalised investigations and pending lawsuits, so it may become significantly higher). Despite the immense damage caused by the banks' fraudulent practices, in many cases the penalty fine amounted to only $300 per home,[275] and more rarely from $1,500 to $2,000. Other allegations made against the banks concern the sale of structured products, made up of toxic mortgage loans (Mortgage Backed Securities) sold by banks to home-loan mortgage companies such as 'Freddie Mac' and 'Fannie Mae' which were then bought up by the US government.

Between 2010 and the end of 2013, on mortgages alone, 26 agreements were made between different US authorities and the major banks.[276]

---

275   Tyler Durden, 'The banks' "penalty" to put robo-signing behind them: $300 Per Person', *ZeroHedge*, 9 April 2013, http://www.zerohedge.com/news/2013-04-09/banks-penalty-put-robosigning-behind-them-300-person/.
276   'Mortgage and credit crisis-related litigation and settlements', http://

All the big banks are involved. Since 2008 they have agreed to pay $86 billion to avoid unfavourable judgements in legal procedures concerning home loans.[277] Bank of America paid $44 billion; JPMorgan Chase $26.4 billion; Wells Fargo $9.5 billion; Citigroup, $4.7 billion; Goldman Sachs almost $1 billion and Morgan Stanley $330 million, to which legal and other expenses must be added. By comparison, in 2012 the net profits of these six banks totalled $59.9 billion, after paying the fines imposed that year. 2013 was even better. After deduction of $18 billion as provision for the fines of the year to come, their net profits progressed by 21% to $74 billion.[278] Had the six banks not had to pay the fines, their profits would have exceeded their record year of 2006, in the thick of the real-estate bubble. It is clear to all that the 'heavy' fines reported in the media did not prevent the bankers popping corks to celebrate the profits they had made by abusing millions of families.

Despite the proof of the banks' fraudulent and deceptive practices, and despite the fact that millions of ordinary people fell prey to those scams, they have not had to face any criminal charges, nor has a single arrest been made. The negotiations and agreements between the banks and the authorities have relieved the banks of their legal and financial responsibilities in previous affairs.[279] Adding insult to injury, Jamie Dimon, the CEO of JPMorgan Chase, was awarded a 74% pay increase in 2013, bringing his annual pay packet up to $20 million.[280]

---

www.ababj.com/images/Dev_SNL/120913_MortgageTimeline.pdf, *SNL Timeline*, consulted 22 February 2014.

277 'Credit crisis and mortgage-related settlements for select bank holding companies', *SNL*, http://www.ababj.com/images/Dev_SNL/CreditCrisis.pdf, consulted 22 February 2014.

278 'Big Six U.S. Banks' 2013 Profit Thwarted by Legal Costs', *Bloomberg*, 9 January 2014, http://www.bloomberg.com/news/2014-01-09/big-six-u-s-banks-2013-profit-thwarted-by-legal-costs.html. See also 'Profits at the Biggest Banks Bounce Back to Post-Crisis Record High', ThinkProgress, 21 January 2014, http://thinkprogress.org/economy/2014/01/21/3184401/banks-profits-2013-record/#.

279 Among critical comments, see 'The Top 12 Reasons Why You Should Hate the Mortgage Settlement', *HuffingtonPost*, 2 September 2012, http://www.huffingtonpost.com/yves-smith/mortgage-settlement_b_1264806.html.

280 'Dimon's pay soars 74% to $20m', see 'Dimon Gets Raise After Rough Year. JPMorgan Chase Chief's 2013 Pay Jumps 74% to $20 Million', *The*

22.
HSBC's drug
money scandal

The British bank HSBC, which employs 260,000 people in 75 countries and claims to have 54 million customers,[281] is another example of the 'Too Big to Jail' phenomenon. Over the past ten years, HSBC has laundered $881 million[282] for Mexican and Colombian drug cartels responsible for tens of thousands of firearms-related murders. Despite dozens of warnings from various US government agencies, including the Office of the Comptroller of the Currency (OCC), the profits from this business are so great that HSBC not only ignored the warnings, but opened a special service in its Mexico offices where drug dealers could simply hand in stocks of cash to be laundered.[283] It has been revealed that HSBC was charged with failing to respect anti-money-laundering regulations on nearly $700 billion of transfers and over $9.4 billion in US currency purchases from HSBC Mexico. The bank also violated sanctions against Iran, Sudan and Burma, amongst others. Despite HSBC's open contempt for the law, it has had to face almost no legal consequences. In

Wall Street Journal, 24 January 2014.
281   See official HSBC site: http://www.hsbc.com/about-hsbc
282   HSBC has also had dealings with a Saudi bank suspected of financial collaboration with al-Qaida. It is accused by the US judiciary of having transgressed embargo restrictions. See 'HSBC Judge Approves $1.9B Drug-Money Laundering Accord', *Bloomberg*, 3 July 2013, http://www.bloomberg.com/news/2013-07-02/hsbc-judge-approves-1-9b-drug-money-laundering-accord.html and 'HSBC pays record $1.9bn fine to settle US money-laundering accusations', *The Guardian*, 11 December 2012, http://www.theguardian.com/business/2012/dec/11/hsbc-bank-us-money-laundering.
283   Matt Taibbi, 'Gangster Bankers: Too Big to Jail. How HSBC hooked up with drug traffickers and terrorists. And got away with it,' *Rolling Stone*, 14 February 2013, http://www.rollingstone.com/politics/news/gangster-bankers-too-big-to-jail-20130214.

December 2012, HSBC was sentenced to a fine of $1.9 billion – about one week of revenue – as the full and final penalty for its money-laundering activities. Although aiding and abetting terrorist organisations and drug trafficking are punishable by a five-year prison sentence, not a single director or employee was prosecuted. Thus bank directors are free to take part in drug trafficking, violations of sanctions or any other crime, with impunity.

The *International Herald Tribune (IHT)* reports what was allegedly said behind the doors of the Justice Department about this case. According to their sources, several prosecutors wanted HSBC to plead guilty and acknowledge that it had broken the law requiring banks to inform the authorities of any transaction of over $10,000 that might be suspicious. The plea would have led to HSBC losing its United States banking licence, putting an end to its activities in that country. After several months of negotiations, it was eventually decided not to press criminal charges in order to avoid the bank's closure. It was even decided to avoid tarnishing the bank's image.[284] There was no conviction. The small fine of $1.9 billion came with a five-year probationary period: should the authorities discover, between 2013 and 2018, that HSBC had not put an end to these practices, the Justice Department could reopen the case. This result may be summed up as: 'Naughty child! Your penance is a fine of one week's pay and a promise not to do it again for five years.' This is clearly an example of a bank that is 'Too Big to Jail'.

During a Senate Committee hearing on HSBC in July 2013, Democrat Senator Elizabeth Warren of Massachusetts grilled David Cohen, who, as the under-secretary responsible for the fight against terrorism and financial espionage, was representing the US Treasury. She made the following points: the United States government takes money laundering very seriously, it is possible to close a bank that engages in this activity, and individuals can be permanently prohibited from conducting banking and financial activities and may be prosecuted.

Yet in December 2012, HSBC admitted to laundering $881 million for Mexican and Colombian drug cartels and also to many sanctions violations over a long period. HSBC has paid a fine, but no individuals

---

284 'HSBC to pay $1.92 billion over money laundering', *International Herald Tribune (IHT)*, 12 December 2012.

were sanctioned and closing the bank down in the US has not been mentioned. 'How many billions of dollars do you have to launder for drug lords [...] before someone will consider shutting down a financial institution like this?' she asked. The Treasury representative dodged the issue, saying the question was too complex to answer.[285] The Senator concluded by saying that when a small-time cocaine dealer gets caught he spends years in prison, whereas bankers who launder billions of narco-dollars can sleep easily in their own beds at night with no fear of prosecution.[286]

Stephen Green, CEO of HSBC then British Minister for Trade and Investment

Stephen Green is a vivid illustration of the symbiotic relationship between finance and government. In this case, it goes ever further, because he does not content himself with serving the interests of big capital as a banker and a minister. His 'ministries' even extended to being an ordained priest of the Church of England. He has written two books on the subject of business and ethics, notably *Serving God, Serving Mammon?*[287] The title alludes to the biblical quotation:

> No man can serve two masters: for either
> he will hate the one, and love the other; or
> else he will hold to the one, and despise the
> other. Ye cannot serve God and Mammon
> (Matthew 6:24).[288]

---

285   Mark Gongloff, 'Elizabeth Warren: Banks Get Wrist Slaps While Drug Dealers Get Jail', *HuffingtonPost*, 7 March 2013, http://www.huffingtonpost.com/2013/03/07/elizabeth-warren-hsbc-money-laundering_n_2830166.html and Ian Fraser, 'HSBC's drugs money laundering settlement a mockery of justice, says Warren', *Shredded*, 7 March 2013, http://www.ianfraser.org/hsbcs-drugs-money-laundering-settlement-a-mockery-of-justice-says-sen-warren/.
286   Part of the hearing is visible in a YouTube video at: http://www.youtube.com/watch?v=fKvGXF7pZAc.
287   Stephen Green, *Serving God? Serving Mammon?*, London: Marshall Pickering, 1996.
288   *The Bible, New Testament*, Matthew 6:24.

Mammon is symbolic of wealth, greed, and profit. The name comes up in Aramaic, Hebrew, and Phoenician. Mammon is sometimes compared to Satan. As for Stephen Green, he has received honorary degrees from the highest university institutions and is clearly untouchable.

Green started his career at the British Ministry of Overseas Development, before going to the private international consultancy company McKinsey. In 1982, he was hired by HSBC, where he was rapidly promoted to positions of high responsibility. He was appointed Executive Director in 2003, and became HSBC chairman in 2006, where he remained until 2010.

The charges brought by the US authorities of laundering $881 million of drug money, and other illicit transactions relate to the period 2003-2010. According to the 334-page Senate report published in 2012, Stephen Green had been informed by an employee in 2005 that HSBC had set up money-laundering operations in Mexico and that numerous dubious transactions were going on. Also in 2005, the financial services company Bloomberg based in New York accused HSBC of laundering drug money. Stephen Green replied that the accusations were 'singularly and wholly irresponsible', casting doubt on the integrity of a great and irreproachable international bank. In 2008, the US federal authorities informed Stephen Green that the Mexican authorities had discovered the existence of a money-laundering operation involving HSBC in Mexico and a branch of HSBC in the Cayman Islands. The agency remarked that such activity could entail criminal responsibility for HSBC.[289] There followed a series of rather soft warnings compared to the gravity of the accusations. HSBC promised to change its behaviour, but continued its criminal practices.

Finally, HSBC was issued a Cease and Desist Order in October 2010 to put an end to these illegal activities.[290] At the end of 2012, follow-

---

289   Ned Simons, 'HSBC: Stephen Green Accused of Hiding from Scandal', *HuffingtonPost UK*, 20 July 2012, http://www.huffingtonpost. co.uk/2012/07/20/hsbc-scandal-stephen-green-hiding_n_1688622.html; see also the previously mentioned article by Matt Taibbi, 'Gangster Bankers: Too Big to Jail.' See fn 283 above.
290   A Cease and Desist Order is an order against a person, corporation or organisation, issued by a court or a US authority, to stop an activity consi-

ing the publication of the Senate Commission's report and months of discussion between different US security agencies, HSBC was fined $1.9 billion.

Stephen Green cannot claim he did not know what his bank was up to, not only in Mexico and in off-shore tax havens, but also in the Middle East and in the US. He was CEO of his group, and had been a director of HSBC Bank Bermuda Ltd.,[291] HSBC Mexico and HSBC Middle East. He had also been president of HSBC Private Banking Holdings (Switzerland) SA and of HSBC North America Holdings Inc.

When the US decision to impose a heavy fine on HSBC for drug-money laundering was made public in 2012, Stephen Green was no longer at HSBC. He was now a minister in the British Cabinet under Prime Minister David Cameron.

With hindsight, Stephen Green's timing was spot on, showing artistic flair. In February 2010, he published a book entitled *Good Value: Reflections on Money, Morality and an Uncertain World.* [292] The foreword asks and answers the following question: 'Can one be both an ethical person and an effective business person? Stephen Green, an ordained priest and the chairman of HSBC, thinks so.' Of course, the 'ethical person' and the 'effective business person' are identifiable in the author, priest and HSBC chairman, Stephen Green. The propaganda was well coordinated, as at the same time Green was made Doctor Honoris Causa by London University's School of Oriental and African Studies (SOAS).

In October 2010, for the second time, the US Justice Department ordered HSBC to cease its criminal activities. Before this information was made public, Stephen Green jumped ship. The following month, at the request of David Cameron, he received honours and was appointed Baron Green of Hurstpierpoint, in West Sussex. How extraor-

---

dered damaging or illegal. The first of these orders was issued in April 2003 and concerned bank accounts and the funding of terrorist organisations such as Al-Qaeda.

291   See 'Bank of Bermuda', *Wikipedia*, http://en.Wikipedia.org/wiki/ Bank_of_Bermuda. The official website of HSBC in Bermuda is http:// www.hsbc.bm/1/2/.

292   Stephen Green, *Good Value: Reflections on Money, Morality and an Uncertain World*, London: Grove Press, 2010.

dinary that on 22 November 2010 a businessman should be made a lifelong peer of the realm, a member of the House of Lords, after having been Chairman of HSBC, which had been accused of facilitating money laundering for drug kings, rogue states and terrorists. Truth is indeed stranger than fiction.

Stephen Green resigned from his position at HSBC in December 2010 to become Minister of State for Trade and Investment in February 2011.[293] He has thus continued to serve the interests of the British corporations, with whom he has very close relations. In May 2010, he became Vice-President of the Confederation of British Industry. He used his know-how to promote London as a candidate for the 2012 Olympic Games, which were held in July, exactly as the US Senate's report on the HSBC affair came out. Stephen Green refused to answer questions from members of the House of Lords on this scandal. He was protected by the leader of the Conservative group in the House of Lords who argued that a Minister is not answerable to Parliament for matters that do not concern his ministerial portfolio.[294]

In 2013, David Cameron commended Lord Green for the 'superb job' he had done in increasing British exports and promoting commercial treaties, especially the EU-US transatlantic treaty (TTIP).[295] He also did a lot to expand British arms sales throughout the world. He finished his term in December 2013, and now devotes his time to speaking at conferences (no doubt for a considerable fee) and to receiving the honours that so many academic institutions heap upon him.

---

293   Stephen Green declared that his position as Minister would be unpaid. His income as CEO of HSBC was £25 million p.a. and he has other assets.
294   Ned Simons, 'HSBC: Stephen Green Accused Of Hiding From Scandal'), *HuffingtonPost UK*, 20 July 2012, http://www.huffingtonpost.co.uk/2012/07/20/hsbc-scandal-stephen-green-hiding_n_1688622.html. See also: 'Lord Green 'regrets' HSBC scandal but still refuses to answer questions. Trade minister breaks silence over money laundering scandal that took place while he was running the bank,' *The Guardian*, 24 July 2012.
295   'Lord Green to retire after reforming UKTI', *The Daily Telegraph*, 19 June 2013, http://www.telegraph.co.uk/finance/newsbysector/banksand-finance/10130551/Lord-Green-to-retire-after-reforming-UKTI.htm 'The Prime Minister said that former HSBC boss Lord Green had done a "superb job" re-focusing Government efforts on export, pushing forward trade agreements, including the planned US-EU trade deal, and had secured "vital investments", including the redevelopment of Battersea Power Station.'

His career is certainly not over. His hypocrisy has no limits. In March 2009 at a press conference about the responsibility for the crisis that started in 2007-2008, precisely when HSBC was involved in the notorious money-laundering affair, he had the gall to declare:

> Underlying all these events is a question about the culture and ethics of the industry. It is as if, too often, people had given up asking whether something was the right thing to do, and focused only on whether it was legal and complied with the rules.

He further added, 'There have been too many who have profoundly damaged the industry's reputation'.[296]

That is how Stephen Green speaks to the lackeys who scurry to repeat his good words all over the mainstream press.

Green and all his HSBC cronies who organised money laundering should answer for their crimes before the courts where heavy custodial sentences along with a period of community service should be handed down. HSBC should be shut down and its directors sacked. The bank should be split into smaller units under public control with a strictly-defined public service objective.

The shameful past of HSBC

From its earliest days, the British bank HSBC was mixed up in the international narcotics trade, having been established in the wake of the British victories in the Opium Wars (1839-1842 and 1856-1860) against China. These two wars played an important role in the consolidation of the British Empire and the marginalisation of China, which lasted for a century and a half. Through the Opium Wars, the British Empire forced China to accept the importation of opium from British India. China had been opposed to this commerce but the force of British arms, with the support of Washington, proved to be stronger.

---

296 'HSBC in bid to raise £12.5bn', *The Independent*, 9 March 2009, http://www.independent.co.uk/news/business/news/hsbc-in-bid-to-raise-pound125bn-1635307.html.

It was in the colony of Hong Kong, set up by the British in 1865, that a Scottish merchant created the Hong Kong and Shanghai Banking Corporation. He specialised in the opium trade, which was the basis of 70% of Hong Kong's trade with the Indies.

From that moment, the bank's history has been closely associated with British interests in Asia. After the victory of Mao Tse Tung's revolution in 1949, HSBC withdrew to Hong Kong, which remained a British colony. Between 1980 and 1997 the bank developed its US and European activities, but only moved its headquarters to London in 1993, in preparation for the transfer of sovereignty back to the People's Republic of China in 1997. HSBC continues to play a significant role in Hong Kong finance, issuing 70% of Hong Kong Dollar banknotes. Hong Kong has now become a major link in the money-laundering chain used by the new Chinese ruling classes.

HSBC and other white-collar crime

In addition to laundering money from drugs and terrorism, HSBC is incriminated in other affairs: manipulating exchange markets (the case was heard in 2013 and focused on a market of \$5.3 trillion a day);[297] rigging the LIBOR interbank interest rate;[298] the abusive and fraudulent sale of interest-rate derivatives; the abusive and fraudulent sale of insurance products to the British public and small companies (the Financial Services Authority prosecuted HSBC for selling policies that were of little or no value);[299] the abusive sale of Mortgage Backed Securities in the US; rigging gold and silver prices, (the case broke in January and February 2014);[300] and large-scale collusion with high-level tax evasion (described below).

Hervé Falciani, the Edward Snowden of HSBC?

Hervé Falciani, a French-Italian, worked at HSBC in Geneva as a systems engineer between 2006 and 2008. Before leaving the company and moving to France, he copied 127,000 documents that clearly linked HSBC to massive fraud and tax-evasion operations. Through Interpol, Switzerland issued an International Arrest Warrant citing data theft, banking and commercial secrecy violations and industrial espionage. Switzerland has not prosecuted HSBC.

In early 2009, armed with a search warrant for his home in Nice, the French police seized the explosive documents which, according to Falciani, named thousands of tax evaders including 8,231 French, 800 Belgians, nearly 600 Spaniards and about 2,000 Greeks on the famous

---

297   See Éric Toussaint, 'Comment les grandes banques manipulent le marché des devises' (How the big banks manipulate the exchange markets), *Le Monde*, 13 March 2014, http://cadtm.org/Comment-les-grandes-banques (in French).
298   See Éric Toussaint, 'Big banks' tampering with interest-rates, CADTM, 28 April 2014, http://cadtm.org/Big-banks-tampering-with-interest (Part 5 of the series 'The banks and the "Too Big to Jail" doctrine').
299   'Cernée par les scandales, HSBC ternit un peu plus la réputation de la City' (Trapped by scandals, HSBC further tarnishes City reputation), *Le Monde*, 1 August 2012 (in French).
300   Madison Marriage, 'Gold price-rigging fears put investors on alert', *Financial Times*, 23 February 2014.

'Lagarde list' given to IMF director Christine Lagarde by the French authorities. There were also many Germans, Italians and Americans. Hervé Falciani then claims to have collaborated with the authorities in Washington, giving them information relevant to their inquiries into HSBC's laundering of money from Mexican and Colombian drug cartels. He went to Spain in 2012 to assist the Spanish authorities. There, he was first arrested under an international warrant instigated by Switzerland, who requested his extradition. This was refused by Spain as he was a principal witness in several major affairs involving fraud and tax evasion.[301] The information provided to the Spanish authorities by Falciani revealed the existence of about €2 billion deposited in Swiss accounts by the family of Emilio Botín, the President of Santander Bank, who was fined €200 million. The scandal of the fraudulent funding of Mariano Rajoy's Popular Party was also brought to light.[302] The Spanish judiciary has placed Falciani under permanent police protection. The Belgian and French authorities used information he provided to conduct tax-evasion proceedings, but it is not certain whether any charges will be brought. Out-of-court tax settlements are much more likely and usual.

Switzerland is not alone in wanting to pursue whistleblowers; Greece, too, has prosecuted the editor of the magazine *Hot Doc*, Kostas Vaxevanis, for having dared to publish, in October 2012, the Lagarde-HSBC-Falciani list that the Greek authorities had been sitting on for three years. He was eventually acquitted under public pressure in Greece and internationally. It is not easy to expose a bank and the rich fraudsters it protects; nor is it easy to denounce the rich fraudsters who protect their banks' sacrosanct code of secrecy.

---

301 'Vol de fichiers bancaires chez HSBC: le récapitulatif' (Theft of bank data at HSBC: an update), *Le Soir*, 8 May 2013, http://www.lesoir. be/239380/article....
302 'Evasion fiscale : le parquet espagnol s'oppose à l'extradition de Falciani, ex-employé de HSBC' (Tax evasion: Spanish courts refuse extradition of ex HSBC employee Hervé Falciani), *Le Monde*, 16 April 2013, http://www.lemonde.fr/europe/articl... (in French); 'A Banker's Secret Wealth', *New York Times*, 20 September 2011, http://www.nytimes. com/2011/09/21/b...: 'The French government passed on to Spain data that it had obtained from Hervé Falciani, a former employee in HSBC's Swiss subsidiary, naming almost 600 Spanish holders of secret bank accounts. Among those was one belonging to the estate of Mr. Botín's father.'

There is a real symbiosis between the big banks and the ruling class-es, as there is between governments and big companies, particularly financial ones.

HSBC finds a loophole in a European Union Directive

In 2013, the EU announced that it was capping bank bonuses for di-rectors and traders at twice the fixed salary. Thus for a salary of €1.5 million, bonuses would be limited to €3 million, which amounts to a total annual income of €4.5 million. Unperturbed, HSBC simply in-creased the fixed salary in order to maintain the level of bonuses.[303]

303   Sharleen Goff and Martin Arnold, 'HSBC plans to sidestep EU bonus cap revealed', *Financial Times*, 24 February 2014.

23.
Tampering
with interest-rates

The third example that illustrates the current situation is the manipulation of the LIBOR (London Interbank Offered Rate) between 2005 and 2010. LIBOR is a benchmark rate used for a market of $350 trillion in assets and financial derivatives, which means that it is the second most important benchmark rate in the world after the dollar exchange rate (see Chapter 18). The rate is based on information provided by eighteen banks on their funding costs in the interbank markets. In 2012, evidence was discovered of collusion among big banks such as UBS, Barclays, Rabobank and Royal Bank of Scotland, in order to manipulate LIBOR in their own interests. They knew they could get away with it. Although steps were taken by regulatory authorities all over the globe (US, UK, EU, Canada, Japan, Australia, Hong Kong), so far no criminal prosecution against the banks has been filed and the fines have been ludicrously small compared with the amounts at stake.[304] They total just under $10 billion and each bank's share is minimal compared with the damage caused. The scandal resulted in the resignation of several bank CEOs, for example at Barclays (the second biggest British bank) and Rabobank (the second biggest Dutch bank), and the sacking of dozens of traders. But, significantly, no banks lost the right to continue operating on the markets they conspired to rig, and no CEO was jailed.

While the banks acknowledged the charge of manipulation and accepted the fines imposed under British law, the US judiciary behaved with outrageous leniency. On 29 March 2013 Naomi Buchwald, a New

---

304   Matt Taibbi, 'Everything Is Rigged: the Biggest Price-Fixing Scandal Ever', *Rolling Stone*, 25 April 2013, http://www.rollingstone.com/politics/news/everything-is-rigged-the-biggest-financial-scandal-yet-20130425?. See also 'Libor scandal', Wikipedia, http://en.Wikipedia.org/wiki/LIBOR_scandal.

York District judge, exempted the banks involved of any legal responsibility towards individuals or institutions that had suffered from the manipulation of the LIBOR.[305] To protect banks from prosecution on the grounds of collusion and monopolistic practices, she argued that laws on competition do not apply to the LIBOR rate, and banks can agree on rates without violating the US antitrust laws. Since rates on swaps and CDS markets are established in the same way – using the average of the rates sent in by participants – such a decision creates a dangerous precedent which opens the door to blatant manipulation of the key rates ruling global financial markets by major financial institutions. In the US, the LIBOR scandal went through a new development in March 2014 when the US Federal Deposit Insurance Corporation (FDIC) filed a law suit against more than a dozen major banks (JPMorgan Chase, Citigroup, Bank of America, UBS, Credit Suisse, HSBC, Royal Bank of Scotland, Lloyds, Barclays, Société Générale, Deutsche Bank, Royal Bank of Canada, Bank of Tokyo-Mitsubishi UFJ, etc.).[306] We will see whether this case will also be dismissed or will result in a fine without the threat of jail.

305 'Judge Dismisses Antitrust Claims in Libor Suits', *The Wall Street Journal*, 29 March 2013.
306 *Agence France Presse*, 'Le scandale du LIBOR rebondit aux Etats-Unis' (The Libor scandal rebounds in the US), 14 March 2014, http://www.rtbf.be/info/economie/detail_le-scandale-du-LIBOR-rebondit-aux-etats-unis?id=8222868 (in French).

The LIBOR is a benchmark interest-rate of considerable importance. It determines the interest-rate at which business and individuals borrow, throughout the world.

HOW IS THE LIBOR RATE FIXED?

Every working day the biggest banks share their estimates of the interest-rate at which they think they can borrow from other banks.

They withdraw the highest and the lowest quarters and calculate the average of the remainder. This becomes the LIBOR rate.

The LIBOR is calculated for 10 currencies and 15 borrowing periods (i.e. short, medium or long term).

WHAT IS THE LIBOR USED FOR?

On the derivatives market
The LIBOR is used to price financial derivatives such as insurance - a sector that represents at least $350,000 bn.

Interest-rates
The LIBOR is often the reference-rate when calculating interest-rates. When the LIBOR increases, the cost of loans increases.

Property mortgages
45% of mortgages and 80% of subprime loans have interest-rates linked to the LIBOR.

There is more...
The LIBOR also affects business, public and consumer borrowing such as student loans at variable interest-rates.

In the context of the LIBOR scandal, the European Commission fined eight banks a total amount of €1.7 billion for forming a cartel that manipulated the derivatives market.[307] Four banks manipulated rates for

307   'Antitrust: Commission fines banks € 1.71 billion for participating in cartels in the interest rate derivatives industry', European Commission, press release issued 4 December 2013, http://europa.eu/rapid/press-release_IP-13-1208_en.htm.

derivatives on the euro exchange market, while six manipulated rates for derivatives on the yen exchange market. The logic of not actually taking them to court was applied again.

Moreover, since the accused banks agreed to pay a fine, the amount was reduced by 10%. The banks fined were JPMorgan Chase and Citigroup (the first and third-ranking US banks), Deutsche Bank (the leading German bank), Société Générale (France's third-largest bank), Royal Bank of Scotland (the third-ranking British bank), and RP Martin. In return for informing on their colleagues, two banks, namely UBS (Switzerland's leading bank) and Barclays (the second-ranking British bank), were exempted from paying the fine.

To sum up, we are back to medieval indulgences: if you pay to redeem your sins you can stay in the paradise of finance. If you repent of your misdeeds and inform on the other thieves, then you will be let off paying the indulgence, or fines.

The Australian government took the farce one step further: they scolded BNP Paribas for 'potential misconduct' (*sic*) relating to Australian interbank rates between 2007 and 2010. BNP Paribas sacked traders and promised to donate AU$ 1 million to promote financial literature!

24.
Tax evasion
and fraud by UBS

UBS (Union de Banques Suisses) was rescued from bankruptcy in October 2008 by massive injections of Swiss public money. It was involved in the LIBOR manipulation scandal, the currency markets manipulation scandal (the subject of several inquiries by regulatory authorities in Hong Kong, the US, the UK, and Switzerland) and the abusive sale of structured Mortgage-Backed Securities on the US market. UBS, just like its fellows, HSBC and Credit Suisse in particular, became specialised in large-scale tax evasion for the very rich in the US, Europe and elsewhere.[308]

> The testimony of a former Swiss bank employee to *Le Parisien-Aujourd'hui en France* shows that the largest Swiss banks, which have been under criminal investigation in France since 2012, have established a well-oiled tax evasion machine to encourage the French to defraud. Guillaume Daïeff and Serge Tournaire, the Parisian financial judges examining the case, suspect the Union de Banques Suisses (UBS) of having established an extensive system aimed at illicitly soliciting French clients and encouraging them to open undeclared accounts in Switzerland in the 2000s.[309]

---

308   See, especially, the excellent book by Antoine Peillon, *Ces 600 milliards qui manquent à la France* (The 600 billion that France needs), Paris: Le Seuil, 2012 (in French). See the review in *Alternatives économiques*, http://www.alternatives-economiques.fr/ces-600-milliards-qui-manquent-a-la-france--enquete-au-coeur-de-l-evasion-fiscale_fr_art_1143_58595.html (in French).
309   'Des conseillers d'UBS faisaient la mule entre la France et la Suisse'

A few weeks later, in February 2014, another accusation against UBS appeared in a book written by a former UBS employee in France in charge of organising high-profile leisure events to entice customers.

> The idea was to put UBS representatives into contact with prospective clients, preferably the richest, with a personal wealth of more than €50 million. Millionaires are not attracted by just a cup of coffee; the events had to be sumptuous – golf competitions, regattas, opera evenings – followed by dinner at the table of a renowned chef. Nothing was too good. [...] Each time, there were a large number of Swiss bank representatives present. They came from Basel, Geneva, Lausanne, Zurich; their mission was to get the millionaires, whom we had pre-selected as targets, to deposit their wealth with them. Each year, the Zurich head office wanted a report: how many new clients? How much fresh money? The rule was that an event had to make a profit.[310]

In France, justice is slow and hesitant and in Belgium, where UBS ran the same fraudulent schemes as elsewhere, it does nothing at all; but in Germany, UBS reached an agreement with the authorities in July 2014. UBS agreed to pay a 300-million-euro fine to avoid pros-

---

(UBS representatives go back and forth between France and Switzerland), *Le Monde*, 21 January 2014, http://www.lemonde.fr/Économie/article/2014/01/21/des-conseillers-d-ubs-faisaient-la-mule-en-transportant-eux-memes-ces-sommes-de-l-autre-cote-des-alpes_4351540_3234.html (in French).

310   From an interview published in *Le Parisien*, 6 February 2014, http://www.leparisien.fr/espace-premium/actu/le-livre-qui-derange-les-banquiers-suisses-06-02-2014-3563661.php (in French). See Stéphanie Gibaud, *La femme qui en savait vraiment trop* (The Woman Who Really Knew Too Much), Paris: Le Cherche-Midi, 2014. Gibaud also says in the interview: 'In the small world of private banking I am blacklisted. My job applications go straight into the waste paper basket. I have started legal proceedings against UBS for harassment and I expect the justice system to bring out the truth. I hope my book will enlighten the judges and help me to rebuild my life.'

ecution.[311] The bank is accused of having helped its German clients hide their fortunes behind foundations and trusts in Liechtenstein. According to the prosecutor's office at Bochum, which conducted the investigation and carried out several raids on UBS subsidiaries in Germany, the funds concerned amount to some €20 billion. With the fine set at €300 million, UBS will get off with paying 1.5% of the amounts involved in the fraud.

UBS is the third Swiss bank to be fined by the German authorities. Two other banks, Julius Bär and Credit Suisse, had to pay €50 million and €149 million respectively. In all three cases, the banks avoided proper convictions by paying these paltry fines and having their image only slightly besmirched as the scandal was brushed under the carpet. They must also change their financial strategy; but they can carry on in their own sweet way without the least threat to their freedom to practice banking activities.

Events in the US confirm the 'Too Big to Jail' doctrine. When in 2008 the US authorities started proceedings against UBS, whom they accused of organising a tax-evasion network in their country, UBS was managing the accounts of about 5,000 wealthy US and Canadian citizens to help them avoid paying taxes. Their fortunes were stashed in Switzerland (often after transiting through several tax havens to cover their traces). In the process of their inquiry, the US authorities were able to consult information passed to them in 2007 by Bradley Birkenfeld, a former specialist in tax evasion at UBS.

311 'UBS négocie son amende avec le fisc allemand' (UBS negotiates its fine with the German fiscal authorities), *Tribune de Genève*, 25 February 2014, http://www.tdg.ch/Économie/ubs-negocie-amende-allemagne/story/26256689 (in French). The title of the article is highly significant. For the conclusion of the case in July 2014, see Mathilde Farine, 'UBS met un point final au litige fiscal en Allemagne' (UBS puts an end to its tax fraud case), *Le Temps*, 30 July 2014, http://www.letemps.ch/Page/Uuid/50e70376-1747-11e4-9c88-1cf3650bdf92/UBS_met_un_point_final_au_litige_fiscal_en_Allemagne (in French).

Bradley Birkenfeld: whistleblower or bounty hunter?

Bradley Birkenfeld is a US citizen. He started his banking career in Boston, at State Street (the thirteenth-largest US bank).[312] Before quitting this job he contacted the FBI in 1994 to denounce the wrong-doings that he had found, but the bank was not prosecuted. He was appointed in 1996 by Credit Suisse (the second-ranking Swiss bank) in the US as a wealth manager. In 1998 he moved to Barclays (Brit-ain's second-largest bank). In 2001 he moved to UBS in Geneva, tak-ing wealthy clients' accounts with him. It was here, under the respon-sibility of Raoul Weil, one of the UBS bosses, that he helped establish a network for the evasion of US taxes. According to Birkenfeld, he left UBS in 2005 having realised the seriousness of the activities he was participating in. It is to be noted, however, that these activities were not illegal under Swiss law. In 2007 he decided to contact the US Justice Department in order to denounce the illegal activities of UBS under cover of a US law of 2006 that protects and rewards whistle-blowers who expose tax fraud.[313] An IRS (Internal Revenue Service) Whistleblower Office had even been created. The home page of the official site says:

> The IRS Whistleblower Office pays money to people who blow the whistle on persons who fail to pay the tax that they owe.[314] If the IRS uses information provided by the whistleblower, it can award the whistle-blower up to 30% of the additional tax, penalty and other amounts it collects.[315]

---

312   Two fairly complete biographical sources: 'Bradley Birkenfeld', *Wikipedia*, http://en.Wikipedia.org/wiki/Bradley_Birkenfeld (consulted 3 March 2014) and David Voreacos, 'Banker Who Blew Whistle Over Tax Cheats Seeks Pardon', *Bloomberg*, 24 June 2010, http://www.bloomberg. com/news/2010-06-24/ubs-banker-who-blew-whistle-on-swiss-secrecy-over-tax-cheats-seeks-pardon.html.
313   Birkenfeld also made contact with the Senate Subcommittee on Banking Activities chaired by Carl Levin, where he testified in 2007. This is the same subcommittee that investigated HSBC. See the official subcom-mittee website, http://www.hsgac.senate.gov/subcommittees/investigations
314   In this case it could be called an 'informants'' office.
315   IRS Whistleblower Office official website, http://www.irs.gov/uac/ Whistleblower-Informant-Award, consulted 3 March 2014.

Information that Bradley Birkenfeld communicated to the IRS and the US Department of Justice has allowed the two organisations to build a solid case against UBS. The seriousness of UBS's illegal activities under US law should have meant the withdrawal of their banking licence, but as happened later with HSBC and other big banks, the authorities in Washington merely settled for the payment of fines ($780 million in February 2009 plus $200 million later). The United States also compelled the bank to notify them of US citizens who had stashed their wealth in Switzerland with the help of UBS (a list of 4,450 names). To achieve this, Washington at times used strong-arm tactics – the threat of withdrawing the bank's licence and the temporary arrest of bank executives, such as Raoul Weil, who appeared in court in 2014.[316]

Meanwhile, Birkenfeld at first paid a heavy price for collaborating with the US authorities. Arrested in May 2008 and brought to trial in August 2009, he was sentenced to 40 months in prison for his illegal activities at UBS. During his plea against Birkenfeld, the prosecutor recognised that without his collaboration, the Department of Justice and the IRS would not have been able to gather proof of UBS's wrongdoing. Birkenfeld started his prison sentence in January 2010. He appealed to President Barack Obama. He also requested a revision of his trial from Attorney General Eric Holder and was finally released in 2012, after serving 31 months. But what the international press highlighted was what happened to him after his release: the IRS paid him a $104-million reward for reporting UBS's illegal activities. The IRS concluded that Birkenfeld was entitled to a percentage of the taxes and fines that were collected from rich tax evaders thanks to his information.[317]

It is impossible to analyse Birkenfeld's motives here. Was he a white knight, a whistleblower, or simply an informer and bounty hunter? What matters is the following observation: the bank that takes part

---

316   Zachary Fagenson and Reuters, 'Ex-UBS bank executive pleads not guilty in tax fraud case', 7 January 2014,
http://articles.chicagotribune.com/2014-01-07/business/sns-rt-us-ubs-tax-banker-20140106_1_bradley-birkenfeld-tax-fraud-conspiracy-u-s-clients.
317   The *Wall Street Journal* has made a copy of the decision of the IRS Whistleblower Office available at
http://online.wsj.com/public/resources/documents/birkenfeld-determination-letter.pdf.

in serious illegal activities and its directors – those who manage and plan the misdeeds – enjoy impunity. At most the bank is sentenced to pay a fine.

But those who denounce the illegal activities of a bank do so at their own risk. Indeed, in the eyes of Swiss law, they are guilty of infringing banking secrecy, while in the US they may be rewarded as well as facing a prison sentence.

25.
Impunity

The banks and other international financial institutions often function as cartels, displaying levels of cynicism and abuse of power rarely seen. Today, once governments have put public money into structures that have squandered their resources in speculation, courts (which are supposed to see that the laws are enforced) do all they can to protect these institutions and so generalise, and even justify, sometimes *a posteriori*, the illegal or criminal behaviour of which these banks are guilty.

Such a context, where impunity is the rule, incites financial directors to take ever greater risks. Banks themselves are not prosecuted, and are rarely even called upon to account for their activities. When something goes wrong, they turn upon traders such as Jérôme Kerviel and others, prosecuted for damages by the banks that employed them. As for top directors, the level of their bonuses increases as their bank's revenue increases, regardless of the origin of the revenue, whether from illegal or from highly speculative operations. Bonuses can increase even when a bank's revenue falls. At the very worst, they leave the bank with a golden handshake, no prosecution and keep all their personal gains.

As long as this perverted system continues, the abuse and pillage of public resources by the financial system will also continue. It is not only the bank directors who are not bothered by the authorities, but also the banks themselves to whom the 'Too Big to Jail' doctrine is applied. This demonstrates the complicity and the mutual vested interests that exist between banks, their major shareholders, high level authorities and central government institutions. This is only the tip of the iceberg revealed through the mist of financial scandals and out-of-court settlements. A large number of these affairs are never made public by the authorities.

In the case of serious breaches, firm disciplinary action must be brought to bear: certain activities must be prohibited, banking licences permanently withdrawn from establishments guilty of criminal offences, and the cost of loss and damages claimed against the directors and major shareholders who are responsible.

Finally, it is urgent to break up big banks into smaller units to limit the risks, for the banks to be socialised and placed under popular control in order to create a public banking service that will give priority to satisfying social needs and protecting the environment.

26.
Governments' and central banks' collusion

Since 2007, governments and central banks of the most industrialised Western countries – which have been hit by the greatest economic crisis since the 1930s – have given top priority to the rescue of private banks and the financial system (insurance companies, mutual funds, private pension funds, etc.).[318] We first analyse the measures that have been implemented to achieve this goal and then examine the broader policy framework. Bank bail-outs happen at the expense of the overwhelming majority of the population. Governments have done their utmost to maintain private banks' main privileges and to keep their power intact. The cost is enormous – explosion of public debt, loss of tax revenue, tight restrictions on loans to households and small businesses, and further speculative and adventurous activities, which in some cases have required expensive new rescue plans.

Central banks lend massively to private banks

Since the banking bubble burst in 2007, the major central banks of the most industrialised countries (the ECB, the Bank of England, the Fed in the US, the National Bank of Switzerland, the Bank of Japan) have lent massively to banks in order to avoid bankruptcy. Without this source of unlimited credit, many banks might have found themselves insolvent, as the usual funding sources declined – the interbank market had seized up as the banks lost confidence in each other, sales of banks' covered bonds became weak and the Money Market

---

318   In Japan the government and central bank did the same when their real-estate bubble burst at the beginning of the 1990s. See Daniel Munevar, 'Décennies perdues au Japon' (Lost decades in Japan), in Damien Millet and Éric Toussaint, *La dette ou la vie* (Life or Debt), Brussels: Aden-CADTM, 2011, Chapter 15 (in French).

Funds became erratic. The total amount loaned by central banks to the private sector since 2007 is more than $20 trillion. As this has been made available at very low interest-rates, the big banks have been able to greatly reduce interest repayments.

Along with direct cash injections, central banks have other ways to assist private banks. Between 2008 and 2014, the Fed purchased huge quantities of Mortgage Backed Securities, totalling $1.5 trillion.[319] In 2012-2013 alone it bought up to $40 billion worth every month from banks and mortgage agencies.[320] Towards the end of 2013, the Fed started to reduce its purchases, which were no more than $35 billion in March 2014. As of October 2014, the Fed held $1.7 trillion's worth of MBS, about 21% of the total value of this kind of toxic product.[321]

The ECB does not purchase these products itself but allows banks to deposit them as collateral, that is, as guarantees for the loans they are granted. During the period from 2010 to 2013, the 'value' of Asset Backed Securities (ABS) on deposit at the ECB varied between €325 billion and €490 billion.

The ECB also purchased covered bonds issued by private banks to finance their activities.[322] Such assistance from the ECB is extremely important to the private banks, which, as we saw in Chapter 19, had serious difficulty finding funding on the financial markets. The media has quite simply ignored the extent of this aid. Since the beginning of the crisis, the ECB has purchased €76 billion in covered bonds, €22 billion on the primary market and €54 billion on the secondary

319 By the end of January 2014, the volume of the Fed's balance-sheet was over $4 trillion: $2.228 trillion in treasury bonds and $1.586 trillion in Mortgage Backed Securities (MBS).
320 Fannie Mae, Freddie Mac and Ginnie Mae.
321 Since the beginning of the crisis the Fed has bought back more than $2.4 trillion of US Treasury bonds (in October 2013 the Fed held US bonds worth $2.45 trillion), which is about 18% of all current US Treasury bonds. The Fed does not purchase them directly from the US Treasury but on the open market from banks who themselves had purchased them from the US Treasury. See US legislation on the matter. The Bank of England has done the same.
322 Natixis, which, like other banks, supports these purchases, published an enthusiastic report on this question. See 'Que penser des achats de covered bonds par la BCE ?' (What of the ECB's purchases of covered bonds?) *Natixis Special Report*, 2005. http://cib.natixis.com/flushdoc.aspx?id=46663 (in French).

market, including bonds rated as badly as BBB-, expressing lack of confidence in the issuing bodies. On 18 March 2014 the ECB held €52 billion's worth of covered bonds – a very large proportion of the total quantity of covered bonds that banks have issued. (For the record, in 2013 the amount issued was €166 billion.)[323]

Banks cumulate aid from central banks and governments

Government aid is made up of guarantees and injections of capital in order to recapitalise the banks. In the period from October 2008 to December 2011, €1.174 trillion (9.3% of EU GDP[324]) of guarantees were underwritten by European governments as a contingency measure. To these guarantees must be added €442 billion (3.5% of EU GDP) of public capital support to banks. During 2012 and 2013 the recapitalisations continued – about €40 billion in Spain in 2012 alone, more than €50 billion in Greece, about €20 billion in Cyprus, €4 billion more for Dexia bank in Belgium, €3.9 billion for Monte dei Paschi in Italy, €3.7 billion for the Dutch bank SNS, €4.2 billion in Portugal on top of the Portuguese bail-out of Banco Espírito Santo in July 2014, not forgetting Ireland, Slovenia and Croatia. In each case this assistance was granted without any government supervision of the use made of the funds.

A quick calculation can give an idea of the extent of the capital injections if we compare their total to that of the banks' hard capital. The twenty largest European banks in 2012 had assets of about €23 trillion; considering that on average their hard capital represents 3% in assets, the total hard capital was roughly €700 billion. In recent years, European governments have advanced an impressive €200 billion of capital to these banks. A precise calculation would also include the injections into banks such as Fortis, which were acquired by BNP Paribas.

Some authors refer to state guarantees granted to 'Too Big to Fail' banks as implicit subsidies and expose their perverse consequences.

---

323   See Christopher Thompson, 'Europe covered bond sales hit decade low', *Financial Times*, 26 November 2013.
324   'State aid: crisis-related aid aside, scoreboard shows continued trend towards less and better-targeted aid', European Commission press-release, 21 December 2012, http://europa.eu/rapid/press-release_IP-12-1444_en-.htm?locale=EN.

Big banks enjoy implicit subsidies

The systemic banks are aware that, because of their size and the repercussions that would result from a failure ('Too Big to Fail'), they can count on the unfailing support of states.

The banks' creditors know this as well. They are thus inclined to lend to banks knowing there is, supposedly, no risk involved for them. They know full well that should one of these banks go down, they would avoid the losses because the state would take them on as lender of last resort. This gilt-edged situation permits banks to negotiate their borrowing at the lowest rates of interest, the interest-rate being proportional to the risk involved. If the banks did not enjoy this guarantee from the state they would have to pay higher interest-rates. The difference between these two rates of interest represents an implicit state subsidy to the banks.

A rigorous study by the European Green Party has worked out that for 2012 the implicit state guarantees to the big banks amounted to €233.9 billion.[325]

This implicit guarantee has perverse consequences:

- It encourages the big banks to take ever greater risks;
- It encourages the centralisation of big banks. Smaller establishments that do not have the same level of guarantee must find their funding at higher interest-rates and in

---

325   See 'EU systemic banks capture huge amount of implicit subsidies', the Greens, January 2014. http://www.greens-efa.eu/eu-systemic-banks-capture-huge-amount-of-implicit-subsidies-11525.html; complete study at: http://www.philippelamberts.eu/wp-content/uploads/2014/01/ImplicitSubsidy-of-Banking-sector_Greens-in-the-EP-study_January-2014.pdf .

case of sharp competition may be forced to close down or be bought out by their competitors;

- These gains are entirely private and do not benefit the population.

Other forms of government aid to banks are:

- Reductions in taxes effectively paid on banks' profits. They declared losses in 2008-2009 (and sometimes for other years too) that exempted them from paying tax over several years. In fact losses are carried forward to subsequent years, thus permitting substantial tax savings.
- The refusal to take measures forcing the banks that receive ECB loans to, in turn, grant loans to households and small businesses (which are the principal private employers) to stimulate the economy. The banks freely use this money as they see fit without bringing any benefits to the real economy.
- The refusal to take strict measures against financial institutions that would avoid repeated banking crises (see Chapters 9, 10 and 13).
- The refusal by governments to prosecute the banks that are considered 'Too Big to Fail'. Since 2007-2008, not one bank in the EU, North America or Japan has had its banking licence revoked. Out-of-court settlements have permitted the banks to carry on business as usual, avoiding being properly prosecuted and convicted. Not one bank director has been imprisoned (except in Iceland, which is not an EU member) or barred from banking activities. The only judgements have been against bank employees, in most cases condemned for having damaged their bank's image. This refusal to prosecute the banks themselves is obvious in the actions taken against traders such as Jérôme Kerviel, who have served as scapegoats.
- The Eurozone banks have the monopoly of lending to the public sector. It is prohibited for the ECB and the Eurozone's central banks to grant loans to public authorities (see Box

on the ECB). However the governments in the Eurozone are free to borrow from publicly-owned banks where they still exist, but they do not do so.

- Since 2008, private banks get most of their funding from public sources (the ECB and the central banks of the Eurozone) at very favourable interest-rates. From November 2013 they could borrow from the ECB at 0.25% while the inflation rate over the same period was 0.8%, which means that the real interest-rate is, in fact, negative. That rate was cut to 0.15% in June 2014 and to 0.05% in September 2014. The banks then lent funds to peripheral European countries like Cyprus, Greece, Ireland, Italy, Spain, Portugal and the East European members of the Eurozone at high or even exorbitant interest-rates (between 4% and 10%); while they lent to Belgium, France and the Netherlands at 2% and to Germany at 1.6% (figures for March 2014).

- Borrowing on the financial markets by issuing sovereign debt bonds. The sale of these bonds is entrusted to a group of big private banks called 'primary dealers' (generally chosen among the group of the thirty biggest international banks)[326] for whom this activity is a source of income. Then, through their central banks, the governments repurchase on the secondary market a part of the bonds they have themselves issued through the primary dealers. In January 2014 the US central bank's balance-sheet included $2.228 trillion worth of Treasury bonds that it had purchased from different banks. The Bank of England had £371 billion of gilts on its books on 13 March 2014,[327] that is, British Government bonds that were purchased on the secondary market. By 31 December 2014 the ECB held €185 billion of Greek, Irish, Italian, Spanish and Portuguese sovereign bonds all of which had also been purchased on the secondary market.[328]

---

326   The same banks have been involved in the different kinds of abuse and manipulation examined in other chapters.

327   See 'Asset Purchase Facility - Results', Bank of England. http://www.bankofengland.co.uk/markets/Pages/apf/results.aspx.

328   Sovereign bonds of Ireland €9.7 billion; Greece €27.7 billion; Spain €38.8 billion; Italy €89.7 billion; Portugal €19.8 billion.

The European Central Bank

Created in 1998 on the model of the German Bundesbank and located in Frankfurt-am-Main in Germany, the European Central Bank (ECB) is the European institution responsible for applying monetary policy in the Eurozone.[329] The Treaty on European Union, commonly known as the Maastricht Treaty (1992) created the ECB and defined its missions as laid out in Article 105:

- To define and implement the monetary policy of the Community;
- To conduct *foreign-exchange* operations;
- To hold and manage the official foreign reserves of the member states;
- To promote the smooth operation of payment systems.

Its principal mission along with that of the national central banks of the Eurozone is to maintain price stability[330] around an annual inflation level of 2%.

The Eurozone's national central banks' monetary competences have been transferred to the ECB.

Proclaimed independent, the ECB is governed by bankers according to pure banking logic. If European populations were democratically to demand different monetary choices, the ECB could quite simply ignore them and continue its dogma, which is favourable to big business and the wealthiest in-

329 Eleven countries founded the Eurozone in 1999 (Austria, Belgium, Finland, France, Germany, Ireland, Italy, Luxembourg, the Netherlands, Portugal and Spain); they were joined by Greece in 2001, Slovenia in 2007, Cyprus and Malta in 2008, Slovakia in 2009, Estonia in 2011 and Latvia in 2014. See: Civitas, Eurozone map, http://www.civitas.org.uk/eufacts/eurozonemap.html.
330 *Treaty of Lisbon*, Article 282.

dividuals. This so-called independence is no more than a façade to suggest that the ECB's choices may not be questioned. In fact, it is the big banks and financial institutions that have the ear of the ECB, along with the European leaders who impose neoliberal policies on their peoples. Although labour-market policies are not under the control of the ECB, it regularly intervenes to promote an increase in casual labour and the interests of big business.

The ECB does not directly buy the public bonds that are issued by governments. The governments that created the ECB chose to give the private sector the exclusive right to finance public borrowing. Since 2010 the ECB has been buying public bonds on the secondary market from the bankers who bought them on the primary market and are having trouble unloading those they no longer want. This is another way in which the ECB finances the banks. If the ECB bought public bonds on the primary market it could directly finance public services or governments. It should also be noted that the ECB only buys public debt bonds on the secondary market that have been issued by countries which accept brutal austerity policies.

The Lisbon Treaty and the ECB statutes prohibit the ECB, and indeed the national central banks, from lending directly to states. They lend to the private banking sector, which in turn lends to states at higher interest-rates. Article 101 of the Maastricht Treaty, reproduced as Article 123 of the Lisbon Treaty, states:

> Overdraft facilities or any other type of credit facility with the European Central Bank or with the central banks of the member states (hereinafter referred to as 'national central banks') in favour of Union institutions, bodies, offices or

agencies, central governments, regional, local or other public authorities, other bodies governed by public law, or public undertakings of member states shall be prohibited, as shall the purchase directly from them by the European Central Bank or national central banks of debt instruments.

This is one of the reasons why this treaty must be abrogated in favour of a truly democratic European Union.

27.
The Fed
bails out Wall Street

Since 2008, the Fed has granted unlimited credit to banks at an official rate of 0.25%. In fact, as the General Accounting Office (GAO)
has revealed, the Fed has lent close to $16 trillion at an interest-rate
below 0.25%.[331] The report shows it has not followed its own prudential rules and has not notified Congress. According to an enquiry by a
US Congress committee, there is clear and evident collusion between
the Fed and the big banks:

> The CEO of JPMorgan Chase served on the
> New York Fed's board of directors at the
> same time that his bank received more than
> $390 billion in financial assistance from
> the Fed. Moreover, JPMorgan Chase served
> as one of the clearing banks for the Fed's
> emergency lending programmes.[332]

According to an independent study by the Levy Institute, which has
the collaboration of economists such as Joseph Stiglitz, Paul Krug-
man and James K. Galbraith, Fed assistance to banks was much more
than the $16 trillion revealed by the GAO; it was $29 trillion.[333]

331   'Federal Reserve System: Opportunities Exist to Strengthen Policies and Processes for Managing Emergency Assistance', US Government Accountability Office (GAO), July 2011, http://www.gao.gov/
assets/330/321506.pdf. This report was made possible by an amendment
to the Dodd-Frank act that had been introduced by Ron Paul, Alan Gray-
son and Bernie Sanders in 2010. Bernie Sanders, an independent senator,
made it public: http://www.sanders.senate.gov/imo/media/doc/GAO%20
Fed%20Investigation.pdf.
332   Senator Bernie Sanders, 'The Fed Audit', http://www.sanders.senate.
gov/newsroom/news/?id=9e2a4ea8-6e73-4be2-a753-62060dcbb3c3.
333   See James Felkerson, '$29,000,000,000,000: a Detailed Look at the

The big European banks had access to Fed funds until the beginning of 2011. Dexia got a loan of $159 billion,[334] Barclays $868 billion, Royal Bank of Scotland $541 billion, Deutsche Bank $354 billion, UBS $287 billion, Credit Suisse $260 billion, BNP Paribas $175 billion, Dresdner Bank $135 billion and Société Générale $124 billion. Under pressure from Congress, the end of this funding was one of the reasons that from May-June 2011, the US Money Market Funds started to block their loans to European banks, considering that without support from the Fed, the European banks incurred too high a risk.

The Federal Reserve System of the United States

The Federal Reserve System, called simply 'the Fed', is the United States' central bank. It is an independent structure within the US government, which participates actively in the private sector and has the responsibility for US monetary policy and thus has a strong influence on the world's financial markets. Under US law, the mission of the Fed is to guarantee price stability and full employment and to ensure the stability of the financial system by taking the necessary measures to predict and attenuate financial crises and panics. To achieve this, the Fed has three important powers:

- It controls interest-rates that influence consumption, investment and inflation;
- It controls the money supply, which permits the stability of prices in times of crisis;
- It supervises and regulates financial institutions.

Fed's Bail-out by Funding Facility and Recipient', Levy Institute of Economics, 2011, www.levyinstitute.org/pubs/wp_698.pdf.
334   See, in particular, page 196 of the above-mentioned GAO report that refers to loans to Dexia amounting to $53.5 billion, which are only part of the total loans to Dexia by the Fed: http://www.gao.gov/assets/330/321506.pdf.

The Fed was created by the Federal Reserve Act of 1913 as a reaction to the growing instability of the North American financial system at the end of the nineteenth and beginning of the twentieth century. Until then the US did not have centralised control and regulation of its financial system. Each state was responsible for regulating and controlling the banks that were within its jurisdiction. The Fed was established to ensure the stability of the US financial system by becoming the lender of last resort and so to be able to supply resources to banks facing difficulties.

The institutional structure of the Fed is made up of twelve regional banks overseen globally by a Board of Governors. These regional banks function as Joint Stock Companies possessing non-negotiable and non-transferable shares in the Federal Reserve System: the stock may not be sold, traded, or pledged as security for a loan; dividends are, by law, 6% per year. These shares enable the banks' participation in the elections of the regional counsellors of the Fed. The councils are made up of nine members. Three are chosen by the banks and represent their interests, three represent industrial and commercial interests and are also chosen by the banks, and the last three members are chosen by the national Board of Governors.

The Board of Governors is charged with overseeing the twelve regional Federal Reserve Banks and with helping implement the United States' monetary policy. It has a maximum of seven members (currently five) who are nominated by the President of the United States and confirmed by the Senate for a fourteen-year term of office. One of the principal functions of the Board is to pilot the Federal Open Market Committee (FOMC), which fixes interest-rates and determines the country's general monetary policy.

There are two basic differences between the Fed and its European counterpart, the ECB. While the Fed's mission is to simultaneously guarantee price stability and full employment, the ECB has as its principal mission to maintain low and stable inflation levels within the Eurozone. The other difference is in their ability to regulate and control their financial institutions. The Fed has the means to regulate and supervise all the financial institutions operating under the Federal Reserve System, while the ECB is dependent on the central bank of each of Eurozone country for the implementation of its regulations and control over its financial institutions. Finally, the European Commission has approved an extension of the ECB's powers, from Autumn 2014, to include responsibility for the direct control of the big banks that are subject to the European system. We shall see what the impact of this change will be.

28.
The ECB
since 2010

In 2010 institutional investors (including banks) and hedge funds attacked Greece, the weak link in the European chain of debt, before turning their attention to Ireland, Portugal, Spain and Italy. In so doing, they made juicy profits by forcing these countries to increase their interest-rates on the bonds they issued in order to refinance their debts. Private banks made the biggest profits compared to other investors, by directly obtaining funds from the ECB at 1%, while at the same time making quarterly loans at 4% or 5%. As for securities, they only agreed to buy Irish and Portuguese ten-year bonds if the interest-rate rose to 10%.

When attacking the weak links, the institutional investors (including banks) were sure that the EU and the ECB would be forced to assist, in one way or another, states that were the victims of speculation by lending them the funds necessary to continue debt repayments. They were quite right: loans were advanced to countries in difficulty. The loan conditions imposed by the Troika (the ECB, the European Commission and the IMF) aimed at producing brutal austerity measures, cuts in wages and pensions and public-sector redundancies.

Despite the help of the ECB, in June 2011 European banks entered a highly critical phase. Their situation was almost as serious as on 15 September 2008, after the failure of Lehman Brothers. Many of them were threatened with asphyxia because their massive need for short-term financing (several hundred billion dollars) was no longer being met by the American Money Market Funds, which, as we saw in the previous chapter, felt that the situation of the European banks was becoming more and more risky. The banks were in danger of being unable to honour their debts.[335]

---

335   In August 2011, a CADTM series entitled 'In the eye of the storm: the

That is when the ECB, following an emergency European summit held on 21 July 2011 to deal with the prospect of a series of bank failures, resumed the massive purchasing of Greek, Portuguese, Irish, Italian and Spanish public-debt securities from the banks, on top of the previously mentioned loans. This was to provide cash flow and to relieve them of a part of the securities they had purchased in huge quantities during the preceding period. Interest-rates, too, were cut on debts of countries in the periphery, but to no avail. The value of bank shares continued to crumble and interest-rates for countries like Italy and Spain remained high. The decisive action that kept the European banks afloat was the extension by the ECB, beginning in September 2011 and in consultation with the Fed, the Bank of England and the Swiss National Bank, of an unlimited line of credit. Banks that were starved of dollars and euros were put on life-support. They began to

---

debt crisis in the European Union', CADTM, 14 June 2012, (http://cadtm. org/In-the-eye-of-the-storm-the-debt), described this situation, at a time when very few financial commentators dared to speak of it: 'They [the European banks] financed, and still finance, their loans to European states and businesses through the United States' Money Market Funds. Since it took fright at what was happening in Europe from June 2011, this source of low-interest-rate financing has almost dried up, precipitating, principally, the major French banks into a stock-market plummet, which increased the pressure on the ECB to redeem their shares and thus provide them with money. To summarise, we have another demonstration of the interaction between the economies of the United States and the EU. Hence the constant contact between Barack Obama, Angela Merkel, Nicolas Sarkozy, the ECB, the IMF and big bankers Goldman Sachs, BNP Paribas, Deutsche Bank. A breakdown in the access to dollars enjoyed by European banks can cause a very serious crisis in Europe, and difficulties for European banks to pay US lenders may precipitate Wall Street into new crises.'
A study by the bank Natixis confirms the distress of French banks during the summer of 2011. In 'Les banques françaises dans la tourmente des marchés monétaires' (French Banks in turmoil in the money markets), *Flash Economie*, October 29, 2012, we read: 'De juin à novembre 2011, les fonds monétaires Americains ont subitement retiré la plus grande part de leurs financements aux banques françaises. (...) C'est jusqu'à 140 Mds USD de financements à court terme qui ont fait défaut aux banques françaises à fin novembre 2011, sans qu'aucune ne soit épargnée.' (From June to November 2011, U.S. Money Market Funds suddenly withdrew most of their funding for French banks. (...) French banks were short of almost $140 billion of short-term financing at the end of November 2011, with none of them spared.), http://cib.natixis.com/flus-hdoc.aspx?id=66654 (in French, trans. CADTM). This shut-down also affected most other European banks, as is also shown in this study by Natixis.

breathe again; but this treatment was insufficient. Their share prices continued to plunge. Between 1 January and 21 October 2011,
the price of shares in France's BNP Paribas dropped by 33.3% and
in Deutsche Bank 28.8%; Barclays dropped 30.5% and Credit Suisse
36.7%, and Société Générale plummeted 52.8%. The ECB was forced
to deploy the heavy artillery.

A Long-Term Refinancing Operation (LTRO), a long-term loan mechanism for banks, was created. Between December 2011 and February
2012, the ECB lent over €1 trillion (that is, €1,000 billion) to more
than 800 banks for a period of 3 years at an interest-rate of 1% (at
a time when inflation was about 2%). In fact, the gift to banks was
even more generous than is suggested by an interest-rate of only 1%,
already very advantageous, for two simple reasons. First, the interest
is not due until the repayment date of the loan. If a bank borrows over
three years for the full period it has no repayments to make, interest
or capital, until the end of the three-year period. And second, this rate
has since been lowered several times, to 0.15% in June 2014 and to
0.05% in September 2014.[336]

Consider a bank such as Dexia, which borrowed more than €20 billion from the ECB for three years at the beginning of 2012. It will
not be asked for repayment until the beginning of 2015, when it will
also be called upon to repay the totality of the interest which will be
calculated as follows: a 1% interest-rate until July 2012, 0.75% for
the period from July 2012 to May 2013, 0.50% from May 2013 to November 2013, 0.25% from November 2013, 0.15% from June 2014
to September 2014, and 0.05% interest from in September 2014.[337]
It is clear that when the time comes, Dexia, or Intesa Sanpaolo (ISP.
MI), the Italian bank which drew €24 billion on the same terms, will
be unable to repay unless they draw a new loan more or less equal to
the previous one. Now, the only place they can borrow from is ... the
ECB. Its president Mario Draghi has announced that at the end of the
3 years, the ECB will grant new loans of unlimited size for periods of
six months or more.

---

336 See Éric Toussaint, 'To the Bankers, he's "Super Mario 2.0" Draghi', CADTM,
8 September 2014, http://cadtm.org/To-the-Bankers-He-s-Super-Mario-2
337   See 'In this longer-term refinancing operation, the rate at which all
bids are satisfied is indexed to the average minimum bid rate in the main
refinancing operations over the life of the operation', on the ECB website.
http://sdw.ecb.europa.eu/servlet/desis?node=100000133

Imagine what would have happened if Dexia, and many other banks that were in trouble, had not had access to ECB loans: they would have had to close down. In fact, had they found lenders (which would have been far from easy, given the amounts needed), the banks would have had to pay more than 8% interest, and to pay it regularly. It would have been better to let the banks fail while guaranteeing savings by putting the toxic assets into a 'bad bank' guaranteed by the major shareholders, and putting the healthy assets into a truly public structure. We will return to this issue in the final chapter on alternatives.

What happened to €1 trillion of ECB liquidities

From 2012, the banks were overflowing with cash and made massive purchases of the bonds issued by their own countries. We have already seen that sovereign debt securities do not require equity, as they are not considered to be a risk. In Spain, for example, Spanish banks borrowed as much as €300 billion for three years at a rate of 1% from the ECB within the LTRO framework.[338] Part of this sum has enabled them to increase their purchases of debt securities issued by the Spanish Treasury. The evolution is quite striking. Towards the end of 2006, the Spanish banks only held €16 billion of public securities from their own country. By 2010, they had increased their purchases of Spanish public securities to a level of €63 billion. In 2011 they again increased their purchases, and their holdings in Spanish securities amounted to €94 billion. But thanks to the LTRO, their acquisitions literally exploded – the volume of their holdings doubled in a few months to reach €184.5 billion in July 2012.[339] Clearly the operation was very profitable for them. Whereas they were borrowing at 1%, they could buy 10-year Spanish securities with an interest-rate that varied between 5.5 and 7.6% in the second semester of 2012. In early 2014 Spanish banks could still borrow at 0.25% and then lend to the Spanish at around 4%.

---

338   Mary Watkins, 'Lenders plot early LTRO repayments', *Financial Times*, 14 November 2012.

339   According to the Spanish financial daily El Economista, 'La deuda del Estado en manos de la banca se duplica en siete meses' (Government debt held by banks doubles in seven months): http://www.eleconomista.es/espana/noticias/4252377/09/12/La-deuda-del-Estado-en-manos-de-la-banca-se-duplica-en-siete-meses.html (in Spanish).

In Italy, between late December 2011 and March 2012, the Italian banks borrowed €255 billion from the ECB within the LTRO framework.[340] Whereas in late 2010 the Italian banks held €208.3 billion in bonds from their country, that amount increased to €224.1 billion in late 2011, a few days after the start of the LTRO. They then used the credits they received from the ECB for massive acquisitions of Italian securities. In September 2012 the total value of the securities amounted to €341.4 billion.[341] As in the case of Spain, it was a very profitable operation – they borrowed at 1% and by purchasing 10-year Italian securities, obtained an interest-rate that varied from 5% to 6.6% in the second semester of 2012. In March 2014, Spanish banks could still borrow from the ECB at 0.25% and then lend to the Italian state at about 3.4%.

The same phenomenon was repeated in most Eurozone countries. Some of the assets of the European banks were relocated to their countries of origin. Concretely, what happened is that the share of public debt of a given country held by the financial institutions in that same country increased very perceptibly during 2012. That development reassured the governments of the Eurozone, in particular those of Spain and Italy, since they found that they had less difficulty in selling their bond issues. The ECB seemed to have found the solution. Lending massively to the private banks saved them from a critical situation and spared certain governments the pain of launching new bank bail-out plans. The money lent to the banks was used in part to purchase public debt securities from Eurozone states. This stopped the increase in interest-rates in the most fragile countries and even resulted in lower rates for others.

It is easy to see that, from the point of view of the interests of the people of the countries concerned, a very different approach should have been adopted – the ECB should have lent directly to the governments at less than 1% or even without interest. The banks should also have been socialised under popular control.

---

340   *Financial Times*, ibid.
341   Banca d'Italia, Supplements to the Statistical Bulletin: Monetary and Financial Indicators - Money and Banking, November 2012, http:// www.bancaditalia.it/statistiche/stat_mon_cred_fin/banc_fin/pimsmc/ pimsmc12/sb58_12/en_suppl_58_12.pdf, Table 2.1a.

Instead, the ECB put the private banks on life-support again by extending an unlimited line of credit at a very low interest-rate (between 0.75 and 1%). The banks used this windfall of public financing in different ways. On the one hand, they purchased sovereign-debt securities from countries like Spain and Italy who, under pressure from the banks, granted them high rates of remuneration (between 5% and 7.6% at 10 years, between 3.4% and 4% in the first quarter of 2014). On the other hand, they deposited a part of the credit that had been extended to them by the ECB... in the ECB! From €300 to 400 billion were deposited by the banks with the ECB as call money at an interest-rate of 0.25% in early 2012, and 0% since July 2012. In February 2014 more than €50 billion was deposited as call money at the ECB at 0%.

Banks did this because they needed to show other bankers and private suppliers of credit (Money Market Funds, pension funds, insurance companies) as well as the shareholders and regulatory authorities that they had ready cash to face the potential explosion of the time-bombs (see Chapter 14) in their accounts. Without this, potential lenders would shun them, or else demand very high interest-rates, the shareholders would pull out and their stock-market quotations would crumble.

With the same objective of reassuring private lenders, they also purchased sovereign bonds from governments that are free of risk in the short or middle term – Germany, Holland, France and so on. The demand was such that the two-year bonds of the governments in question sold at a rate of 0% or even with a slightly negative yield (not including inflation). The rates paid by Germany and the other countries that are considered financially sound dropped significantly thanks to the ECB's policy and the increasing seriousness of the crisis affecting the periphery countries. This resulted in a flight of capital from the European periphery towards the centre. German securities are so safe that if cash is needed, they may be negotiated overnight without loss. Banks acquire them, not with a view to earning money but to have deposits or highly liquid securities in the ECB that are immediately available. This enables them to create an (often false) impression of solvency and thus to deal with unforeseen events. By lending to Spain and Italy at a higher rate they can compensate for certain losses they might take on the German securities. Borrowing at 0.05% and lending at 1.6% yields comfortable profits.

29.
The European Central Bank's priorities

We have seen that since the beginning of the 2007-2008 crisis, the ECB has played a vital role in saving the big private banks, their owners and directors, while at the same time guaranteeing the continuity of their privileges. We can clearly see that without the ECB, the big banks would have sunk and that would have forced the authorities to take very severe action against them. Beyond bank bail-outs, the ECB is charged with maintaining an inflation rate of around 2%. From this point of view the ECB has failed because the Eurozone has a rate of less than 1% and borders on deflation.[342] The ECB has three more objectives, which can be summarised as follows:

- To defend the euro, which is a straitjacket for the weaker European economies and for all the people of Europe. The euro is an instrument that serves the big private companies and the European elites (the richest 1%). If Eurozone countries could devalue they would improve their competitiveness against the Austrian, Benelux, French and German economic giants.[343] Countries like Greece, Italy, Portugal and Spain are re-

---

342 On the consequences of a very low inflation rate or deflation and the dangers they represent in the view of many economists, including those at the ECB, see Martin Wolf, 'The spectre of Eurozone deflation', *Financial Times*, 12 March 2014.

343 An alternative project to neoliberal capitalism cannot be based on competition. Other relationships of exchange must be developed, with large transfers aimed at reducing economic differences between countries. Also, a maximum number of short producer-to-consumer circuits should be developed.

stricted by their membership in the Eurozone. So the European authorities and governments implement 'internal devaluation',
which means pay-cuts for the workers.

- To consolidate the domination of Europe's
  strongest economies (Benelux, France,
  Germany) where the big European corporations have their bases, thus maintaining
  important differences between the strong
  European economies and the others.
- To actively support the attacks of Capital
  against Labour in order to increase business profitability and to make the big European companies more competitive on the
  global market.

What impact have these three objectives had on the situation in Europe since 2011?[344]

How the ECB affects the richest 1%
and the big private companies

To appreciate the work of the ECB, imagine being one of the richest
1%. The official line has it that in 2011 the ECB successfully managed
the transition from the former presidency of the Frenchman Jean-
Claude Trichet to the new presidency under the Italian Mario Draghi,
former governor of the Bank of Italy and former vice-president of
Goldman Sachs Europe.[345] The ECB and the leaders of major Euro-

---

344   We have analysed the evolution of the crisis in Europe, since 2007,
in numerous articles and in the following French-language works: Damien
Millet, Éric Toussaint, *La Crise, quelles crises ?* (The Crisis – which Crises?),
Brussels: Aden, 2010; *La Dette ou la Vie* (Life or Debt), Aden, 2011; *AAA,
Audit, Annulation, Autre politique* (Audit, Abolition, Alternative Policies),
Paris: Le Seuil, 2012.
345   From 1991-2001, Mario Draghi was Director General of the Italian
Ministry of the Treasury in charge of privatisation. From 1993 to 2001, he
chaired the Committee on Privatisation and was thus a member of the board
of directors of several banks and companies undergoing privatisation (Eni,
IRI, Banca Nazionale del Lavoro, BNL and IMI). From 2002 to 2005, Draghi
was Vice-President of the European branch of the US investment bank Goldman Sachs. On 16 January 2006, he became Governor of the Bank of Italy,

pean countries negotiated a reduction of about 50% of Greek debts with private banks.[346] At the same time, the Troika got the Greek government to implement a radical new austerity plan including mass privatisation and the surrender of a large part of its sovereignty. By March 2012, Troika representatives were permanently installed in Greek ministries in order to closely monitor Greek finances. New loans to Greece now travel through an account, which the European authorities can block if necessary. Equally advantageous for the creditors, new Greek debt securities no longer come under the legal jurisdiction of the Greek courts but are framed within English law; disputes between the Greek government and private creditors will be referred to Luxembourg courts.[347]

George Papandreou's government, led by the Greek socialist party, PASOK, enacted neoliberal dogma and as a result became increasingly unpopular. Finally, under pressure from the ECB and the European leaders, it was replaced, without any democratic election, by a new government of national unity made up of a coalition between PASOK and New Democracy, with key portfolios in the hands of ministers coming directly from the banks.

Just before the G20 meeting in Cannes at the end of October 2011, George Papandreou announced a referendum on the latest plan to be imposed by the Troika; it never happened. It was clear that if the Greek people were consulted they would reject austerity. So the Troika, supported by the G20, forced Papandreou to abandon this basic democratic initiative.

---

appointed by Prime Minister Silvio Berlusconi, with a renewable term of six years. Mario Draghi became President of the ECB on 1 November 2011.
346   Greek bonds were sold on the secondary market at 20% of their value; the 50% discount allowed the banks to limit the losses they would have taken if they had sold the securities on the secondary market. In addition, for the banks that had acquired the shares at 20% of their value, unloading them at said 50% was a real windfall.
347   See 'Greek government-debt crisis', *Wikipedia*, http://en.Wikipedia. org/wiki/Greek_government-debt_crisis. See also Alain Salles and Benoît Vitkine, 'Fatalisme face à un sauvetage échangé contre une perte de souveraineté' (Greeks resigned to swapping sovereignty for a bail-out), *Le Monde*, 22 February 2012: http://www.forumfr.com/sujet448690-fatalisme-face-a-un-sauvetage-echange-contre-une-perte-de-souverainete.html (in French).

To complete the picture we can add three other items of good news for the ECB and its directors. The Italian Prime Minister, Silvio Berlusconi, was forced to resign in late 2011 and was replaced, without elections, by Mario Monti, a former European Commissioner and very close to the banking community, who formed a government of technocrats to impose severe neoliberal policies. [348] In Spain, the head of government, Mariano Rajoy, President of the People's Party, has radicalised the neoliberal policies initiated by his predecessor, the Socialist José Luis Zapatero. Lastly, European leaders[349] came to an agreement in March 2012 on a Treaty on Financial Stability, Coordination and Governance (TSCG) that further supported fiscal austerity, sanctioned member states, scraped away more of their national sovereignty and injected an extra dose of submission to the logic of private capital.[350] Finally, the European Stability Mechanism (ESM) has come into effect to better help states and banks through the next banking crises, and to help member states struggling to find finance.

In March-April 2012 Mario Draghi, along with most European leaders and bank officials, had much to celebrate. The richest 1% were not feeling the pinch despite the crisis.

---

348   Prime Minister from 16 November 2011 to 28 April 2013, Mario Monti was appointed Senator for Life by the President of the Italian Republic, Giorgio Napolitano. On this occasion, he left various positions of responsibility: the Presidency of the most prestigious Italian private university, Bocconi; the European Department of the Trilateral Commission, a circle of the international oligarchic elite; the steering committee of the powerful Bilderberg club; and the Presidency of the neoliberal think-tank Bruegel. Monti was an international advisor to Goldman Sachs from 2005 to 2011 (as a member of the Research Advisory Council of the Goldman Sachs Global Markets Institute). He has been European Commissioner for the Internal Market (1995-1999) and European Commissioner for Competition (1999-2004). He has been a member of Moody's European Senior Advisory Council, an advisor to Coca-Cola, a member of the Business and Economics Advisors Group of the Atlantic Council (a US think-tank that promotes US leadership) and a member of the Praesidium of Friends of Europe, an influential think-tank based in Brussels.
349   With the exceptions of the UK and the Czech Republic.
350   *Treaty on Stability, Coordination and Governance (TSCG)*, March 2012. The text is available at http://european-council.europa.eu/media/639235/st00tscg26_en12.pdf

However from May 2012 dark clouds appeared on the horizon, when Bankia, the fourth-largest Spanish bank (headed by former IMF Managing Director Rodrigo de Rato) went virtually bankrupt. There are reports that Spanish banks are in need of between €40 billion and €100 billion of recapitalisation, and that Mariano Rajoy does not want to ask for help from the Troika. Added to these difficulties, a series of international banking scandals broke out, of which the two most important were the manipulation of the LIBOR, involving a dozen major banks, and HSBC's laundering of drug money.

At the same time, in France a majority of voters no longer wanted President Nicolas Sarkozy. François Hollande was elected on 6 May 2012. International finance looked on, knowing it could count on the leaders of the French Socialist Party, like other European socialist parties, to pursue austerity.

Since the 13 July 2015 'agreement' with Greece, the ECB and other proponents of austerity measures can breathe more freely, though obviously only in the very short term. Those who have followed the dramatic events of the last months know that SYRIZA, the left-wing coalition that had promised to repeal austerity measures, suspend repayment of debt and challenge the European authorities, has not lived up to expectations. It had won the 25 January 2015 elections and formed a coalition government with the nationalist party ANEL. However it never really considered challenging the terms in which the European institutions and the IMF had trapped the Greek population. For example, in spite of the conclusive findings of the Truth Commission on Greek Public Debt, created by the Greek Parliament, SYRIZA did not question the legitimacy of the debt. This was apparent when Prime Minister Alexis Tsipras, by signing the agreement, flouted the overwhelming 61.3% referendum victory rejecting the Troika's bailout conditions announced on 25 June.

In July-August 2012 the Eurozone was once again under extreme pressure and, to reassure the markets, Mario Draghi declared in September that he would do everything to save the euro. The ECB started buying massive amounts of government bonds, mainly Italian and Spanish. The main subject of discussion of the European Commission, the governments and the mainstream media was the sovereign debt crisis, diverting attention away from the euro – and once again, from the private banks, which are really the cause of the crisis.

The situation began to ease after the ECB purchased Italian and Spanish bonds from the banks and made massive liquidities available to them. Interest-rates charged by these banks to lend to weaker countries gradually began to decline, particularly in Spain and Italy. But it is clear that the banks are not out of danger: Belgian and French taxpayers bailed out Dexia – whose earlier rescues are reported in Chapter 16 – for the third time. In December 2012, Italy came to the aid of the Western world's oldest bank, Monte dei Paschi (the fourth-largest bank in the country). Spain had to recapitalise several banks. In February 2013 the Netherlands had to inject €3.7 billion into SNS, a mortgage bank, and in March 2013, the two main Cypriot banks were on the verge of bankruptcy.

In February 2013, the Italian Prime Minister, Mario Monti, suffered a crushing electoral defeat. The ballot-box protest carried a new political movement centred on the comedian Beppe Grillo. The vast million-strong anti-austerity protests that had taken place in Portugal in September 2012[351] were revived in March 2013 with over a million demonstrators.[352] People expressed their rejection of austerity policies and at the same time, signs of crisis were evident among the elites. On three occasions in 2013, the Portuguese Constitutional Court invalidated the austerity measures taken by the government, and in July, the finance minister resigned, causing significant turbulence.

In September 2013, Angela Merkel was elected for another term in Germany but her even more neoliberal political partner, the FDP, was rejected by the voters and lost all parliamentary representation. Arithmetically, a centre-left government could have been established by a coalition of the Social Democrats (SPD), the Greens and the Radical Left (Die Linke), but the SPD preferred an alliance with Angela Merkel, more pleasing to German employers, the European Commission and the ECB.

---

351   Maria da Liberdade, 'Portugal : 15 septembre 2012, le peuple était en masse dans la rue!' (Portugal: a sea of people in the streets), CADTM, 28 September 2012, http://cadtm.org/Portugal-15-septembre-2012-le (in French or in Portuguese).
352   Maria da Liberdade, 'Les Portugais dans la rue contre la Troïka, le gouvernement et le régime' (The Portuguese demonstrate against the Troika, the Government and the regime), CADTM, 5 March 2013, http://cadtm.org/Les-Portugais-dans-la-rue-contre (in French or in Portuguese).

Also in 2013, the Netherlands, which had long given an impression of stability and economic success, went into profound crisis when its real-estate bubble finally burst and caused an economic recession. In a country where the pension scheme is largely privatised, several pension funds reduced the level of pensions.

Eliminating the *demos*

This rapid retrospective of the management of the Eurozone crisis between the end of 2011 and the end of 2013 shows that by being at the service of big capital, the European leaders increasingly choose to override the legislative bodies and side-track the voters' choices. The European leaders have gradually eliminated the *demos*[353] from democracy, replacing it with banks and thus creating a bankocracy.

Where is democracy when people no longer have the possibility of expressing their massive rejection of austerity policies by voting, or when the voters' choices are ignored or swept aside because they did not make the choice the elites had decided on? Examples abound: in 2005 in France and the Netherlands after the 'No' vote on the Treaty for a European Constitution; in Ireland and Portugal after the 2011 elections; in Greece on several occasions between 2010 and 2012; in France and the Netherlands again after the 2012 elections. Then there was the previously mentioned abandonment of the Greek referendum of early 2012, promised by Prime Minister George Papandreou at the end of October 2011. Everything is done to reduce the power of national governments and public authorities within a restrictive European contractual framework. This is a very dangerous trend. The power of the ECB and the European Commission is growing under the supervision of the governments of the strongest EU and Eurozone countries.

The process is not irreversible. Under pressure from their populations, governments can decide to disobey the European Commission, the ECB and the bosses of the big European companies. It is clear that

353 *Demos* (in Greek: δῆμος, 'people') is the Greek root to be found in 'democracy'. In its primary sense, the *demos* represents all members of the civic community in the Greek city. In a democracy, power of decision lies in the assembly of the *demos*. In literary and rhetorical prose, *demos* represents the common people, as opposed to the rich (*ploutos*) and powerful.

governments, when supported by popular mobilisation, can retrieve the power to act. Indeed, the strength of the EU rests on the docility of the governments and the people.

30.
Policies
that fail

If governments' intentions were truly what they claim – that is, to reduce unemployment, boost economic activity, clean up the banking sector, increase and stimulate lending to small businesses and consumers, increase investment, reduce debt, and so on – then their policies have clearly failed. But were these ever their true intentions?

The mainstream media often mention the dangers of the Eurozone falling apart, the failure of austerity policies to fan the embers of the economy, tensions between Paris and Berlin, or even London and the Eurozone, disagreements between ECB directors, the enormous difficulty in agreeing on the EU budget or the grimaces of certain European governments concerning IMF remarks about austerity levels. These problems are real but they should not overshadow the essential issues.

The leaders of the strongest European countries and of big business alike are delighted to have created a common economic, commercial and political zone in which European transnational corporations and the major Eurozone economies benefit from the collapse of the Eurozone's southern economies. The stronger economies derive a competitive advantage over their North American and Chinese competitors from this. Their objective at this point is not to revive growth to reduce the difference between the stronger and weaker economies of the EU.

Furthermore, the European elites see the economic collapse in the south as an opportunity to privatise public companies on a large scale and acquire common goods, public services and national assets at give-away prices, helped by the Troika with the active complicity of the peripheral governments. Big Capital in the southern European countries is in favour of this prospect, hoping to get a piece of the cake it has been ogling for a long time. The grabbing of public sector companies in Greece and Portugal foreshadows what will happen in Spain and Italy where public companies are relatively bigger in respect to the size of their economies.

The collusion between governments and big business has gone public. At the head of several governments, in important ministerial posts and at the presidency of the ECB, we find men and women who are part and parcel of the world of high finance, in particular former directors of Goldman Sachs. Certain high-profile politicians are rewarded with jobs in big banks once they have fulfilled their loyal service to Big Capital. This revolving-door complicity is not new; it is just more obvious and systematic than at any time over the last fifty years.

Politicians who have done well out of business

The French Socialist Dominique Strauss-Kahn ('DSK'), who was France's Minister of Finance and the Economy towards the end of the 1990s, then Managing Director of the IMF (2007-2011), from which he was compelled to resign, has been on the board of the Anatevka Group, now known as Leyne, Strauss-Kahn and Partners (LSK) since 2013. The group employs about one hundred people in several European countries (Luxembourg, Belgium, Monaco, Switzerland and Romania) and Israel, and in tax havens. DSK is advisor to several foreign governments, including Serbia and South Sudan, and several corporations, such as the Russian Regional Development Bank, the Russian Direct Investment Fund, the National Credit Bank and a consortium of Moroccan Banks. In March 2014 he launched the DSK Global Investment Fund, a hedge fund set up to speculate on the commodity markets and on interest-rates.[354]

---

354   Miles Johnson, 'Strauss-Kahn is to launch a $2bn hedge fund', *Financial Times*, 20 March 2014.

Tony Blair, former Prime Minister of the UK, is also doing well. In 2013 his personal fortune was estimated at somewhere between £30 and £60 million. He directs a group of small companies that all have their head offices in the same five-storey building in Grosvenor Square in London's diplomatic district. A hundred or so people have their offices there, including an ex-director of Barclays Investment Bank, David Lyon, who runs Firerush Ventures, the financial branch of what has come to be known as 'Tony Blair Inc.' Among Blair's collaborators are former managers from Lehman Brothers and JPMorgan Chase. Tony Blair also sits on the international advisory board of JPMorgan Chase.[355]

On the other side of the Atlantic, Tim Geithner, President Obama's former Secretary of the Treasury, has been president of Warburg Pincus, a Wall Street investment bank, since 2013.

His predecessor Robert Rubin, ex-Secretary of the Treasury under Bill Clinton, joined Citigroup in 1999 after having repealed the Glass-Steagall Act, thus enabling the creation of Citigroup. Between 1999 and 2008, Citigroup paid him $166 million in different forms of remuneration.[356]

To imagine that the policies imposed by the European elite have failed because economic growth has not recovered would be to totally miss the point. The goal of the board of the ECB, the European Commission, the governments of the strongest EU economies, the boardrooms of the banks and other big companies is neither a quick return to growth, nor the reduction of inequalities in the Eurozone

---

355   'Fine dining for Dimon at the Palace', *Financial Times*, 23-24 November 2014.
356   See Damien Millet and Éric Toussaint, *La Crise, quelles crises ?* (The Crisis — which Crises?), Brussels: Aden, 2009, Chapter 4, pp. 58-59.

and the EU that would favour a more coherent system and the return of prosperity.

One fundamental issue is paramount, and that is the capacity of the elites, who have meekly put themselves at the service of the multinationals, to manage crises, even chaotic situations, in the interests of these big companies. The crisis is presented as the motive justifying the biggest offensive since the Second World War against the economic and social rights of the people of Europe. The panoply of weapons includes rampant unemployment, repayment of public debt and the constraint of a balanced budget, all of which are pretexts for severe cuts in social and public spending and the pursuit of ever greater competitiveness between EU member states and in the face of worldwide competition.

Capital's objective is to further threaten stable employment, radically reduce the capacity of workers to organise, and substantially push down direct and indirect wages while at the same time maintaining enormous disparities between workers within the EU so as to exacerbate competitiveness between them and force them into debt. First, there are the inequalities between women and men, between workers with permanent or temporary jobs, between full-time and part-time workers, between generations who have gained pension rights based on universal and compulsory systems and younger generations faced with ever more individualised and uncertain systems; not to mention over-exploited clandestine workers who have no benefits or work-related social rights.

The inequality gap has widened over the last twenty years, pushed by employers' initiatives and helped along by successive governments (including left-wing governments). There are also the inequalities between workers in the different EU countries. In Germany, for example, there are 7.5 million workers who must make ends meet on €400 a month, whereas the normal monthly rate is €1,500. The recently agreed national minimum wage will not come into effect until 2017, will not be index-linked and will be riddled with exceptions.

Secondly, there are inequalities between workers in the different EU countries. The differences between workers in the principal and secondary economies within the EU complement those found within national boundaries. Workers' wages in the stronger countries (Austria, Denmark, Finland, France, Germany, the Netherlands and Sweden) are two or three times higher than the wages of Greek, Portuguese, or Slovenian workers, ten times higher than Bulgarian workers and seven or eight times higher than those earned by Romanian, Lithuanian, or Latvian workers.[357] In South America, although there are great disparities between the stronger economies (Argentina, Brazil, and Venezuela) and the weaker ones (Bolivia, Ecuador, and Paraguay), there is no more than a fourfold difference in the legal minimum wage there – which is much less significant than in the EU. This difference clearly shows how strong competition is among European workers today.

The major corporations in the stronger European economies profit greatly from this wage disparity. German corporations have chosen to increase their production in the EU countries where wages are lowest. Partly finished goods are then reintroduced into Germany, without paying import/export taxes, for assembly and re-exportation, mainly to other European countries. This reduces production costs, puts the German workers into competition with their foreign comrades and increases company profits. In addition, these assembled and re-exported goods appear, of course, in Germany's export figures, whereas they are to a great extent produced from imported goods.

Corporations in the other strong European countries are doing the same thing, but proportionally speaking the German economy profits most from the low wages and precarious working conditions of the Eurozone workforce (including within Germany's national boundaries) and the EU. In 2007, 83% of German exports went to other EU countries: €145 billion to Eurozone countries, €79 billion to non-Eurozone EU countries, and €45 billion to the rest of the world.[358]

357 'Minimum Wage Statistics', Eurostat, http://epp.eurostat.ec.europa.eu/statistics_explained/index.php/Minimum_wage_statistics (2013 data). See also, 'Le salaire minimum en Europe' (The minimum wage in Europe), *Observatoire des inégalités*, http://www.inegalites.fr/spip.php?article702 (in French; unfortunately, data are given only up to 2011).
358 OECD, *International Trade by Commodity Statistics (SITC Revision 3)*, cited by ATTAC and Fondation Copernic, *En finir avec la compétitivité* (Doing away with competitiveness), Paris: ATTAC/Fondation Copernic, October 2012, https://france.attac.org/IMG/pdf/en_finir_avec_la_competitivite.pdf (in French).

31.
The German model

German employers, in collusion with Gerhard Schröder's socialist government, imposed heavy sacrifices on workers during the 2003-2005 period. This meant massive privatisations in the former East Germany, attacks on the job security of ex-GDR workers and, combined with the increase of Germany's public debt due to the take-over of the GDR, new retrograde labour laws for German workers, both West and East.

For today's German leaders and bosses, the Eurozone crisis and the brutal attacks against the Greek people and other populations on the periphery of Europe are opportunities to reproduce the success of the German offensive on a European scale.

Real labour costs were reduced by 10% in Germany between 2004 and 2008. In the rest of Europe these costs also decreased, but to a lesser extent. Since the 2008-2009 crisis, the Eurozone has been severely affected by a clear drop in real wages in the most exposed countries. The reduction of wages is aimed at weakening workers' capacity to resist in the countries concerned, while increasing profit margins and dismantling what is left of the 'social contract' established between the end of the Second World War and the neoliberal offensive of the 1980s.

Between 2003 and 2005, Gerhard Schröder's socialist government gave German employers a helping hand in imposing sacrifices on the workers. The paper *En finir avec la compétitivité* (Doing away with competitiveness), published jointly by ATTAC and the Fondation Copernic, sets out the measures taken and the attacks on social and economic rights:

The Hartz Acts (named after Volkswagen's Human Resources Director, who was also Schröder's advisor) were adopted between 2003-2005. Hartz I compels the unemployed to accept any job that is proposed to them, even if the pay is less than unemployment benefits. Hartz II created the mini-job at less than €400 a month (exempt from social contributions). Hartz III limits the right to unemployment benefits for older workers to one year and makes access more difficult. Hartz IV merged long-term unemployment and other welfare benefits, and imposed a ceiling of €345 a month. There were also successive retirement and healthcare reforms – the capitalisation of pension schemes (Riester-Pensions), increased contributions, and later retirement ages (reaching 67 by 2017).[359]

The authors of the paper mention in particular that:

Together these reforms have contributed to a considerable rise in social inequalities. This point is often forgotten in the 'German example', as may be demonstrated by some precise figures. Germany has become a divided country: a parliamentary draft report on wealth and poverty[360] has recently established that the poorest half of the population possess only 1% of the assets, compared to 53% for the richest. Between 2003 and 2010, the purchasing power of the average salary

---

359 ATTAC and Fondation Copernic, *En finir avec la compétitivité* (Doing away with competitiveness), Paris: ATTAC/Fondation Copernic, October 2012, https://france.attac.org/IMG/pdf/en_finir_avec_la_competitivite. pdf (in French).
360 German government report, Lebenslagen in Deutschland. Entwurf des 4 Armuts- und Reichstumsberichts der Bundesregierung (Aspects of Daily Life in Germany. Draft 4 of the Poverty and Wealth Report of the Federal Government), drafted 17 September 2012, http://gesd.free.fr/arb912.pdf (in German).

decreased by 5.6%, but the effect was very unequally spread, with the lowest-paid 40% seeing a fall of 12% while the highest-paid 40% lost only 4%.[361] Official statistics show that the proportion of low salaries increased from 18.6% in 2006 to 21% in 2010. It should be emphasised that West Germany was worst hit.

According to the same study, the number of employees rose by 1.2 million between 1999 and 2008, reflecting an increase of 1.9 million casual jobs corresponding to the loss of half a million full-time permanent jobs. A quarter of today's wage-earners occupy precarious jobs and this proportion is 40% for women, as it is in the US.

The majority of precarious jobs (70%) are considered women's jobs.[362] The proportion of unemployment benefit claimants dropped from 80% in 1995 to 35% in 2008, and all those receiving unemployment benefit for over a year have been transferred to welfare benefits.

As noted by Arnaud Lechevalier, this trend lies within the general framework of a context of erosion of the collective bargaining agreements protecting employees: the percentage of employees covered by these agreements decreased from 76% to 62% in ten years, and by 2008 they existed in only 40% of German firms. In addition, the unions have had to make many exemptions to sector-based and/or company-wide collective agreements.[363]

A possible explanation of German leaders' current attitude towards the Eurozone crisis might lie in the lessons they learned from the absorption of East Germany at the beginning of the 1990s – in particular that significant wage disparities between employees can be exploited to the advantage of employers. The massive East German privatisations,

361   Karl Brenke and Markus M. Grabka, 'Schwache Lohnentwicklung im letzten Jahrzehnt' (Weak wage growth over the last decade), *DIW Wochenbericht*, #45, 2011, http://gesd.free.fr/brenke11.pdf.
362   Source: German Federal Office of Statistics, https://www.destatis.de/EN/Homepage.html.
363   Arnaud Lechevalier, 'Un modèle qui ne fait guère envie' (An unenviable example), *Alternatives économiques*, #300, March 2011 (in French), http://gesd.free.fr/allmodel.pdf, cited by ATTAC and the Fondation Copernic.

the attacks on the job security of ex-GDR workers, along with the increase of German public debt due to the costs of this absorption (used as the pretext for austerity programmes), have enabled the employers to erode the situation of East as well as West German workers. German workers have been strictly divided between those in the big industrial sectors where many advantages have been maintained and other, more precarious, sectors including small to medium-size businesses.

IG Metall, one of the big German industrial trade unions, has published a text in defence of the Eurozone, which helps explain why unitary action against the employers has been abandoned. It provides an interesting advocacy of German economic interests and the single currency. In this document, entitled *Ten Reasons for the Euro and the Currency Union*, published on 19 August 2011, we read:

> The German economy depends more than any other on its exports. Our foreign clients are the source of millions of jobs in Germany. The biggest market for German products is Europe. [...]. The single currency has played a huge role in the competitiveness of German products. If indebted countries are excluded from the single currency, they will devalue their own currencies to improve their competitiveness. This would then place considerable pressure on the remaining Eurozone, which would be composed exclusively of those countries of the European Union with the strongest economies, to revalue the euro. A return to the Deutsche Mark would entail a revaluation of at least 40%.[364]

For today's German leaders and employers, the Eurozone crisis and the brutal attacks against the Greek people and the other peripheral populations are opportunities to push the offensive further and to reproduce, on a European scale, the success of the German offensive.

---

364 IG Metall, *10 Gründe für den Euro und die Währungsunion* (10 Reasons for the Euro and Currency Union), 19 August 2011, cited in Cédric Durand (ed.), *En finir avec l'Europe*, (No More Europe), Paris: Editions La Fabrique, 2013, p. 68. (In German or French).

Not to be outdone, the leaders of the other strong European countries and the CEOs of their major corporations are making the most
of the common European political, commercial and economic zone.
The northern European economies and transnational companies
are exploiting the strife in the Eurozone's southern economies to
improve their profitability and to gain a competitive advantage over
their North American and Chinese competitors. Their objective at
this point, as mentioned above, is not to revive growth and reduce
differences between the EU's stronger and weaker economies. Southern capital-holders and the governments themselves approve of these
policies, looking to seize long-coveted privatised sectors at give-away
prices with the help of the Troika.

Europe – the new battleground for wage cuts

According to Michel Husson, real labour costs per unit were reduced by 10% in Germany between 2004 and 2008.[365] In the rest of
Europe these costs also decreased, but to a lesser extent. Since the
2008-2009 crisis, the Eurozone has been severely affected by a clear
drop in real wages in the most exposed countries. As Patrick Artus, a
researcher for the bank Natixis, points out, 'We notice a significant
reduction in real income in the Eurozone countries having the most
difficulties (Greece, Italy, Portugal, and Spain)'. Artus claims that European leaders are imposing a deliberate pay reduction policy, and
adds that this has neither boosted investment in these countries nor
helped their exports to become more competitive. The favourable effects of pay reductions 'are not showing in competitiveness, foreign
trade, or business investments', he writes. He adds that lower wages have two clear effects: on the one hand they have raised profits
(in Marxist terms, a reduction in variable capital investment leaves
a greater margin of absolute surplus value; see boxed article 'Wages
and absolute and relative surplus value'); on the other hand, it has reduced consumer demand, which in turn has resulted in a contraction
in the economy. [366]

365   Michel Husson, 'Economie politique du "système-euro" ' (The political
economy of the 'euro-system') , CADTM, June 2012, http://cadtm.org/Eco-
nomie-politique-du-systeme-euro or http://hussonet.free.fr/eceurow.pdf
(in French).
366   Patrick Artus, 'La baisse des salaires dans les pays en difficulté de la
zone euro est-elle utile?' (Is the wage decrease in the Eurozone's peripheral

Artus's report confirms that the goal of the European leaders is neither to revive economic activity, nor to improve the situation of the countries in the periphery relative to those in the centre. The pay reductions aim to weaken workers' resistance in the countries concerned, while increasing profits and progressively destroying what is left of the welfare states built up over the three and a half decades following the Second World War and before the neoliberal turn of the late 1970s and early 1980s.

In the *Global Wage Report 2012-2013* published by the International Labour Organisation in December 2012, the authors notice that 'in developed economies, the crisis led to a 'double dip' in wages: real average wages fell in 2008 and again in 2011, and the current outlook suggests that in many of these countries wages are growing marginally, if at all, in 2012'.[367] This is the only part of the world, along with the Middle East, where wages have fallen since 2008. In China, the rest of Asia, and Latin America, wages have increased. In Eastern Europe they have recovered to a certain extent after plummeting in the 1990s. This report confirms that Capital's offensive against Labour has been displaced towards the developed countries.

Wages: absolute and relative value[368]

When a worker does her or his day's work at the factory s/he adds value to the raw materials s/he uses. This added value becomes incorporated in

---

countries any use?), *Flash Economie #289*, 18 April 2012 (in French). Artus writes, 'Il ne reste que les effets sur la demande des ménages, d'où une forte contraction de l'activité dont le seul effet positif est de réduire le déficit extérieur (puisque les importations diminuent'. (All that is left is the demand, which has suffered a strong reduction, having only one positive effect – to reduce the trade deficit (through reduction of imports). (Trans. CADTM). Artus demonstrates clearly that business profitability has improved in four countries that were studied.

367   *Global Wage Report 2012-2013*, Geneva: ILO, December 2012, http://www.ilo.org/wcmsp5/groups/public/---dgreports/---dcomm/---publ/documents/publication/wcms_194843.pdf .

368   The contents of this box are liberally arranged extracts from Ernest Mandel's *Introduction au Marxisme* (Introduction to Marxism), Brussels: Fondation Léon Lesoil, 2007, p. 59, p. 68, p. 66-67.

the products s/he produces. After a certain number of hours s/he has reproduced an amount of value that is exactly equal to her/his daily or weekly wage. If s/he stopped working at this moment the capitalist would not make a penny of extra value but neither would s/he have any interest in employing the worker. Like Medieval money-lenders or merchants, s/he buys for reselling. S/he buys the worker's labour to obtain a product worth more than s/he originally spent on it. This 'extra worth' is her/his gain, or profit. It is therefore clear that if the worker produces the equivalent of her/his wages in working for four hours, s/he will work not for only four hours, but for six, seven, eight, nine or more additional hours. During these additional hours s/he produces profit for the capitalist and receives naught in return.

So the origin of profit is excess unpaid labour that is appropriated by the capitalist. Are we going to cry out 'Stop thief!'? The reply is both 'yes' and 'no': 'yes' from the worker's point of view, and 'no' from that of the capitalist and the laws of the market. The capitalist has not in fact purchased 'the value produced or to be produced by the worker' on the market. S/he has not purchased the work that the worker will do (if s/he had done that, s/he would have simply committed theft: s/he would have paid less than the purchase was worth). What s/he has purchased is the worker's capacity to work. This working capacity has its own value, like any other merchandise, which is determined by the inputs necessary to reproduce it, in other words the subsistence (in the wide sense) of the worker and her/his family. Profit finds its origin in the difference between the value produced by the worker and the value of the goods necessary for her/his subsistence.

Labour power has a particular characteristic that sets it apart from other merchandise: it is made up of both a measurable element and a variable element. The stable part is the value of goods, containing nourishment, calories and vitamins and meeting the labourer's basic needs to reconstitute her/his capacity to work and meet the employer's expectations. The variable part is the value of the goods, at a given time and place, that are paid to the worker over and above her/his basic subsistence needs. Marx calls this the 'historico-moral' part. It is not fortuitous, but the result of a historical process and the balance of power between workers and capitalists. In Marxist economic analysis, it is here that the past and present class struggles become part of the determining factors of capitalist economics.

Wages are the market price of labour, which, like all market prices, fluctuates around the value of the merchandise concerned. Wage fluctuations are strongly determined by levels of inactive reserves such as the unemployed or undocumented workers and women.

To make maximum profit and to accumulate a maximum of capital, the capitalist reduces to a minimum the part of new value in the form of work put into the productive process that should go to workers in the form of wages. The two principal means of doing this at the capitalist's disposal are firstly, to increase the length of the working day and to reduce the real value of wages and the minimum subsistence needs – this is what Marx called the growth of absolute surplus-value; and secondly, to increase the intensity and productivity of work without applying a proportional increase in wages. This is increased relative surplus-value.

As it is difficult for the employers in the developed countries to increase working hours, it is the increase in intensity of work and its productivity that are the privileged means of increasing profits.

'Benchmarking'[369] and 'Lean Management'[370] are two such processes, with disastrous consequences on workers' health and social conditions.

---

369   Benchmarking is a marketing method of studying, analysing and comparing the production, management and organisation practices of different companies in the same activity so as to appropriate them in order to improve performances. These methods are applied internally to corporations to put different branches, departments and employees into continual competition with each other. This has the consequence of seriously deteriorating working conditions. In France, the trade union Sud BPCE won legal actions against benchmarking. The courts recognised that such practices were 'seriously detrimental to employees' health' (decision by the Tribunal de Grande Instance of Lyon, 9 September 2012, confirmed by a decision of the Lyon appeals court on 21 February 2014).

370   Lean Management is a method of production management that results from the permanent seeking of gains in productivity, quality, lead times and costs. The expression 'lean' is associated with 'downsizing', which is synonymous with redundancy plans. This headlong race for performance has a very negative effect on workers, causing psycho-social risks and Repetitive Strain Injuries.

32.
Capital's global offensive against Labour

The workers, pensioners and social beneficiaries in Cyprus, Greece, Ireland, Portugal and Spain are subjected to the same attacks today as those that took place against the workers of developing countries during the 1980s and 1990s. The offensive was also launched against workers in North America during the Reagan regime, in the UK whilst in the iron grasp of Margaret Thatcher, and in the Old Continent where she had her followers. The workers in the former Eastern-bloc countries have also suffered the brutal policies imposed by their governments and the IMF. To quote the *Global Wage Report* again, 'In Russia, for example, the real value of wages collapsed to less than 40% of their value in the 1990s and it took another decade before wages recovered their initial level'. Then, between 2003 and 2005, German workers were the next victims of the offensive, although in a less brutal manner than was forced on the workers of the Third World (whether in the poorest countries or the so-called emerging economies). A large part of the German working population still feels its harmful effects today, even though the success of German exports[371] has curtailed unemployment and though part of the working class has not felt the effects directly. The offensive, which has intensified since 2007-2008, started at the beginning of the 1980s.[372] The ILO looks at a shorter period and makes an interesting remark:

---

371   Germany has continued to register economic growth carried by buoyant exports whilst most of its EU partners, particularly in the Eurozone, have been hard hit by the crisis. As all the EU is feeling the pinch of decreased consumption as described above, exacerbated by a decrease in public consumption, the market for German exports has become seriously restricted. The boomerang effect is already hitting the German economy.
372   See Éric Toussaint, 'In the South as well as the North: from the great transformation in the 1980s to the current crisis', CADTM, September 2009, http://cadtm.org/In-the-South-as-well-as-the-North.

Between 1999 and 2011 average labour productivity in developed economies increased
more than twice as much as average wages (see figure 11). In the United States, real
hourly labour productivity in the non-farm
business sector [has] increased by about
85% since 1980, while real hourly compensation increased by only around 35%. In
Germany, labour productivity [has] surged
by almost a quarter over the past two decades while real monthly wages remained
flat.[373]

Further on the ILO comments:

The global trend has resulted in a change
in the distribution of national income, with
the workers' share decreasing while capital income shares increase in a majority of
countries. Even in China, a country where
wages roughly tripled over the last decade,
GDP increased at a faster rate than the total
wage bill – and hence the labour share went
down.[374]

---

373 *Global Wage Report 2012-2013*, analytical summary, Geneva: ILO,
December 2012, pp. VI-VII.
374 *idem*, p. VII. The *Report* also shows the spread between highest and
lowest salaries in each country.

Evolution of the share of revenue
from labour in % of GWP from 1980 to 2011

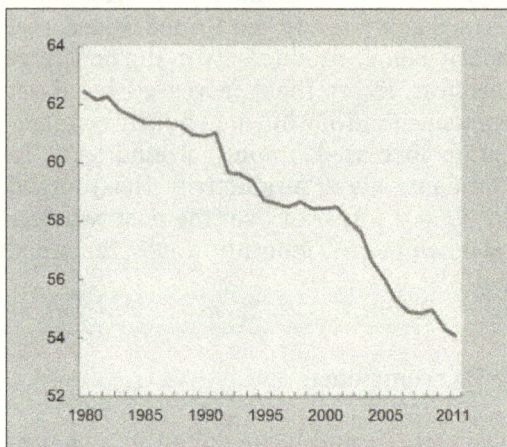

Source:
UNCTAD secretariat calculations, using UN Global Policy Model,
based on UN-DESA, National Accounts Main Aggregates
database; and ILO, Global Wage database.

This strong worldwide tendency is the consequence of the increase of surplus value extracted from labour by capital. It is important to note that during much of the nineteenth century, the principal means of increasing surplus value was by increasing absolute surplus value (lower wages, longer working hours). Progressively, in the developed economies, during the second half of the nineteenth century and throughout the twentieth century (except under Nazism, Fascism, and other dictatorial regimes that imposed wage reductions) this was replaced or outstripped by increases in relative surplus value (i.e. productivity increases without corresponding wage increases). After several decades of neoliberal offensive, increases in absolute surplus value have become, once again, a major element in the extraction of surplus value and are added to the relative surplus value. The employers, using the excuse of the crisis, are now increasing the extraction of both forms of surplus value, thus showing the magnitude of the current offensive.

In a European Commission document entitled *The Second Economic Adjustment Programme for Greece* published in March 2012,[375] it was clearly indicated that Greek wages must be reduced. This study compares the minimum wage in Greece with that of its neighbours: it was five times the average minimum wage of Romania and Bulgaria, triple that of Hungary and the Baltic States, double the minimum wage in Poland and the Czech Republic and higher than in Portugal or Spain.[376] The goal is to make Greek wages more 'competitive', in other words, lower. Of course, if Greek wages are cut as the Troika and the employers want, the wages in Ireland, Portugal and Spain as well as in the stronger economies will have to rapidly follow suit.

European leaders obey a logic that increases the surplus value extracted from European labour for capital, and which permits them to score points against their Asian and North American competitors. They want to reduce European trade unions' room for manoeuvre by scaling down the negotiating options they have enjoyed for decades. In most of the EU countries, the offensive against social rights by governments and the European Commission has succeeded in radically reducing the scope of labour laws, collective bargaining and agreements. This is particularly the case in the ex-Eastern Bloc countries, Ireland, Italy, Spain and Portugal. They have also cut the minimum wage and pensions in several countries, radically reduced protection against redundancy, and raised the age of retirement.

During 2012, the crisis worsened in Greece, Ireland, Portugal and Spain as a result of the brutal austerity policies implemented by their governments in line with the requirements imposed by the Troika. In Greece, the aggregate drop in GDP since the crisis has reached 25%. The purchasing power of the great majority of the population has fallen by 30% to 50%. Unemployment and poverty have literally exploded.[377] In Portugal, austerity measures have become so violent that the

---

375   See European Commission, Directorate General Economic and Financial Affairs, *The Second Economic Adjustment Programme for Greece*, March 2012, http://ec.europa.eu/economy_finance/publications/occasional_paper/2012/op94_en.htm.

376   *idem*, Chart 17, p. 40.

377   From the beginning, the CADTM has denounced the disinformation campaign by the Troika and the Greek government. See 'The CADTM condemns the disinformation campaign on the Greek debt and the rescue plan by private creditors', CADTM press release 10 March 2012, http://

flow of Portuguese people into economic exile has reached the same volume as fifty years ago when large parts of the population fled dictatorship and poverty. In the same year of 2012, 10,000 Portuguese left the country each month (out of a population of about 10.5 million), more than emigrated in 1966. The Portuguese government shamelessly encourages its citizens to leave the country and gloats over the resulting fall in unemployment. Nevertheless, youth unemployment is nearly 40%. The 'discovery' of sixty Portuguese workers working for €2.06 per hour even moved the Belgian Prime Minister, who cried, 'wage dumping!' as though this phenomenon were not the result of European measures prohibiting social harmonisation.[378]

In Ireland, unemployment has taken on enormous proportions, with 150,000 young people having left the country since 2008, according to the country's Central Statistics Office.[379] Since the 2008 crisis,[380] one young worker in three who had a job before the crisis is now unemployed. Bailing out the banks has so far cost 40% of GDP (approaching €70 billion out of a GDP of €156 billion in 2011).[381] Economic activity has declined by 20% since 2008. The government in Dublin has confirmed that it will cut 37,500 public-sector jobs by 2015. The rise in water rates is causing shortages for many families. In Spain, the level of youth unemployment has reached 50%. Since the crisis hit Spain, 400,000 families have had their homes repossessed due to mortgage repayment arrears.[382] In one year, from mid-2011 to mid-2012, the number of Spanish families where all members are unemployed increased by 300,000 to reach 1.7 million, or 10%

cadtm.org/The-CADTM-condemns-the. See also Christina Laskaridis, 'Greece already defaulted on the creditors' terms; what they fear is default on the debtor's terms', CADTM, 31 May 2012, http://cadtm.org/Greece-already-defaulted-on-the .

378   Cristina Semblano, 'L'exode portugais' (The Portuguese exodus), *Libération*, 3 February 2014 (in French).

379   'Emigration at record high as 87,000 people left the country last year - CSO', *Irish Independent*, 27 September 2012, http://www.independent.ie/irish-news/emigration-at-record-high-as-87000-people-left-the-country-last-year-cso-28814646.html

380   Jamie Smyth, 'Ireland's emigration highest for 25 years', *Financial Times*, September 30, 2012.

381   Jamie Smyth, 'Bailed-out Irish banks edge towards stability', *Financial Times*, 29 December 2011.

382   Miles Johnson, 'Suicides spark call for Madrid to halt evictions by banks', *Financial Times*, 13 November 2012.

of all the families in the country.[383] The situation in the countries of the former Eastern Bloc is in continuous decline, particularly in those that have joined the Eurozone.

A report published on 3 December 2013 by Nils Muižnieks, European Commissioner for Human Rights, entitled *Safeguarding Human Rights in Times of Economic Crisis*,[384] shows the unforgivable consequences of the austerity policies currently being applied to Europe. Education, health, employment, justice, housing, water and food are all sectors that have been hit hard by these policies.

Nils Muižnieks points out in this report the inefficiency and the counter-productive nature of austerity programmes, particularly concerning health services, and the dire long-term consequences of the increased public spending to counter the effects:

> What began as a meltdown of the global financial system in 2008 has been transformed into a new political reality of austerity, which threatens over six decades of social solidarity and expanding human rights protection across Council of Europe member states.
> [...]
> Many of these austerity measures – characterised by public expenditure cuts, regressive tax hikes, reduced labour protection and pension reforms – have exacerbated the already severe human consequences of the economic crisis marked by record levels of unemployment. The whole spectrum of human rights has been affected – from the rights to decent work, an adequate standard of living and social security to access to justice, freedom of expression and the rights to participation, transparency and accounta-

---

383 Tobias Buck, 'Spain's deepening lack of hope takes its toll', *Financial Times*, 6 November 2012.
384 Nils Muižnieks, *Safeguarding Human Rights in Times of Economic Crisis*, Council of Europe, 2013, http://www.enetenglish.gr/resources/article-files/prems162913_gbr_1700_safeguardinghumanrights_web.pdf

bility. Vulnerable and marginalised groups of people have been hit disproportionately hard, compounding pre-existing patterns of discrimination in the political, economic and social spheres. Poverty, including child deprivation, is deepening and is likely to have long-term effects.

Another report, published on 17 February 2014 by Professor Andreas Fischer-Lescano of the Centre of European Law and Politics (ZERP) at the University of Bremen for the Austrian Trades Union Congress (BAK), the European Trade Union Confederation (ETUC) and the European Trade Union Institute (ETUI), also denounces the choices made by the European Union. Fischer-Lescano claims that 'austerity policies in the EU are illegal' because they do not respect fundamental Human Rights.[385]

Yet another report, this time from the European Parliament on the role and activities of the Troika, was adopted on 13 March 2014. It points out the opacity of the Troika's mandate and is particularly critical of the lack of transparency in the negotiations for the Memoranda of Understanding.[386]

In short, it is clear that Capital has launched a worldwide offensive against Labour. It is in Europe since 2008 that the offensive has been most systematic, starting with the peripheral countries. Meanwhile the banks, that form the spearhead of the capitalist system and are responsible for the crisis, are systematically protected. Everywhere, the repayment of public debt is the leaders' leitmotiv used to justify policies that trample the economic and social rights of the vast majority of the population. If social movements, especially the unions, are really serious about overcoming this devastating attack, they must get

385   Andreas Fischer-Lescano, *Human Rights in Times of Austerity Policy*, (Legal opinion commissioned by the Austrian Chamber of Labour), Bremen: ZERP (Centre of European Law and Politics), 17 February 2014, http://www.etui.org/content/download/13817/113830/file/Legal+Opinion+Human+Rights+in+Times+of+Austerity+Policy+(final).pdf
386   'Le Parlement européen questionne (à moitié) la Troïka' (The EU Parliament halfway questions the Troika), CADTM, 28 February 2014, http://cadtm.org/Le-Parlement-europeen-questionne-a (in French)

to grips with the question of public debt and expose the ruling elites and the falsity of their principal argument. The cancellation of the illegitimate part of the public debt and the expropriation of the banks, so that they are integrated into a democratically controlled public service of savings and credit, are essential measures in any alternative to the capitalist management of the crisis.

33.
Discord between
IMF and EU?

In October 2012, the IMF provided a key explanation of why the crisis was getting worse in Europe. Its Research Department wrote that every euro cut from public spending would result in a drop of €0.9 to €1.7 in GDP. Wolfgang Münchau, an editor at the *Financial Times*, concluded that in this time of crisis a 3% fiscal adjustment (that is, a 3% decrease in public spending) would produce a 4.5% drop in GDP.[387] Thus the policies currently pursued by European governments have been causing a drop in economic activity, making it impossible to reduce the amount of public debt. As Wolfgang Münchau writes, the IMF's motivation should not be misconstrued:

> The IMF does not say that austerity is too hard, too unfair, causes too much pain in the short term or hits the poor more than the rich. It says simply that austerity may not achieve its goal of reducing debt within a reasonable amount of time.

Meanwhile, if IMF Director General Christine Lagarde has hinted that the introduction of some austerity measures should be spread over a longer period of time, and that it might be possible to increase some public spending in order to stimulate the economy, this is because she is under pressure from IMF members from emerging countries. The BRICS countries especially, led by China and Brazil, are fearful of the boomerang effect of the drop in European imports, and criticise the degree of the IMF's financial engagement in Europe. The IMF's Man-

---

387   Wolfgang Münchau, 'Heed the siren voices to end fixation with austerity', *Financial Times*, 15 October 2012, http://www.ft.com/cms/s/0/07f74932-13bb-11e2-9ac6-00144feabdc0.html#ixzz2BOFHZGDg.

aging Director expressed this point of view in Tokyo, at the annual assembly of the IMF and World Bank in October 2012. European leaders were clearly not happy with the IMF document or Christine Lagarde's recommendations. For example in Tokyo, Wolfgang Schäuble, the Finance Minister of Merkel's government, publicly criticised Christine Lagarde for her untimely remarks.

Wolfgang Münchau considers that the reservations expressed by the IMF on the depth of the austerity measures will in no way modify the attitude of European leaders who are sticking to a hard-line position: 'European policy makers are paranoid about their credibility, and I expect them to hold on to austerity until the bitter end, when the policy implodes'.

The tension between the IMF and the European Commission was expressed publicly again on 14 November 2012. Christine Lagarde contradicted the optimism expressed by Jean-Claude Juncker (Luxembourg), the president of the Eurogroup, concerning the outlook for Greece. The IMF seems to want to put pressure on the Commission in order to increase its influence on the direction that Europe should take. Emerging countries and the United States have been taking action within the IMF to influence the solutions adopted concerning the European crisis, especially since they are being asked to make a financial contribution.

A chapter in the IMF *World Economic Outlook* report published just before its annual assembly in October 2012, studies public debt crisis episodes since 1875 in which public debt was greater than 100% of GDP. It analyses the measures taken to resolve these crises. One such case was that of the United Kingdom after the First World War. British public debt stood at 140% of GDP. The British government imposed a radical policy of fiscal austerity combined with a stringent monetary policy. By making large cuts in expenditure, the government attained a primary fiscal surplus of nearly 7% of GDP (before payment of interest) throughout the 1920s, in order to reduce British debt by strictly paying it back. However, public debt did not decrease: by 1930, it was 170% of GDP, and three years later in 1933, it was more than 190% of GDP.

Martin Wolf, the chief economics commentator at the *Financial Times*, states that the real objective of British government policy 'was to break organised labour. These policies resulted in the general strike of 1926. They spread bitterness that lasted decades after the Second World War'. This is exactly what is being done in Europe today. Wolf suggests that European policymakers and the Spanish government of Mariano Rajoy want to drastically push down wages by using unemployment as a weapon. He writes, 'Meanwhile, Spain's real GDP is shrinking. Efforts to tighten fiscal policy are sure to reduce it further.'[388]

Wolf goes on to assert that the Italian government has been inspired by the same policy, and concludes with a statement that may seem unusual coming from a star journalist at one of the principal financial dailies on the planet: 'But fiscal austerity and efforts to lower wages in countries suffering from monetary strangulation could break societies, governments and even states.' In fact, as Martin Wolf has been insisting for months, it is because of austerity measures that countries are heading straight for disaster. To support his analysis, he points to the overwhelming electoral defeat of Mario Monti in March 2013 in Italy.

Since the 2007-2008 crisis erupted, several papers produced by the IMF support arguments that criticise the neoliberal political approach. In addition to the two IMF studies cited above, another one by Luc Laeven and Fabián Valencia is worth mentioning.[389] It focuses on the impact of the banking crisis on public debt. According to these authors, over the 1970-2011 period the increase in public debt in the advanced economies due to the banking crisis averaged 21%, with 20% in the Eurozone and 24% in the US. The loss of economic growth because of the banking crisis is estimated at around 33%. It was 23% for the Eurozone and 31% for the US.

In another study published by the IMF, Fabian Bornhorst and Marta Ruiz Arranz demonstrate that private indebtedness has more serious effects than public debt.[390] This well-argued thesis totally undermines

388   Miles Johnson, 'Spain's growth weaker than first thought', *Financial Times*, 27 August 2012.
389   Luc Laeven and Fabián Valencia, *Systemic Banking Crises Database: An Update*, IMF Working Paper 12/163, 2012, http://www.imf.org/external/pubs/ft/wp/2012/wp12163.pdf.
390   Fabian Bornhorst, Marta Ruiz Arranz, 'The perils of private-sector

the policies promoted, and sometimes imposed, by the IMF, the Western leaders and all the neoliberals.

Studies by IMF researchers contain the following disclaimer:

> This Working Paper should not be reported as representing the views of the IMF. The views expressed in this Working Paper are those of the author(s) and do not necessarily represent those of the IMF or IMF policy. Working Papers describe research in progress by the author(s) and are published to elicit comments and to further debate.

Thus, although the results of studies by IMF researchers should lead it to adjust its objectives, the institution stubbornly goes its own sweet ideological way, demolishing the social advances achieved after the Second World War.

However, we must not mistake the deeper meaning of the IMF's declarations. Although it has shown itself at variance with European policymakers, this is not to convince them to abandon the structural adjustment policies that are favourable to privatisation and a more intense offensive against the social rights won after the Second World War. The IMF would like to have more influence on the decisions made, and to impose its own. While the research produced by some IMF departments contains arguments that contradict mainstream policies more or less clearly, the IMF's actions throughout the world have not changed at all. These are the actions which we must combat because they have disastrous effects on the vast majority of the populations concerned.

---

deleveraging in the Eurozone', *Vox*, 10 November 2013, http://www.voxeu. org/article/private-deleveraging-eurozone. See also Fabian Bornhorst, Marta Ruiz Arranz, 'Indebtedness and Deleveraging in the Euro Area', In: Selected Issues Paper: Euro Area Policies 2013 Article IV Consultation, *IMF Country Report 13/231*, Washington: IMF, 2013, p. 46, https://www.imf. org/external/pubs/ft/ scr/2013/cr13231.pdf

34.
The central banks' dilemma

A complete overview of the actions of the central banks of the industrialised countries since the beginning of the crisis and their possible consequences requires an understanding of the dilemma they now face, a dilemma of their own creation.

To put it simply, the central banks are asking themselves how long they can continue injecting massive amounts of liquidity into the banking system and at the same time maintain near-zero interest-rates or, at least, interest-rates that are lower than inflation rates. They know very well that this policy, which is designed to protect the banks and big non-financial corporations, threatens to produce new speculative bubbles. The question is not whether these bubbles will burst, but when.

At the same time, they know that if they seriously reduce liquidity injections they will be endangering the big banks, and recently formed speculative bubbles will burst. If, on top of that, they increase interest-rates, this will make the banks even more fragile and result in more bubble-bursting. An additional difficulty is that higher interest-rates would automatically increase the cost of servicing public debt and thus aggravate state deficits.[391]

---

391 Note that increases in prime interest-rates will have very negative effects on the treasuries of developing countries, who will have greater difficulty in refinancing their debts and will see capital flee to safer industrialised countries. Central bankers do not care about this: the president of the Fed said as much in February 2014. This brings to mind the events of 1980-1981 when interest-rates rebounded following Fed decisions. Several authors have analysed the effects of the change in Fed policies that took place in October 1979 (see especially Gérard Duménil, Dominique Lévy and Éric Toussaint's many articles published in coordination with the CADTM).

We will see in the final chapter that there are alternatives. They imply radical political choices and changes, namely to stop favouring the richest 1% and to make reforms in the interests of the 99%. However the central bankers do not have the will to change the class content of their policies. They are at the service of the 1%, the hand that feeds them.

This brings us to the horns of their dilemma: whether to continue in the error of their present policies – high liquidity injections and low interest-rates – or to make the error of changing them while adhering to the same logic.[392]

The present policy of low interest-rates and high liquidity injections has produced the following effects:[393]

1. Banks, with a few notable exceptions, are managing to stay afloat because the central banks provide funds that are no longer available on the financial markets. Interbank lending has been severely reduced and the unloading of long-term bank securities such as covered bonds and others has become very difficult. The fresh money gives the banks access to the Money Market Funds for their day-to-day finance. This access can dry up overnight, as was the case in 2011. Banks are clearly dependent on state support.

2. Banks have continued their speculative activities by entering into other highly lucrative markets, eschewing, for the time being, the property market to speculate on commodities and food (peaking in 2008-2009); sovereign bonds (since 2009); corporate bonds, stocks and shares (since early 2013); and *foreign-exchange*. Thus their trading activities have not diminished. Speculation techniques have changed – in some cases for the worse, as in the increase in high-frequency trading.

---

392   The Fed started a cautious change of direction in December 2013 by reducing its monthly volume of purchases of MBS and US Treasury bonds.
393   As well as banks' crimes and misdemeanours that are discussed in Chapters 17, 18 and 20 to 25.

3. Banks have reduced their lending to consumers and to small and average businesses, which create the majority of jobs. In 2013, consumer bank loans in the Eurozone dropped by 2% and loans to business by around 3.5%. The peripheral EU economies are the worst affected. Contrary to the wishes of the central banks, which want more money injected into the economy, banks have toughened their conditions for granting loans to the real economy. In the US, the situation is not much different from that of Europe and Japan, where, since 2013-2014, the banks have gone back to the business of making risky loans via structured products, in particular containing mortgages and car purchases. However the central banks are taking no action at all to impose lending on banks for the purpose of investment in the real economy, to create demand and foster growth or support the little there is.

4. Big non-financial companies in search of finance can issue their own corporate bonds. Banks and other institutional investors buy them because they give a good return and are easily sold on the secondary market. The losers are small and average businesses, which do not have this possibility. Mario Draghi proposes that the banks should offer businesses structured loans to enable bankers to take the entailed risk off their balance-sheets as Asset Backed Securities (ABS). This is because banks that grant loans to small businesses can include them in a mixed bag of the same kind as the Collateralised Debt Obligations (CDO) that caused the subprime crisis. They may then be deposited at the central bank as ABS and removed from their balance-sheets. These ABS are then considered to be collateral for loans at 0.05% from the central bank. Banks are lending to businesses at 5 to 6% in Italy and in Spain, and between 3 and 4% in France and Germany. Whenever he gets the chance, Mario Draghi, President of the ECB, hastens to point out the opportunity for banks to make good profits. In

spite of such attractive encouragement the banks remain shy of increasing loan offers, structured or otherwise, to local enterprises.[394]

5. Banks' policies concerning sovereign debt are both complementary and contradictory. On the one hand they have no qualms about speculating on the sovereign debt of certain countries they have helped put into difficulty. When they do not intervene directly they use their other financial structures, such as hedge funds, SPV (Special Purpose Vehicles) or pension funds. At the same time the banks have increased their stock of sovereign debt as a source of high returns, Italian and Spanish bonds being the most significant examples. Bonds from other countries, such as the US, the UK, Germany and other strong Eurozone countries, are used as guarantee and are easily negotiable securities that can be quickly transformed into liquidity if needed. It is no surprise that the banks' policies seem to be contradictory: they are caught between the rock of their speculative activities (seeking high returns) and the hard place of their other investments.

6. Nevertheless, the banks have by no means cleaned up their activities, and have barely reduced their use of leverage, as discussed in Chapter 13.

7. Generally, central bank and government policies have had very negative effects on the health of the economies while contenting the banks and the rest of the financial sector, along with the big non-financial corporations. Millions of jobs have been lost, millions of families evicted from their homes, poverty and inequality have greatly increased, the quality of public services has been seriously and purposely downgraded and new speculative bubbles are in preparation.

---

394 In 2013 in Europe, all types of ABS fell by 38% from 2012. See *Financial Times*, 18 February 2014. In 4 years, the drop had been of more than 80%! See *Financial Times*, 3 September 2013.

8. Here is a list of known speculative bubbles in preparation, which for the moment are generating high returns:
   - The corporate bonds bubble: the last big crashes took place in 1994 and 1987 (see Chapter 14).
   - The stock exchanges are expanding too fast (the last bubble burst in 2007-2008).
   - The commodities bubble: there was a minor commodities crash caused by high-frequency trading in May 2010; the last big commodities crash happened in 1981-1982 (see Chapter 17).
   - Some economists warn of a property speculation bubble forming in Germany and perhaps in the US. On 18 May 2014 the Governor of the Bank of England, Mark Carney, warned that a housing bubble was forming in Britain.[395]

The bursting of even one of these bubbles can have far-reaching effects.

Patrick Artus of the bank Natixis warns of the possibility of a crisis due to the return of speculative capital placed in Italy, Portugal and Spain during the second half of 2013, where investors were promised greater returns than in the emerging countries such as Brazil, India, Indonesia, South Africa and Turkey from which they had withdrawn.[396] This speculative capital can flee as quickly as it had ar-

---

395   'Bank of England's Mark Carney warns on housing market', *BBC News*, 18 May 2014, http://www.bbc.com/news/business-27459663.
396   Patrick Artus, 'Où peut se localiser la prochaine crise financière?' (Where will the next financial crisis come from?), Natixis, Flash Marchés #181, 26 February 2014, http://cib.natixis.com/flushdoc.aspx?id=75383 (in French). In this report, Patrick Artus also mentions the possibility of a financial crisis being caused by the UK: 'Le Royaume-Uni est un candidat possible, avec l'ouverture très rapide de son déficit extérieur due à l'asymétrie entre progression de la demande et progression de l'offre, ce qui est une cause habituelle des crises' (The UK is a possible candidate because of the deepening external deficit caused by the very rapidly widening gap between supply and demand, a situation that is often at the origin of crises) (in French).

rived if the situation deteriorates in these countries or if other countries offer higher returns.

What is new about current bubbles is that they occur in situations of stagnation or weak economic growth in the industrialised countries, whereas previous bubbles developed during periods of economic euphoria and fairly high growth.

9. Because of central bank and government policies, the economies of the industrialised countries have fallen into what Keynes called the 'liquidity trap'. While central banks inject liquidities and reduce interest-rates, the big banks prefer to keep their resources stashed away in readiness for the explosion of the time-bombs they see on their books, and to hedge against the bursting of the new bubbles they are creating. The industrial and service companies do not invest because demand, whether private or public, is anaemic. They either sit on enormous reserves of liquidities or use them to speculate. At the end of 2013, Apple (the computer company) held $150 billion in cash or equivalent. This amount represents the annual budget of the whole EU (more than 500 million people). At the same time, the world's biggest non-financial companies have $2.8 trillion.[397] According to another estimate, European companies are withholding the unprecedented sum of €2.4 trillion in their treasuries – that is, sixteen times the annual budget of the whole EU![398]

397   Anousha Sakoui, 'Huge cash pile puts recovery in hands of the few', *Financial Times*, 21 January 2014.
398   Alexandra Stevenson, 'European Corporate buybacks hit lows', *Financial Times*, 1 November 2012. The article refers to studies by Thomson Reuters. According to *The Economist*, Canadian companies held $300 billion in cash in 2012, 25% more than in 2008. This phenomenon is happening in all the industrialised countries: in Japan in 2012 corporations had the equivalent of $2.8 trillion in liquid assets, 75% more than in 2007! ('Dead money. Cash has been piling up on companies' balance-sheets since before the crisis', *The Economist*, 3 November 2012).

10. This situation is unheard of. The big corporations
    are sceptical about investing their resources in the
    economy of production and/or lending to consum-
    ers or small businesses. According to Keynes, to
    escape from the liquidity trap, the authorities must
    increase public spending to stimulate demand, and
    so stimulate the economy. Investment spending
    could be directed towards renewable energy, big
    public engineering projects, public buildings (es-
    pecially schools and hospitals) and a massive effort
    could be made towards an ecological transition.
    More staff could be taken on in public services,
    particularly in health, education and social servic-
    es, and they could have higher salaries. Pensions
    and benefits could be increased. Of course, central
    banks and governments dismiss such proposals.

11. As a result of their policies, the central banks' bal-
    ance-sheets have considerably increased in volume.
    That of the ECB has tripled in the five years from
    2007 to 2012 and that of the Fed has quadrupled
    between 2006 and 2014. This enormous expansion
    in such a short period has enabled the big private
    banks to remain as powerful as ever without bring-
    ing relief to economies in crisis. Despite dramatic
    announcements, no radical measures have been
    taken to truly clean up the banking system. Thanks
    to the actions of the central banks, and the govern-
    ment decisions that follow in their wake, the big
    private banks continue their extremely speculative,
    often fraudulent and even criminal, activities. They
    are helped by a permanent mechanism of trans-
    fer of resources (unlimited public lending at very
    low and sometimes negative interest-rates). Some
    of them, even among the bigger ones, are simply
    on life support: in addition to the unlimited public
    lending, they have been recapitalised with public
    funds and their obligations guaranteed by the gov-
    ernments.

The same policies applied by the central banks and governments have caused a huge increase in public debt. This is due to several connected factors:

- The cost of bank bail-outs;
- The multiple costs of the crisis for which the central banks, governments, private banks and big corporations are responsible;
- Ever more tax breaks for big business and the wealthy.

These are all clear indications of the illegitimate character of a large part of public debt. The cancellation of this debt is one of the essential proposals for ending the crisis.

The central banks and crises in the capitalist system

In the capitalist system, crises serve as regulators. Speculative bubbles burst, then asset prices approach their real value; profitable companies sink; capital is destroyed; unemployment increases and wages are reduced. Crises are part of the metabolism of capitalism. This is not to justify crises or capitalism, but simply to indicate that crises are an essential part of the way capitalism works. Until now public intervention, meekly responding to the demands of the employers, has managed to avoid or prevent the crisis from fulfilling its normal function of purging the capitalist system.

While among the population, the victims of the crisis are counted in tens of millions: those responsible for it have made no attempt to clean up capitalism. The bankruptcies of big companies have been very few, the banks have not cleaned up their books and new speculative bubbles have formed or are forming. Productive investment has not been relaunched.

The fact that only a small number of banks in Japan, the UK and the US have collapsed is entirely due to the assistance given to private banks from the central banks and the governments of the EU. Those in power have considered that private banks were 'Too Big to Fail'. Government policies that persistently favour the interests of big business and attack the population's social and economic rights, along with insufficient or reduced public and private investment and the continual bursting of speculative bubbles, are the ingredients of a prolonged crisis. Unless a radical reversal of policies in favour of social justice is undertaken, the crisis is going to last for many years to come.

35.
Banks from Karl Marx's day to the present

> At their birth the great banks, decorated with national titles, were only associations of private speculators who placed themselves by the side of governments, and, thanks to the privileges they received, were in a position to advance money to the state.[399]

Since Karl Marx wrote those lines in 1867 the banks, to put it politely, have not kept to the straight and narrow. The way they, along with the rest of the financial sector – insurance companies, pension funds and others – have developed over the last two centuries is quite extraordinary.

In the middle of the nineteenth century in the UK, the world's dominant financial and banking power, the assets of the financial sector represented less than 50% of GDP; those of the three biggest banks no more than 5% of total GDP.[400]

In 2012, still in the UK, the total assets of the financial sector represented more than 1000% of GDP and the assets of the three biggest banks (HSBC, Barclays and Royal Bank of Scotland) were together worth 350% of GDP.

---

399   Karl Marx, *Capital, Volume One: A Critique of Political Economy* [1887] trans. Ben Fowkes, Harmondsworth: Penguin Classics, 1992, Chapter 31; online version https://www.marxists.org/archive/marx/works/1867-c1/ch31.htm
400   Much of the data used in the beginning of this chapter is from a speech by Andrew Haldane, Chief Executive of the British Financial Stability Authority (FSA), wittily entitled 'Control Rights (and Wrongs)', 24 October 2011, http://www.bis.org/review/r111026a.pdf.

The growth in the volume of the balance-sheets of those three banks compared to the GDP of the country was as follows: 5% in the mid-nineteenth century, 7% at the beginning of the twentieth century, 25% at the beginning of the 1950s, 75% at the end of the 1990s, reaching 350% in 2012.

These figures are a clear and irrevocable indication of how the sum value of financial assets has exploded over the last twenty years. Other noteworthy developments have also taken place.

One is the significant reduction of hard capital on banks' balance-sheets and the concomitant increase in leverage coefficients. In the middle of the nineteenth century, hard capital usually represented between 25% and 50% of a bank's resources (more often 50% than 25%). In 2014, this hard capital represents between 3% and 5% of a bank's resources. This situation is not specific to the UK; the same phenomenon is found in the other industrialised countries of Europe and North America.

Leverage has thus increased considerably. To put it simply, in the mid-nineteenth century a bank's shareholders provided between 25% and 50% of the bank's resources and the bank borrowed the rest, an amount about equal to the owners' investment, thus doubling its resources. In 2014 investors bring no more than 3% to 5% and the bank borrows 20 to 30 times that amount to complete its resources.

Another development is that limited liability companies have come into existence. Until the beginning of the nineteenth century in Britain, and afterwards in other European countries, the estate of company-owners was fully liable if their businesses (which they either fully or partially owned) went under. In legal terms this was called the unlimited liability of owners or shareholders.

Take a bank that has assets of 1,000 with ten shareholders each holding 5%. Each would hold 50 parts. The company goes bankrupt and the creditors claim 900 parts. The capital of 500 would be insufficient to pay the creditors in full. To ensure full payment, it would be possible to draw the difference from the total of the estates of all the shareholders.

All over the world in the nineteenth century laws were modified to allow capitalists to limit their risks and liabilities.[401] This is what is meant by limited liability companies. In case of liquidation, the investors and shareholders only lose the amounts they put into the company. Returning to our example above, a capitalist who has wealth of 10,000 will only be liable for a maximum of 50; his property is safe from being seized in order to cover full indemnity to creditors.

This is where we see the interest of controlling a company of which one owns only 3% to 6% of the stock. If the capital brought into the company by the shareholders is only 5% of the balance-sheet and the principal shareholder owns 5% of this equity, his risk is limited to 0.25% of the balance-sheet!

In the example given, imagine that the principal shareholder is Black-Rock, which also owns 5% of JPMorgan Chase. The principal shareholder risks, in this case, 5% of 50, or a mere 2.5 parts, even if he is fully responsible for the bankruptcy, while 900 are needed to indemnify the other beneficiaries. It is easy to understand that the lawmakers who created the conditions for limited liability companies have guaranteed non-accountability and immunity to major shareholders. Before limited liability, speculators risked much more than their own stake and so tended towards prudence. Now, while the losses of big shareholders who invest a small part of their wealth in the bank are limited leaving the rest of their wealth that is invested in other companies intact, the small shareholders of Fortis in Belgium, Royal Bank of Scotland, Dexia in France or Lehman Brothers who had entrusted a large part of their savings to these shares lost far more, relatively. Of course, their liability is also limited, but if they put all their savings into shares in one of these companies, they lost everything.

The legal limited liability of shareholders encourages risk-taking by the big shareholders because their potential losses are limited in proportion to their entire estates. Such laws encourage moral hazard and should be repealed. The costs of corporate bankruptcies and all the damage they cause should be supported by the controlling shareholders and paid from their estates. This matter will be mentioned again in the final chapter.

---

401   See Thomas Piketty, *Capital in the Twenty-first Century*, trans. Arthur Goldhammer, Cambridge (MA): Harvard University Press, 2013, p. 320. See also Andrew Haldane, 'Control Rights (and Wrongs)', (referenced in footnote 400), pp. 3 and 4.

Because the total equity in the balance-sheet of the banks is much re-duced compared to the assets that are involved, and since the profits are in relation to the amount in assets, the Return on Equity is that much higher (see Chapters 4 to 6). At the beginning of the twenti-eth century, ROE was around 4% to 6%; by the end of the twentieth century it was at 20%, reaching 30% in 2007 at the dawning of the banking crisis.

Shares circulate ever more rapidly. In the nineteenth century it was not uncommon for big shareholders to keep their shares for life – their own life or that of the company or bank. This is no longer the case. In economics textbooks of the 1960s-1980s, one could read that shareholders held their stock for an average period of eight years. By 1998 this average period had fallen to three years and in 2008 it was around three months.[402] It was for this reason that banks started an-nouncing quarterly results. Bank directors thus came under pressure to have positive results at all costs so that shareholder interest was maintained.

This situation had another consequence: institutional investors (in-vestment funds, insurance companies, hedge funds, banks) were able to push shares downwards themselves and make profits by specu-lating on this trend. They could make short selling or short buying, high-frequency trading transactions. According to Laurence Scialom and Gaël Giraud, 'the average period a hedge fund holds a share is ten minutes'.[403] Long-term investors such as small shareholders or public institutions are the losers; it is the short-term speculators who control the situation and can make profit on almost every occasion. This situation causes erratic price swings, which serve the interests of speculation, which in turn, triggers more volatility.

Bank directors' incomes have rocketed. In 1989, the chairmen of the seven biggest US banks made on average $2.8 million per annum, about a hundred times the median household income. In 2007, while they were bringing their banks to the brink of ruin, their average in-

---

402   Andrew Haldane, ibid., p. 12.
403   Laurence Scialom and Gaël Giraud, 'Pour une réforme bancaire plus ambitieuse: vous avez dit *Liikanen*? Chiche' (For a more ambitious banking reform. The *Liikanen Report*? Go for it), p. 12, *Terra Nova*, Note 22/22, 28 February 2013 (in French), http://tnova.fr/etudes/pour-une-reforme-ban-caire-plus-ambitieuse-vous-avez-dit-liikanen-chiche.

come was $26 million, about five hundred times the median household income. Of the top five US banks that in 2006 had paid their directors the highest rewards in Stock-options, four went to the wall in 2007-2008.[404]

A look in the rear-view mirror: Adam Smith, Karl Marx and banks

In 1776, Adam Smith wrote:

> Merchants and master manufacturers are, in this order, the two classes of people who commonly employ the largest capitals, and who by their wealth draw to themselves the greatest share of the public consideration. The interest of the dealers, however, in any particular branch of trade or manufactures, [author's note: Adam Smith included bankers here] is always in some respects different from, and even opposite to, that of the public. To widen the market, and to narrow the competition, is always the interest of the dealers.

The following sound advice from Adam Smith (concerning merchants and master manufacturers) has never been followed:

> The proposal of any new law or regulation of commerce which comes from this order, ought always to be listened to with great precaution, and ought never to be adopted till after having been long and carefully examined, not only with the most scrupulous, but with the most suspicious attention. It comes from an order of men whose interest is never exactly the same with that of the public, who have generally an interest to deceive and even to oppress the public,

---

404   Andrew Haldane, *idem*, p. 13.

and who accordingly have, upon many occasions, both deceived and oppressed it.[405]

Judging by what we have seen of the evolution of banking legislation,
it is clear that governments have ignored Adam Smith's recommendation: the laws have evolved according to the interests of bankers. In
his time Adam Smith recommended that governments severely limit
bankers' freedom:

> But those exertions of the natural lib-
> erty of a few individuals, which might
> endanger the security of the whole so-
> ciety, are, and ought to be, restrained
> by the laws of all governments; of the
> most free, as well as or the most despoti-
> cal. The obligation of building party walls,
> in order to prevent the communication of
> fire, is a violation of natural liberty, exactly
> of the same kind with the regulations of the
> banking trade, which are here proposed.[406]

By knocking down the wall that separated the commercial banks from
investment banks,[407] governments have removed the firewall. The
lawmakers' refusal to oblige the banks to rebuild the wall is an ad-
mission of the collusion between government and the big bankers.[408]

Nearly 150 years after Marx wrote the lines that introduced this chapter, it is evident that bankers are indeed only associations of private
speculators, who place themselves at the side of their governments.
Taking advantage of the privileges that accrued to them, they are indeed in a position to collect the deposits of the public and borrow

405   Adam Smith, *An Inquiry into the Nature and Causes of the Wealth of Nations* [1776], Book I.1, New York: Bantam, 2003, http://www.econlib.org/library/Smith/smWN5.html.
406   Adam Smith, op. cit., Book II, 2.94.
407   The abolition of the Glass-Steagall Act in 1999 by the Clinton Administration.
408   The reference is of course to the many on-going banking reforms in
Europe and North America.

from the central bank at reduced rates in order to make substantial profits re-lending to the governments at much higher rates. With the active support, or at least the passive complicity, of governments, banks can freely engage in financial delinquency (insider trading, breach of trust, deception, conspiracy to defraud, fraud, embezzlement, manipulation of exchange and interest-rates and commodity prices, money laundering, tax evasion and corrupting civil servants), overthrow governments, take over whole sections of the economy and put people out of their homes.

To quote Karl Marx once again, 'The national debt has given rise to joint-stock companies, to dealings in negotiable effects of all kinds, and to agiotage',[409] in a word, to stock-exchange gambling and the modern bankocracy.

It is high time to return to the original meaning of democracy and put the banks back to serving the community under popular control.

---

409   Karl Marx, *Capital*, Vol. 1 [1867] (referenced in footnote 400), Chapter 31'Genesis of the Industrial Capitalist'; online version https://www.marxists.org/archive/marx/works/1867-c1/ch31.htm

36.
Alternatives

Our final chapter proposes a series of concrete alternatives to counter the current crisis shaking Europe. It presents nineteen immediate measures concerning finance in general and the banking sector in particular. In addition to these measures, it proposes to socialise the banking and insurance sectors and to place them under citizens' control. It then examines ten further measures to reverse the crisis in the interests of the majority of people: stopping austerity plans; repudiating all illegitimate, unsustainable, odious and illegal public debt; cancelling all illegitimate and illegal private debt; increasing the resources of public authorities; reducing inequality by establishing fiscal justice; setting up legitimate government borrowing; developing and extending public services; strengthening the pension system based on intergenerational solidarity; radically reducing working hours to guarantee jobs for everyone and adopting an income policy that will bring about social justice; questioning the basis of the euro and taking action to build a different Europe, which would mean replacing the current treaties through true democratic process involving all the peoples of Europe. These are the proposals the CADTM is putting forward for discussion and debate.

From the 1980s, the private banking sector succeeded in freeing itself from the constraints that the public authorities had established and maintained for several decades, in order to prevent another banking crisis like the one that occurred in the 1930s. Regulators and governments who believed in neoliberal ideology gave free rein to capitalist bankers, who took full advantage of the situation. These events took place in a context in which the major financiers won back their advantage by undermining the social rights gained by workers, which were in the interests of the vast majority of people. The current crisis, which began in 2007-2008, has not induced the public authorities to impose strict rules on private capital. The few measures adopted and the paltry mechanisms envisaged to clean up the private financial sector are completely inadequate for preventing new financial crises or curbing the dangerous, speculative behaviour of the financial institutions. Economic, social and cultural rights laid out in the Universal Declaration of Human Rights and codified in an international covenant in 1966[410] are being seriously undermined.[411] Civil and political rights are being attacked on a daily basis by governments and international institutions[412] to favour major capital owners: the people are not consulted on vital issues such as the bailing out and future use of private banks, the privatisation of public corporations and public services or the ratification of European treaties. The choices made by voters are not respected, the constitutions of various countries are trampled on[413] and the legislative bodies are marginalised or relegated to simply rubber-stamping decisions made by others.

---

410   *The International Covenant on Economic, Social and Cultural Rights* was adopted in New York on 16 December 1966 by the United Nations General Assembly in its resolution 2 200 A (XXI). It came into force on 3 January 1976. See the full text of the Covenant and the list of countries that signed it at http://treaties.un.org/Pages/ViewDetails.aspx?src=TREATY&mtdsg_no=IV-3&chapter=4&lang=en&clang=_en. Brief presentation at 'International Covenant on Economic, Social and Cultural Rights', Wikipedia, http://en.Wikipedia.org/wiki/International_Covenant_on_Economic,_Social_and_Cultural_Rights.
411   See Nils Muižnieks, op. cit.: 'What began as a meltdown of the global financial system in 2008 has been transformed into a new political reality of austerity which threatens over six decades of social solidarity and expanding human rights protection across Council of Europe member states. [...] Many of these austerity measures – characterised by public expenditure cuts, regressive tax hikes, reduced labour protection and pension reforms – have exacerbated the already severe human consequences of the economic crisis marked by record levels of unemployment. The whole spectrum of human rights has been affected – from the rights to decent work, an adequate standard of living and social security to access to justice, freedom of expression and the rights to participation, transparency and accountability'.
412   The European Commission, ECB, and IMF.
413   This was clearly the case in Greece in 2010, when the Troika imposed its structural adjustment programme. Another example is the unconstitutional decision made by the Belgian government to grant a more than €50-billion guarantee to Dexia Bank in October 2011. The Belgian government adopted the measure by means of a simple royal decree, even though the Belgian constitution and laws stipulate that this kind of action must be decided by the legislative body.

The financial crisis falls within a much broader systemic crisis of global capitalism and is multi-faceted, with economic, environmental, social, political, moral and institutional dimensions.[414] We need to make a radical break with the mind-set of today's leaders, and take urgent measures. Those who are responsible for bank meltdowns must be obliged to pay for the bail-outs, as opposed to the current system of giving golden handshakes to those responsible for the economic disasters instead of holding them accountable.

The measures announced to regulate the banks are superficial. As well as new banking rules there are proposals to centralise supervision of Eurozone banks, create a European deposit guarantee scheme, prohibit certain operations (concerning only 2% of global banking activities), cap bonuses and render banking activities transparent. Yet all are mere recommendations, promises, or at best, completely inadequate for the task, in view of the scale of the issues to be resolved. What are needed are strict, universally applicable rules.

To get beyond this crisis, measures that would affect the very structure of the financial world and capitalist system should be implemented. The banking business is too crucial to be left in the hands of the private sector. The banking sector must be socialised, which means expropriating the banks and placing them under popular control – by bank employees, customers, associations and representatives of local public institutions — because banks should be run as a public service,[415] and the revenues generated by banking activities used for the common good.

The public debt incurred to save the banks is clearly illegitimate and must be repudiated. A citizens' audit must be conducted to determine the other illegitimate, illegal, odious or unsustainable debts, and to help to create mobilisation through which a credible anti-capitalist alternative can emerge.

These two measures must be part of the broader programme outlined in this chapter, which should start with the measures to be taken immediately in the financial sector.

---

414   The different aspects of the present systemic crisis were presented by Damien Millet and Éric Toussaint in *La crise, quelles crises ?* (The Crisis – which Crises?), Brussels: Aden, 2009.
415   The banking sector should be entirely public except for a small cooperative sector with which it could coexist and collaborate.

Popular mobilisation and social self-organisation are essential for achieving the different objectives proposed below. Without them, there will be no truly liberating solution to the current crisis.

I. Immediate measures for finance in general and banks in particular

As mentioned in the introduction, the socialisation[416] of banks everywhere is our ultimate goal. However, already today, minimal but real measures aiming to expropriate the financial sector can unite movements, unions, political parties and individuals that do not necessarily share the same vision, around a common platform.

There follows a list of 18 concrete measures proposed by the CADTM.

1. **Radically reduce the size of banks** so there are no longer banks that are 'Too Big to Fail' which represent a risk for the whole system.

2. **Separate commercial banking from investment banking.** This implies the splitting up of universal banks (which engage in commercial banking, investment banking, and insurance activities at the same time) into different legal entities.[417] Commercial banks would be the only institutions authorised to collect deposits and savings from people and obtain support from public authorities (a public guarantee on deposits and access to central bank liquidities).[418]
Only these banks would be allowed to make personal loans to depositors and savers, loans to businesses and loans to local and national public authorities. They would be forbidden entry to the financial markets.

---

416   The term 'socialisation' rather than 'nationalisation' is used in this book. See Section II of this chapter for further discussion of the term.
417   This would mean resuscitating the Glass-Steagall-type laws adopted in the US from 1933.
418   Philippe Lamberts and Gaspard Denis, *The Seven Deadly Sins of Banks*, The Greens/EFA, 2013, http://bankingsins.eu/en/.

They would be prohibited from engaging in any kind of securitisation: loans may not be converted into tradable securities, and must be retained on their books until the loans granted have been fully paid off. A bank that grants a loan must bear the risk it entails. On the other hand, investment banks must use the financial markets when issuing bonds, shares, and other financial instruments.[419]

We also support the proposal made by the Belgian MEP Philippe Lamberts to limit the weight of security-backed instruments in investment-bank portfolios by making them retain, say, 60%[420] of the tradable securities on their own books and thereby bear more of the risk. On the other hand, it would be safer to simply prohibit securitisation of any kind, as we propose for commercial banks.

It is important to point out that investment banks should not enjoy any kind of public underwriting. In the case of bankruptcy, all losses should be fully assumed by the private sector, starting with the shareholders (on all of their assets; see below).

3. **Prohibit derivatives**. This would mean that investment banks and other financial actors wishing to hedge against risks (such as exchange and interest-rate fluctuations or payment defaults) would have to go back to using traditional insurance policies.

4. **Impose pre-commercialisation compliance controls** on all new financial products proposed to the markets. Philippe Lamberts proposes to do this and to subject the products to 'marketing authorisations' before commercialisation. As said before, we prefer the complete prohibition of derivatives. Nevertheless, we support this proposal, as well as a similar one put forward by the Fondation Copernic.[421]

---

419 This was part of the Glass-Steagall Act already mentioned.
420 This percentage is the author's proposal.
421 For the Fondation Copernic, it is 'just as important to stop [invest-

5. **Prohibit credit relationships between commercial and investment banks**. We agree with FrédÉric Lordon, who supports the total separation of commercial banks and investment banks. A commercial bank must in no way be involved in a credit relationship with an investment bank.[422]

6. **Prohibit speculation**. As Paul Jorion proposes, speculation should be prohibited.
Speculation has been authorised in France since 1885 and in Belgium since 1867. Speculation was clearly defined by the law, which aimed to 'prohibit bets on the rise or fall of the price of financial instruments'. With such a restriction, whoever practised speculation would be violating the law, whichever bank was involved.[423]

---

ment banks] from taking ill-considered risks (on their own behalf and on behalf of local authorities) as it is to prevent these risks from being passed on. The same authorities should have the power of pre-commercial examinations of the new, sometimes exotic, financial products and to prohibit operations that are not very well understood even by the financiers themselves or speculative interventions on public debt (CDS markets, national bond futures, and securitisation), commodities and foodstuffs. The granting of a commercialisation licence presupposes the competence of the supervisors to understand banking innovations and in case of doubt have the capacity to refuse them.' (in French, trans. CADTM), Fondation Copernic, *Changer vraiment ! Quelles politiques économiques de gauche ?* (Real change! What economic policies for the Left?), Paris: Syllepse, June 2012, http://www. fondation-copernic.org/spip.php?article684.

422 Frédéric Lordon, 'La régulation bancaire au pistolet à bouchon' (Banking regulations enforced with a pop-gun), *Le Monde Diplomatique blog*, 18 February 2013, http://blog.mondediplo.net/2013-02-18-La-regulation-bancaire-au-pistolet-a-bouchon (in French).

423 Paul Jorion in *Financité*, November 2013. Elsewhere, Jorion refers to two articles of French criminal law prohibiting speculation that were abrogated in 1885 under the influence of the business sector. According to Article 421, 'Speculation on the rise or fall in the prices of government securities will be punished by imprisonment for not less than one month and not exceeding one year.' Article 422 specifies that: 'Shall be considered to be speculation of this kind, any agreement to sell or supply government securities that sellers cannot establish to have had in their possession at the time of the agreement or that should have been in their possession at the time of delivery.' http://www.pauljorion.com/blog/?p=57581. Paul Jorion also

271

It would be illegal for a bank to speculate either for itself or for its clients. The purchase by a bank – or any other financial institution – of physical goods (raw materials, foodstuffs, land and real-estate) or a financial product (shares, bonds, and so on) with the intention to speculate on its price would be prohibited.

7. Who should be liable for bank losses?
The unlimited liability of major shareholders must be reinstated. In case of bankruptcy or liquidation, the cost must be paid for by seizing the assets of the major shareholders (natural persons and companies/moral persons). Globally, small investors/savers must be fully protected – up to €300,000, let us say, as a basis for discussion. According to Thomas Piketty, in several European countries comparable to France the 50% least wealthy have an average wealth of €20,000, while many of these households either have no wealth at all or are in debt.[424] The wealthiest 40% possess an average wealth of €175,000 (from €100,000 to €400,000). Therefore, the vast majority of people, that is, around 80%, possess less than €300,000. So the above proposition would not affect 80% of the population. As for commercial banks, the Copernic Foundation proposes that '[in] case of failure, bank customers must continue to enjoy national guarantees on their deposits, limited to a reasonable 'savings' bal-

mentions Article 1965 of the French *Code Civil* that states 'The law makes no provision to incriminate the payment of gaming debts or of wagers.' This measure is in harmony with Article 138 of the royal decree by Louis XIII dated 15 January 1629, known as the Code Michau, which says: 'We declare that all gaming debts are non-existent, and all guarantees and promises on gaming, in whatever form they may take, are null and void, and devoid of any civil or natural obligations.'
424   According to a report by ING Bank, three Belgians out of ten have no savings: Arnaud Lefebvre, 'ING: près de 3 Belges sur 10 déclarent n'avoir aucune épargne' (ING: nearly 3 out of 10 Belgians say they have no savings), *Express* (Belgium), 30 January 2014, http://www.express.be/sectors/fr/finance/ing-pres-de-3-belges-sur-10-declarent-navoir-aucune-epargne/201690.htm (in French).

ance of an upper-middle-class household (about €150,000)'.[425] This proposal should also be the subject of democratic debate.

8. **Prohibit Over-the-Counter (OTC) trading**. All financial market transactions should be registered, traceable, supervised and controlled. Currently, all the major markets, such as currency markets ($5.3 trillion a day),[426] derivatives markets and commodity markets,[427] are OTC and are subject to no form of control.

9. **Put an end to banking secrecy**. Banks must provide all the requisite information about their directors, subsidiaries, branches, customers, activities and the business they handle for themselves and for their customers. Their accounts must be transparent and consistent. The removal of bank secrecy must become a minimal democratic imperative in all countries. To that effect, banks must provide fiscal authorities with the following information on request: lists of persons who earn interest, make dividends and capital gains or other financial revenues; details of the opening, closure and modification of accounts in order to establish national registers of bank accounts; details of all inward and outward capital flows, with identification of the beneficiary.

10. **Prohibit transactions with tax havens**. All transactions with tax havens are to be prohibited. The penalty for violating this restriction should be heavy – revocation of the banking licence and heavy fines.

---

425   Fondation Copernic, ibid., http://www.fondation-copernic.org/spip.php?article684.
426   See Éric Toussaint, 'Comment les grandes banques manipulent le marché des devises' (How the big banks manipulate the currency markets), *Le Monde*, 13 March 2014 and available at CADTM, http://cadtm.org/Comment-les-grandes-banques (in French, Spanish, and Portuguese).
427   Éric Toussaint, 'Banks speculate on raw materials and food,' CADTM, 7 March 2014, http://cadtm.org/Banks-speculate-on-raw-materials.

11. **Prohibit high-frequency trading, shadow banking, short selling and naked short selling** and strictly limit what may be retained 'off-balance-sheet'.[428]

12. **Require banks to radically increase their equity-to-assets ratio**.[429] Whereas this ratio is generally below 5%, we propose increasing it to 20%.

13. **Working conditions and hours, pay and employment**. Guarantee working conditions and the number of jobs in the banking sector. Implement gender equality, including in pay scales. Create a pay scale that increases the lowest wages and puts a limit on the highest. Plato's recommendation of limiting the highest incomes to four times the lowest could be applied, or Aristotle's, with the upper limit of income at five times the lowest.[430] This clearly means a radical reduction in the level of highest authorised incomes (fixed salaries and other income advantages) paid to top executives.[431]

---

428 For example, restrict off-balance-sheet to guarantees and signature engagements only. This measure requires further discussion.

429 This requires eliminating the risk-weighted assets system.

430 'Now the legislator should determine what is to be the limit of poverty or wealth. Let the limit of poverty be the value of the lot; this ought to be preserved, and no ruler, nor any one else who aspires after a reputation for virtue, will allow the lot to be impaired in any case. This the legislator gives as a measure, and he will permit a man to acquire double or triple, or as much as four times the amount of this.' Plato, *The Laws, V, 744 d - 744 e* in *Works by Plato*, http://classics.mit.edu/Plato/laws.5.v.html. Aristotle broaches the question in *Politics, Book 2*, chapter III § 8 and chapter IV § 3, referring to Phaleas and Plato; see http://classics.mit.edu/Aristotle/politics.2.two.html. Philippe Lamberts proposes an upper limit of remuneration (salary + bonuses) of 10 times the average of the lowest incomes, while the bank-workers' union Sud BPCE proposes to eliminate bonuses, stock-options, retirement compensations and other unjustified advantages and exceptional practices, and to set up an MAI (Maximum Authorised Income).

431 Should corporations exceed this limit the revenue would be taxed at 100%.

Non-fixed incomes indexed on sales figures and other bonuses that encourage bad counselling, even misinformation, and mismanagement must be abandoned in favour of fixed incomes. In addition, the reduction of working hours recommended further on must evidently be applied to the banking sector, so that new jobs will be created. 'Benchmarking' and 'Lean Management' must also be prohibited.

14. **Prohibit the transfer of the losses of banks** and other private financial institutions to the public sector. Public authorities cannot be permitted to transfer private debts to the public sector.

15. **Systematically prosecute directors guilty** of financial and other crimes and misdemeanours. Cancel the banking licences of institutions that try to override restrictions and misappropriate funds.

16. **Tax banks**. Bank profits must be strictly subjected to the normal framework for taxing corporate profits. The current tax rate paid by banks is very much lower than the usual corporate-tax rates, which are already too low. Currency and financial securities transactions must be taxed. Short-term bank debts must also be taxed in order to encourage long-term investment.

17. **Use a different method to save banks**. In addition to the three measures mentioned above – unlimited liability of the biggest shareholders, guarantee of deposits up to €150,000, and prohibiting the transformation of private banking debt into public debt – a well-ordered liquidation process made up of two structures must be put into place. These would be a private 'bad bank', at the owners' expense and at no cost to the public authorities, and a public bank to which all the deposits and remaining safe assets will be transferred.

Some recent experiences, such as Iceland's since 2008, may serve as a source of inspiration.

18. **Existing public banks must be strengthened** and new ones created where banks have been privatised (of course, under the same strict control mentioned above). A collective was created in France in 2012 for a 'Public Finance Unit'.[432] In Belgium, where the government privatised the last public banks during the 1990s, the state has taken over the banking activities of Dexia by acquiring 100% of its stock at a cost of €4 billion, a price that the European Commission itself considered to be excessive. Dexia Bank has been renamed Belfius and is run as a private company. Belfius must truly become a public bank, and the above measures must be implemented. Belfius should have been set up as a public financial institution, at no cost to public finance, to take over the deposits of Dexia customers and all the safe assets. The bank should have been placed under popular control. The jobs, working conditions, and wages of the personnel should have been guaranteed while the remunerations of the directors and other board members should have been seriously reduced. They should have been prohibited from managing other private financial institutions, prosecuted by the authorities and held to account for the infractions they have committed.

---

432   See Fondation Copernic's petition 'Pour un Pôle Public Financier' (For a public finance division), 'http://pourunpolepublicfinancier.org/ (in French). This collective brings together various public financial institutions (Banque de France, Caisse des Dépôts and its financial subsidiaries, OSEO, Société des participations de l'État, Banque Postale, UbiFrance, Agence Française de Développement, Institut d'émission des départements d'Outre-Mer, and CNP Assurance), and institutions that provide a public service (Crédit foncier, Coface), including any bank or insurance company in which the State has a majority holding or to which a public-service mission has been entrusted. In Belgium, a website created by the PTB is dedicated to promoting awareness of the necessity for a public banking structure. http://www.banquepublique.be/ (in French or Dutch).

Implementing these concrete measures would be an advance in banking reform even if the private banking sector were to retain the dominant position. Recent experience shows that we cannot trust capitalists to own and run banks. If, through a strong social movement, we can impose the above measures (which, of course, can be further improved), the capitalists will still look for all possible ways to regain lost ground. They will strive to find ways around the rules, they will use all the powers at their disposal to win over lawmakers and government officials to the cause of a new deregulation of the banking and financial sectors, to maximise their profits once again with no consideration of the interests of the majority of the people.

II. Socialising the banking sector under popular control

There are a number of compelling reasons to socialise the banking sector. First of all, capitalists have repeatedly shown the crimes they are capable of perpetrating and the risks they are ready to take to increase their profits, without ever taking responsibility for the consequences. In addition, their irresponsible behaviour regularly results in a heavy burden on society. Thirdly, the society we want to build together must be based on the common good, social justice and the restoration of equitable relationships among humans, and between humans and the rest of nature. What we are trying to achieve is a 'complete deprivatisation of the banking sector.'[433]

Socialising the banking sector means:

- Expropriating without compensation (or with symbolic compensation) the assets of the major shareholders (small shareholders will be compensated);
- Granting the public sector a monopoly on banking activities with the exception of a small-sized co-operative banking sector (subject to the same rules as the public sector);
- Creating a public service for savings, loans and investments, which will be organised in a network of

---

433   Frédéric Lordon, 'L'effarante passivité de la "re-régulation financière"' (The shocking passivity of 'financial re-regulation'), in *Changer d'économie !* (Changing the economy), Les économistes atterrés, Paris: Les liens qui libèrent, 2012, p. 242 (in French).

      small neighbourhood branches;
- Defining a charter of goals and missions to be fulfilled (with popular participation in debates and decisions);
- Ensuring transparency in accounts, which must be submitted publicly in a way that makes them easy to understand.

We use the term 'socialisation' rather than 'nationalisation' to indicate how crucial popular monitoring is and the sharing of decision-making among executives, representatives of the employees, clients/users and associations, local officials, and representatives of national and regional banking institutions. We must democratically define how active popular control can be implemented. Similarly, we must promote the close monitoring of banking activities by employees in the banking sector as well as their active involvement in deciding what has to be done and how. The boards of banks must account for their management on a yearly basis. We must place the priority on high-quality local services, which would be contrary to current outsourcing policies. Employees in financial institutions should be encouraged to provide genuine advice, and move away from an aggressive sales approach, which amounts to forcing people to buy financial products they do not need.

Socialising the banking sector and integrating it into public services will make it possible to:

- Free populations and governments from the grip of financial markets;
- Finance projects proposed by popular and public bodies;
- Dedicate the banking activity to common welfare, including the task of facilitating transition from a productivist capitalist economy to a social and environmentalist economy.

As Patrick Saurin rightly observes, 'The time has come when it is no longer bank losses that must be socialised, but the banks themselves, lock, stock and barrel.'[434]

434   Patrick Saurin, 'Socialiser le secteur bancaire' (Socialising the banking sector), 2 February 2013, www.cadtm.org/Socialiser-le-syste-

III. Socialising the insurance sector and making it a public service

Considering how interdependent the banking and insurance sectors have become within the mammoth universal banks that have developed; and also that large insurance groups are as irresponsible in their decision-makings as banks while being even less accountable, it is also necessary to socialise the private insurance sector. Following the programme drafted by the Conseil National de la Résistance (the National Council of the Resistance),[435] French insurance companies were nationalised in April 1946 after large banks were nationalised at the end of 1945.

IV. Further measures for a recovery that favours the great majority

Reducing the public deficit is not an end in itself. Indeed, in some circumstances, the deficit can be used to stimulate economic activity and invest in improving the living conditions of those who are suffering from the crisis. Once the economy has recovered, public deficits must be reduced, but not through cuts in social expenditure; rather through an increase in tax revenue by fighting tax evasion and imposing higher rates of taxation on profits of major companies and on the income and assets of rich households, as well as by taxing financial transactions. In any case, it is definitely possible to increase tax revenue while decreasing the tax burden on the poorest 50% of the population.

To reduce the deficit, we must also radically reduce the expenses resulting from repaying the public debt. To start with, the portion that is illegitimate, unsustainable, odious and illegal must be cancelled.

---

me-bancaire. See also: 'Projet bancaire alternatif' (Alternative banking project), by Sud BPCE (the trade union for workers in the banking group BPCE), June 2012, http://www.sudbpce.com/files/2013/01/2012-projet-bancaire-alternatif-definitif.pdf or http://cadtm.org/Projet-bancaire-alternatif .
435   The National Council of the Resistance directed and coordinated the different movements of the French Resistance. In 1944, it adopted a programme proposing nationalisations, a social security system and a planned economy.

Expenses that have to be cut are those related to the army and other socially useless and environmentally dangerous projects such as building new airports or new motorways.

On the other hand, it is essential to increase social spending, especially to counter the consequences of the economic depression. We must also increase investments in renewable energies and in infrastructure, such as public transport, schools and hospitals. Stimulating the economy through public spending and household demand also results in more tax revenue.

Beyond stimulating employment and the economy, the crisis must be an opportunity to break with the capitalist mindset and radically change society. This new way of thinking must move away from productivism and incorporate respect for the environment, do away with all forms of oppression and promote the common good.

To accomplish these goals, we have to organise a massive movement against austerity, both locally and internationally, to bring together the energies needed to tip the balance of power in favour of such radical changes centred on social and environmental justice.

V. Ending unfair austerity measures

Putting an end to antisocial austerity measures is an absolute priority. Through street mobilisation and strikes and by refusing to pay unpopular taxes, people must force their governments to cancel austerity policies.

VI. Identifying illegitimate, unsustainable, odious and illegal public debt

Citizens' audits that are under way in several countries[436] have resulted in rich and stimulating debates that clarify what may be defined as public debt that does not have to be repaid. Without claiming to be exhaustive, we can propose the following definitions:

---

436   Spain, Portugal, Greece, France, Belgium and Brazil are among them. See the ICAN website: http://www.citizen-audit.net/

- **Illegitimate public debt**: debt contracted by a government which is not in the public interest or undermines the general interest.
- **Illegal debt**: debt contracted in violation of the current legal or constitutional system.
- **Odious public debt**: loans to authoritarian regimes or granted on conditions that violate the social, economic, cultural, civic and political rights of the people concerned.
- **Unsustainable public debt**: debt that can only be paid back with dire consequences for the people, such as a dramatic decline of living conditions, health care and education, or an increase in unemployment, or even starvation. In short, debt whose repayment makes it impossible for governments to guarantee basic human rights.

A popular audit of public debt under public control, combined in some cases with a unilateral, sovereign refusal to continue repaying the public debt, will make it possible to cancel / repudiate the illegitimate, odious, unsustainable and illegal portion of public debt and to greatly reduce the rest. Public debt that results from bailing out banks is clearly illegitimate debt. In some countries, it may even be illegal. It can certainly be unsustainable, as is the case for Greece, Cyprus, and Ireland.

The debts claimed by the Troika from Greece, Portugal, Ireland and Cyprus are illegitimate (they go against the general interest), odious (they entail the infringement of contractual relations and of economic and social rights), unsustainable (considering the dramatic deterioration of the living conditions of a significant part of the population) and in some cases illegal (as is the case of Greece, where the constitution was violated because of pressure exerted by the Troika with the collusion of the Greek government).

Why should public debt be reduced? Why should our indebted governments radically reduce their public debt by cancelling their illegitimate debts?

First, in the name of social justice, but also on economic grounds that everybody can understand.

To move beyond the crisis in a way that meets the legitimate expectations of the people, stimulating economic activity through public spending and household spending, would simply not be enough. Even with the added tax revenue, repayment of public debt would totally absorb any surplus. What the richer households and big private companies would pay as taxes would be compensated by the return they would get from the public bonds of which they are the main shareholders (which is why they fiercely resist the notion of debt cancellation). Therefore a large portion of public debt must be cancelled.

The extent of the cancellation will depend on the specific features of the debt in each country and the level of awareness of the people it affects (in this respect popular audits play a major role), as well as the way the economic and political crisis develops. Especially important is the balance of power that will evolve through popular mobilisation in the street, the workplace and all public spaces, now and in the future. In some countries, such as Greece, Portugal, Ireland, Spain and Cyprus, the issue of debt cancellation is urgent. In countries such as Germany, the Netherlands, France, Belgium, Austria, the United Kingdom and the United States, it is not yet such an urgent matter. Nevertheless, eventually, most countries will have to face the unsustainable nature of debt repayment.

Suspending payment. Countries that have already been blackmailed by speculators, the IMF and other bodies such as the EC, should call for a unilateral moratorium on debt repayment. This proposal has become quite popular in the countries that are the most severely affected by the crisis. The unilateral moratorium must be combined with a citizens' audit of government borrowing, which should bring forth evidence and arguments to justify repudiation of the part of the debt that has been identified as illegitimate. The CADTM has shown in several of its publications that a legal basis for a unilateral, sovereign decision of this nature exists in both international and national law.[437]

---

437   Cécile Lamarque, Renaud Vivien, 'How debts can legally be declared void,' CADTM, 16 May 2011, http://cadtm.org/How-debts-can-legally-be-declared. Cécile Lamarque, Renaud Vivien, 'Plaidoyer juridique pour la suspension et la répudiation des dettes publiques au Nord et au Sud' (A plea for the suspension and repudiation of public debt in the North and South), CADTM, 1 June 2011, http://cadtm.org/Plaidoyer-juridique-pour-la (in French).

Refusing debt relief tied to antisocial measures. We cannot accept debt relief as decided by creditors because of the heavy demands they make in return. The reduction plan for part of the Greek debt in effect since March 2012 is conditioned upon the country enforcing more measures that infringe the Greek people's economic and social rights as well as the country's sovereignty.[438] Its real intent is to enable foreign private banks, mainly in France and Germany, to cut their losses; for private Greek banks to receive fresh money from the Treasury; and for the Troika to tighten its grip on Greece. The Greek public debt amounted to 130% of the country's GDP in 2009, then 157% in 2012 after a partial cancellation of the debt, to reach 175% in 2013. We must expose the fraud of Greek debt reduction as it was implemented and put forward our alternative: cancellation of the debt (that is, its repudiation by the indebted country), which is a legitimate act of unilateral sovereignty.

Audit to identify those responsible for odious, unsustainable, illegitimate or illegal debt. Popular audits make it possible to determine responsibilities in the process of contracting debts and to demand that those who are responsible (whether at the national or international level) face the consequences of their acts. If audits reveal illegal actions related to illegitimate debts, their perpetrators (whether natural or moral persons) must be convicted and made to pay compensation. They should be banned from any jobs related to credit institutions (banks could have their banking licences withdrawn), and must not be exonerated from prison sentences if the gravity of their acts merits such punishment. It is time to bring legal action against public authorities that enter into illegitimate debts.

Who will pay the bill for debt cancellation? It is logical that the private institutions and the rich who hold debt securities should bear the burden of cancelling illegitimate sovereign debt, since they are largely responsible for the on-going crisis and have actually profited from it. Making them pay is only a small step towards more social justice.

It is therefore important to identify security holders in order to compensate those who are low- or middle-income earners. The way to identify debt security holders is to stop paying, since they will then

---

438   See 'The CADTM condemns the disinformation campaign on the Greek debt and the rescue plan by private creditors', CADTM, 12 March 2012, http://cadtm.org/The-CADTM-condemns-the.

have to come forward and claim repayment. That will help the state to compensate small holders of public debt securities. Furthermore,

> When public debts are cancelled, small savers who have invested in public securities, as well as wage earners and old-age pensioners who had part of their social security contributions (old-age, unemployment, healthcare or family benefits) invested in institutions or bodies that run the same kind of securities, can very well be protected.[439]

The portion of public debt that has been identified as legitimate will have to be reduced by asking for help from those who benefitted from it. One way to make sure they pay the cost of the operation is to levy an exceptional progressive tax on the top 10% of accumulated wealth. The revenue from this tax could be used to anticipate repayment of that part of the debt that has been established as legitimate. There are other possibilities open to debate.

Additional measures for handling debt. The portion of the national budget spent on the repayment of public debt must be capped according to the country's economic capacity and the public authorities' ability to repay while guaranteeing a socially agreed level of social expenditure. We should learn from what was done for Germany after the Second World War: the 1953 London Agreement included a 62% reduction of the German debt stock and stipulated that the debt/export ratio should not exceed 5%.[440]

A legal framework must also be set up to avoid the repetition of the crisis that started in 2007-2008. The socialisation of private debt must be prohibited, and there must be an obligation to organise a permanent audit of the public debt policy with popular participation. The statutory limitations for crimes related to illegitimate debt must be abrogated and illegitimate debt must be considered null and void.

---

439   Thomas Coutrot, Patrick Saurin and Éric Toussaint, 'Cancelling debt or taxing capital: why should we choose?', CADTM, 2 November 2013, http://cadtm.org/Cancelling-debt-or-taxing-capital.
440   Éric Toussaint, *The World Bank: A Critical Primer*, London: Pluto Press, 2008, Chapter 4.

In addition, there must be a golden rule that public spending for fundamental human rights cannot be cut and takes priority over spending to repay debt. There are clearly plenty of alternatives.

VII. Cancelling illegitimate and illegal private debt

All over the world, as the driving force behind real-estate speculation, private banks abused millions of households with mortgages. When the bubble burst and payment defaulting spread they seized the mortgaged properties and evicted the inhabitants. This happened in the USA, Spain, Ireland, Iceland and several Eastern and Central European countries. Illegitimate or even illegal debt, which has dramatic consequences for hundreds of thousands of households or more, must be cancelled and foreclosures prevented where possible.

Banks and private universities have swindled hundreds of thousands of students by pushing them into intolerable and illegitimate debt. As mentioned earlier, student-loans in the US amount to some $1 trillion. These student-loan debts must also be cancelled.

VIII. Taxation to improve public resources and reduce inequalities

Direct taxation of the highest incomes and major corporations has decreased continually since 1980. Thus hundreds of billions of euros in fiscal gifts have essentially been oriented towards speculation and the accumulation of wealth by the richest segment of the population. Since 1975-1980, the trend has been towards increased inequality, with a sharp rise in the share of overall wealth controlled by the wealthiest 1% and 10%. In 2010, the wealthiest 1% possessed 25% of the total wealth in Europe. This corresponds more or less to the capitalist class and an impressive share of the wealth is concentrated there. If we extend the study to the wealthiest 10%, we find that 60% of the total wealth is in the hands of that minority. We can assume that the extra 9% represents the entourage or the allies, in the broad sense, of the capitalist class. The remaining 90% of us had to make do with 40% of the total wealth, and among the 90%, the poorest 50% owned a mere 5% of the wealth.[441]

---

441   See Éric Toussaint, 'What can we do with what Thomas Piketty

What has just been said about the European Union can be extended to the rest of the world; from the North to the South of the planet, we have witnessed an extraordinary increase in the share of the wealth held by the wealthiest fraction.

We could extend the study to an even more infinitesimal minority: the wealthiest 1/20,000,000 of the adult population at the planetary level in 1987 was made up of 150 individuals, each with an average of $1.5 billion. Sixteen years later, in 2013, the wealthiest 1/20,000,000 numbered 225, each with an average wealth of $15 billion – a growth of 6.4% per year.[442] The wealthiest 0.1% (one thousandth of the global population) owns 20% of the world's wealth and the wealthiest 1%, 50%. If we take the wealth of the richest 10% into consideration, Thomas Piketty estimates that it represents 80 to 90% of the world's total wealth, with the least wealthy 50% owning less than 5%. That gives us an idea of the effort towards redistribution that needs to be made. Such redistribution requires confiscating a large share of the wealth held by the richest fraction of the population.

Let us return to Europe. A profound reform of taxation aimed at achieving greater social justice (reducing the revenue and the wealth of the wealthiest segment to increase that of the majority of the population) must be combined with harmonisation at the European level to prevent fiscal dumping.[443] The goal is to increase public funds, partly by a progressive income tax on the revenue of the wealthiest physical individuals (there is no reason why the marginal income-tax rate should not be increased to 90% or even 100%),[444] a tax on wealth above a certain amount, and corporate tax.

---

teaches us about capital in the twenty-first century?', CADTM, 19 January 2014, http://cadtm.org/What-can-we-do-with-what-Thomas.

442   Thomas Piketty, *Capital in the Twenty-First Century* (op. cit.), p. 692.

443   We could take the example of Ireland, where the tax rate on corporate profits is only 12.5%. In France, the actual tax rate on companies on the CAC 40 index is a mere 8%.

444   We should point out that the 90% rate was first applied to the wealthiest individuals under the presidency of Franklin Roosevelt in the United States in the 1930s. In France, it was applied in 1924, then again just before the Second World War.

The gross domestic product of the European Union in 2013 was approximately €14.7 trillion. The total private wealth of European households is approximately €70 trillion. The wealthiest 1% alone possesses roughly €17.5 trillion (25% of €70 trillion). The next-wealthiest 9% hold €24.5 trillion (35%). The 40% in the middle hold €24.5 trillion (35%). The remaining 50% own €3.5 trillion (5%).

The annual budget of the European Commission is approximately 1% of the EU's GDP. Considering that an annual tax of 1% on the wealth held by the wealthiest 1% in the EU would provide €175 billion – more than the current budget of the EU, which is approximately €145 billion, what about a tax of 5%? This gives an idea of what is potentially achievable if social mobilisation were to bring about a radical change of policy at the European level, or even at the level of a single EU country.

An exceptional tax (levied once in a generation) of 33% on the holdings of the wealthiest 1% in the EU would yield nearly €6 trillion (40 times the annual budget of the EU). And what about a confiscatory rate of 80%?

These figures give an idea of what is at stake when considering the issue of taxation of the private wealth of capitalists and the possibilities that arise for developing proposals for using that money in the service of social justice. Many economists endlessly repeat the idea that there is no point in taxing the wealthiest people because there are so few of them that the yield would not be significant. However, over time, the wealthiest 1% have concentrated such large quantities of tangible and intangible assets that a policy targeting the wealthiest 1% or 2.5% (or perhaps the wealthiest 10%) would provide substantial means for breaking with neoliberalism.

To those who claim that wealth is inaccessible, because it can cross borders easily, we must retort that sequestration, the freezing of financial assets, heavy fines and the control of capital movements are powerful tools that can be readily used against banks that collude in the flight of capital.[445]

---

445   A government can prohibit the banks doing business in a country from conducting any transaction in excess of a certain sum without prior authorisation, on pain of a fine equal to the amount transferred (to which

This increase in revenue must be accompanied by a rapid decrease in the cost of access to fundamental goods and services (basic food items, water, electricity, heating, public transport, school supplies, etc.), for example through a sharp and targeted reduction of the VAT (sales tax) on these vital goods and services. Similarly, exemptions from real-estate taxes on residences must be applied to immediately lighten the tax burden on the least wealthy 60 or 70% of the population.

Another need is for a tax policy that encourages protection of the environment through dissuasive taxation of polluting industries.

IX. Legitimate public borrowing

A state must be able to borrow money in order to improve the living conditions of its people – for instance, to finance public utility works. Some of this work may be funded by the current budget if the right policy choices are made. However, government borrowing may be necessary to finance large-scale projects, such as public transport networks that would provide an environmentally friendly alternative to road transport. Or it could be used to replace nuclear power stations with clean alternative sources of energy production, create or reopen local railway lines throughout the country, especially in urban or suburban areas, and construct and renovate public buildings and public housing while making them more energy-efficient and of high quality.

New standards of transparency in public borrowing must be defined: loans must go towards improving living conditions, while breaking away from imperatives that harm the environment; the use of borrowing must contribute to a programme of wealth redistribution so as to reduce inequality. Financial institutions, major corporations and wealthy households must be legally obliged to purchase state-issued, non-indexed bonds at 0% interest in an amount proportional to their overall wealth. Other savers would be offered state-guaranteed public bonds indexed at 3% above inflation. Thus, if a country's annual inflation rate were 3%, the bonds would have a nominal yearly interest-rate of 6%.

could be added the threat of losing their banking licence). Various measures are definitely possible.

This sort of positive discrimination (similar to what is practised in the US in the struggle against racial oppression, in India in favour of the lowest castes, or to advance gender equality) would permit advances towards greater fiscal justice and a more equitable sharing of the wealth.

In addition, the central banks and the ECB (in the Eurozone countries) must provide funding for state budgets at a rate of interest close to 0%.

X. Developing and extending public services

The development of public services during the twentieth century, until the neoliberal turnaround of the 1980s, was a great step forward for social progress. What remains today must be protected, sectors that have been privatised should be re-socialised, and the public/collective service model extended to new sectors. Education, health, public transport, telecommunications, the internet, radio and television, postal services, water works, rubbish collection and processing, local health-care services, local and regional administrative services, fire services and civil protection are sectors in which public services should have the monopoly or play a dominant role. Public/collective service structures should be extended to banking and insurance. We also include the energy sector in that list, because this will be essential for ensuring the ecological transition.

Public services must be allocated sufficient funding to enable them to fulfil their missions and to pay their staff correctly. Wages, personnel rights, job security and working conditions must be improved. Popular control is an essential ingredient for higher-quality services.

XI. Consolidating public pension schemes

Another fundamental victory in the twentieth century was the creation of a universal and compulsory public pension scheme. These structures must be gradually consolidated to become fully comprehensive and replace the private sector. We reject any increase in the age when people become eligible for their pension. This is certainly feasible through a general reduction in working hours, and the corresponding increase in the workforce (including public-service jobs) and thus the number of workers contributing to the pension scheme.

XII. Reducing working hours to guarantee full employment with a socially just wage policy

Sharing the wealth more equitably is the best answer to the crisis. The portion of the wealth going to employees has been seriously reduced over the last few decades, while the financiers and corporations have increased their profits and used them to speculate. Increased wages permit wage-earners to live better and at the same time make more resources available to implement social policies and strengthen retirement schemes.

Reducing working hours without reducing wages but creating the corresponding number of jobs improves living conditions and opens up positions to be filled by others. Substantial reductions in working hours also permit other lifestyle choices than the consumer society with its deleterious effect on social relationships. The free time created would allow more people to take part in political, social and voluntary activities, as well as cultural creativity, 'Products of High Necessity' as a group of West Indian intellectuals called them in a 2009 platform.[446] In fact, a new mindset is needed to replace the rampant alienation and objectification of free market society.

Minimum and average wage levels and benefits must be significantly raised. On the other hand, company directors who receive unacceptably high levels of remuneration should have their income limited, both in the public and private sectors. Stock-options, excessive bonuses and retirement advantages, as well as other abusive gains, must be made illegal. A maximum income must be created. As indicated above, we recommend a maximum pay differential of 1 to 4, taking into account all of a person's income, which would then be subject to taxation.

---

446 'A Plea for "Products of High Necessity" ', *L'Humanité*, 5 March 2009, http://www.humaniteinenglish.com/spip.php?article1163.

XIII. Reconsidering the euro

It is absolutely necessary for some countries, such as Greece, to reconsider their membership in the Eurozone. It is clear that it is a straitjacket for Cyprus, Greece, Ireland, Portugal and up to a point, Spain. If we do not give the question the same attention here as other alternative proposals, it is because this is an overarching debate that tends to be divisive within social movements and left-wing political parties. It is indeed a major topic that would require lengthy discussion to be dealt with adequately. As Costas Lapavitsas has remarked,[447] if countries want to drop the euro, they have the choice of going left or right. Our main concern here is to unite as many people as possible around the vital issues mentioned above, especially the proposals regarding banks and the debt. We must leave the divisive questions for subsequent debate.

XIV An alternative Europe: replace current treaties with a truly democratic constitutional process

Several clauses in EU, Eurozone and ECB treaties must be abrogated; for example, Articles 63 and 125 in the Treaty of Lisbon, prohibiting all controls of capital movements and all aid to member states in difficulty. The Stability and Growth Pact and the European Stability Mechanism (ESM) must also be revoked.

Monetary policy and the status and practices of the ECB must be completely overhauled. The governments and the EU, which created the ECB, have armed themselves with a new tool for destroying social and democratic rights.

The central banks and the ECB must be authorised to directly finance states seeking support for social and environmental programmes that are perfectly adapted to satisfying the fundamental needs of their peoples. The current treaties must be abrogated and replaced by new treaties drawn up within the framework of a truly democratic constitutional process.

This presupposes the election, by universal suffrage, of a Constituent Assembly followed by a referendum to accept a newly drafted Con-

---

447 Costas Lapavitsas in Cédric Durand (ed.), *En finir avec l'Europe* (No More Europe), Paris: La Fabrique, 2013.

stitution. The aim would be to create a pact of solidarity between the peoples for more democracy, better jobs and an ecological transition.

A Europe built on solidarity and cooperation would be able to turn its back on the oppressive competitiveness dragging it down. Neo-liberal policies, at the root of the crisis, have failed miserably. They have pushed down social indicators, slicing away social rights, employment and public services. The handful of people who have bene-fitted the most from the crisis have done so by riding roughshod over the rights of the majority. The crooks have won and the victims must pay the bill! This way of thinking, which underlies all the founding EU texts and treaties, must be routed. An alternative Europe based on cooperation between states and solidarity between peoples must become the priority.

Global policies at the European level, financed by massive public investment to create public jobs in essential sectors (local services, clean and renewable energy, protection of the environment, and the provision of basic social necessities), must be imposed. The creation of a new political system would require the populations of Europe to collaborate in drafting a new constitution that would frame a very different Europe.

This new democratic Europe must strive to impose non-negotiable principles: economic and social justice, gender equality, decisions aimed at improving the quality of life, disarmament and radical re-duction of military spending, sustainable nuclear-free energy options, radical reduction of greenhouse-gas emissions and the prohibition of GMOs. Europe must also put an end to its 'fortress under siege' poli-cies, where immigrants are seen as a menace, and become a true ally and partner of the countries and peoples of the global South. The first step should be the unconditional abolition of Third World debt. The abolition of debt is the common denominator of the struggles in the North and South. A new Europe must emerge that will entirely re-think its attitude and relations with the rest of the world by returning to the peoples of the other continents what was pillaged and stolen from them through centuries of European domination.

These proposals will not become reality unless the peoples of Europe mobilise, rise up and, through their self-organisation and activity, be-come the actors of their own emancipation.

Postscript

What major developments have affected the issues dealt with in the present volume since the original version in French, *Bancocratie*, was sent to press on 31 March 2014?

No measures designed to avoid further crises have been imposed on the private finance system. Governments and the various authorities meant to ensure that the regulations are respected and improved have either shelved or significantly attenuated the paltry measures announced in 2008-2009. The concentration of banks has remained unchanged, as have their high-risk activities. There have been more scandals implicating the fifteen to twenty biggest private banks in Europe and the United States— involving toxic loans, fraudulent mortgage credits, manipulation of currency exchange markets, of interest rates (notably, the LIBOR) and of energy markets, massive tax evasion, money-laundering for organised crime, and so on.

The authorities have merely imposed fines, usually negligible when compared to the crimes committed. These crimes have a negative impact not only on public finance but on the living-conditions of millions of people all over the world. People in charge of regulatory bodies, such as Martin Wheatley, former director of the *Financial Conduct Authority* in London, have been sacked for trying to do their job properly and being too critical of the behaviour of banks.[448] George Osborne, the Chancellor of the Exchequer, dismissed Martin Wheatley in July 2015, nine months before the end of his five-year contract.[449]

---

448   Jonathan Ford, 'Greenspan's capital idea for cutting back on banking angst', *Financial Times*, 23 August 2015, http://www.ft.com/intl/cms/ s/0/59b15ccc-49aa-11e5-9b5d-89a026fda5c9.html#axzz3lL1YX2wK The article reports, 'The UK government recently sacked one of the country's most senior financial regulators, the head of the Financial Conduct Authority, Martin Wheatley. His crime? Annoying too many financiers by the assiduousness with which he approached the task.'
449   'Martin Wheatley still has 'unfinished business' at financial regulator FCA', *The Independent*, 13 September 2015

Although obviously to blame, no bank director in the United States or Europe (with the exception of Iceland) has been convicted, while traders, who are mere underlings, are prosecuted and sentenced to between five and fourteen years behind bars.

As was the case for the Royal Bank of Scotland in 2015, banks that were nationalised at great public expense to protect the interests of major private shareholders have been sold back to the private sector for a fraction of their value. Salvaging the RBS cost £45 billion of public money, while its reprivatisation will probably mean the loss of a further £14 billion.[450] We have seen the same thing happen for SNS Reaal and ABN Amro in the Netherlands, the AIB group (Allied Irish Banks) in Ireland or part of the defunct Banco Espirito Santo in Portugal. In every case, the losses to the public purse are tremendous.

ECB policy has undergone superficial changes, but nothing far-reaching. Since early 2015, the Frankfurt-based institution has embarked upon an active policy of quantitative easing, buying up €60 billions' worth of bonds a month from private European banks. The ECB encourages the banks to create structured products which it then buys. It also buys covered bonds and sovereign debt paper from countries which implement neoliberal policies. At the same time, the ECB lends to private banks at an interest-rate of 0.05% (the rate in force since September 2014).[451]

The Fed has put a stop to quantitative easing, having practised it from 2008 until 2014. It no longer buys structured Mortgage-Backed Securities from banks. Early in 2014, it announced plans to raise interest-rates for the first time since 2006. Theoretically, this should come about before the end of 2015; but potential negative fall-out for the country's economy has led to hesitation. Indeed, raised interest-rates are bound to attract massive capital inflow to the United States, which would push up the value of the dollar against other currencies and

http://www.independent.co.uk/news/business/news/martin-wheatley-still-has-unfinished-business-at-financial-regulator-fca-10409061.html.
450   Christine Berry, 'RBS sale: there is an alternative', The NEF blog, 4 August 2015, http://www.neweconomics.org/blog/entry/rbs-sale-there-is-an-alternative
451   Eric Toussaint, 'To the Bankers, he's "Super Mario 2.0" Draghi', CADTM, 8 September 2014, http://cadtm.org/To-the-Bankers-He-s-Super-Mario-2

thus cause a reduction in US exports, in the present context of a weak global economy. Furthermore, many private companies are likely to run into trouble when the time comes to refinance their debts. Add to this that the cost of repaying the public debt will increase automatically. Although this last factor may count for little in the Fed's hesitations, the impact on emerging economies will be very negative as masses of their capital will be transferred to the United States for better returns and security.

Neither central banks' policies nor those adopted by governments have succeeded in boosting productive investment. The big private corporations are sitting on mountains of liquidities, on both sides of the Atlantic. For non financial companies in Europe, this means that more than €1000 billion remain in company treasuries instead of being used to increase investment and productivity. Corporations use their profits in great quantities, especially to buy up their own shares on the stock market with a view to keeping prices up, or preventing them from falling, and to make sure that their shareholders get juicy returns. At the same time, the share of profits that goes to shareholders in the form of dividends continues to rise, which of course means that there is even less incentive to invest.

Clearly, governments' and central banks' policies are causing a speculative bubble on the stock markets. This bubble may burst at any moment. In 2015 the phenomenon has started in China and is imminent in Europe and the United States.

Meanwhile, the prices of several primary materials are falling (e.g. oil, solid minerals, and more). The dramatic fall in the price of oil put an end to the shale-gas boom in the United States leaving many companies in that sector on the verge of bankruptcy. Large oil-exporting countries such as Venezuela and Nigeria have been badly hit by the fall in oil prices.

A key thesis of *Bankocracy* is that central banks and governments are pursuing two major objectives: first, to rescue the large private banks, their principal shareholders and their top management, while guaranteeing that their privileges will continue. There is little doubt that, had it not been for the actions of the central banks, the big banks would have failed and governments would have been forced to take strong and forceful measures against their directors and principal shareholders. The second objective is to participate and support Capital's offensive against Labour, so that corporate profits increase, making the big European corporations more competitive on the global market. These two objectives are shared by the Fed, the Bank of England, the ECB and the Bank of Japan.

The ECB itself has two further specific objectives which complement each other. The first is to defend the euro, which acts as a straitjacket for the weaker economies of the Eurozone and indeed, for all the populations of Europe. The euro is an instrument that serves both the large private corporations and the ruling classes of Europe, that is, the wealthiest 1%. Having adopted the euro, Eurozone countries cannot devalue their currency. Yet the weaker Eurozone economies would have every interest in devaluing, if they are to become competitive again in the face of Europe's economic giants – Germany, France, the Benelux Union (Belgium, the Netherlands and Luxembourg) and Austria. Belonging to the Eurozone has proved to be a financial snare for countries like Greece, Portugal, Spain or Italy. In times of crisis, the European authorities and their national governments apply what they call internal devaluation: they force salaries down, to the sole benefit of the management of large private corporations. The second of the ECB's specific objectives is to strengthen the domination of Europe's leading economies (especially Germany, France and Benelux) where the largest private European corporations are based. This implies maintaining a markedly asymmetrical relationship between the strongest and weakest economies.

The victory, in January 2015, of an anti-austerity left-wing coalition in Greece was seen as a direct threat by the ECB, the European Commission, the large corporations and all the other governments of the EU (not only those in the Eurozone). Defeating Syriza's project became the main goal of the ECB and all the European leaders; they finally achieved it in July 2015. The ECB literally strangled Greece financially, forcing the Tsipras government onto its knees. To avoid capitulation, the Tsipras government could have turned to alternative solutions[452] such as those described in the final chapter of *Bankocracy*. They should have made use of the results of the audit carried out by the Truth Committee on the Greek Public Debt.[453] Instead, they

452 Eric Toussaint, 'Greece: Alternatives to the Capitulation', CADTM, 16 July 2015, http://cadtm.org/Greece-Alternatives-to-the
453 Truth Committee on the Greek Public Debt, 'Preliminary Report of the

chose a more moderate path, despite the fact that it was bound to lead to failure.

Nevertheless it has become clear over the last few years that since the 2007-2008 crisis, with the ensuing intensification of neoliberal austerity policies, populations are ready to opt for radical solutions. This is evident from the growing popularity of the radical left-wing proposals of Syriza in Greece, Podemos in Spain and even Jeremy Corbyn in the United Kingdom and Bernie Sanders in the USA. One of the central lessons of Greece's capitulation in July 2015 is that we need political forces that are determined to carry through the measures they call for, integrating them into a coherent programme that breaks with the system. Another lesson is that left-wing governments must really get to grips with issues such as illegitimate debt, private banks, taxes and public services. This is the only road to social justice and the way to get the energy and environmental transition started. There are no other ways of solving the crisis for the benefit of the 99%.

Truth Committee on Public Debt', 18 June 2015, http://cadtm.org/Prelimi-nary-Report-of-the-Truth

Acronyms

ABS: Asset Backed Securities
BIS: Bank for International Settlements
BNP: Banque Nationale de Paris
BPCE: Banque Populaire-Caisse d'Épargne (French banking group)
BRICS: Brazil, Russia, India, China and South Africa
CADTM: Committee for the Abolition of Third World Debt
CAIC: Internal Auditing Commission for Public Credit (in Ecuador)
CDO: Collateralised Debt Obligation
CDS: Credit Default Swap
CFTC: Commodity Futures Trading Commission
CMBS: Commercial Mortgage Backed Securities
CoCo: Contingent Convertible (bond)
EBA: European Banking Authority
EBRD: European Bank for Reconstruction and Development
ECB: European Central Bank
EFSF: European Financial Stability Facility
EFTA: European Free Trade Association
ESCB: The European System of Central Banks
ESM: European Stability Mechanism
EU: European Union
EURIBOR: Euro Interbank Offered Rate
FBF: Fédération de Banques Françaises or French Banking Federation
FDIC: Federal Deposit Insurance Corporation (USA)
Fed, The: the Federal Reserve of the United States
FOMC: Federal Open Market Committee (USA)
GAO: Government Accountability Office (USA)
GDP: Gross Domestic Product
GWP: Gross World Product
HFT: High Frequency Trading
HSBC: Hong Kong & Shanghai Banking Corporation
ICAN: International Citizen (Debt) Audit Network
IMF: International Monetary Fund
IRS: Internal Revenue Service (USA)
ISDA: International Swaps and Derivatives Association

LBO: Leveraged Buy-Out
LIBOR: London Interbank Offered Rate
MBS: Mortgage-Backed Securities
MMF: Money Market Fund
NATO: North Atlantic Treaty Organisation
OECD: Organisation for Economic Co-operation and Development
OMT: Outright Money Transactions
RBS: Royal Bank of Scotland
RMBS: Residential Mortgage-Backed Securities
SEC: Securities and Exchange Commission (USA)
SIV: Structured Investment Vehicle
SNS: Samenwerkende Nederlandse Spaarbanken, a Dutch retail bank
SPV: Special Purpose Vehicle
UBS: Union de Banques Suisses
UKTI: UK Trade & Investment (government agency)
UN: United Nations
VAT: Value Added Tax
WTO: World Trade Organisation

Glossary of financial terms

Asset backed security (ABS): a genÉric term designating a security issued by an intermediate entity (SPV) between a transferor and investors in the context of a securitisation operation. This security is a bond. When the assets backing these securities (called underlying assets) are made up of mortgage loans like subprime loans, they are called Mortgage Backed Securities (MBS). MBS are subdivided into Residential Mortgage Backed Securities (RMBS), backed by mortgage loans made to private individuals, and Commercial Mortgage Backed Securities (CMBS). The term Collateralised Debt Obligations (CDO) is used when the underlying assets are bonds issued by companies or banks, and Collateralised Loan Obligations (CLO) when these assets are bank loans.

Asset: something belonging to an individual or a business that has value or the power to earn money. The opposite in assets are liabilities; that is the part of the balance-sheet reflecting a company's resources (the capital contributed by the partners, provisions for contingencies and charges, as well as the outstanding debts).

Balance: end-of-year statement of a company's assets (what the company possesses) and liabilities (what it owes). In other words, the assets provide information about how the funds collected by the company have been used; and the liabilities, about the origins of those funds.

Bank for International Settlements (BIS): the BIS is an international organisation founded in 1930 and charged with fostering international monetary and financial cooperation. It also acts as a bank for the central banks (55 national central banks and the ECB are members).

Banker's guarantee: a banker's guarantee is a commitment by a bank to pay a customer's debt in the case of the customer defaulting. In this case the bank only lends its signature.

Bond market: a market where medium-term and long-term capital is lent/borrowed in the form of bonds. Bonds are creditor stakes issued by companies or states.

Bond: a bond is a stake in a debt issued by a company or governmental body. The holder of the bond, the creditor, is entitled to interest and reimbursement of the principal. If the company is listed, the holder can also sell the bond on a stock exchange.

BRICS countries: Brazil, Russia, India, China and South Africa... five major emerging national economies whose combined GDP is equal to 20% of total Gross World Product. Founded in 2001, the acronym was BRIC until South Africa joined in December 2010.

Contingent Convertible Bonds (CoCo): debts convertible into equity if a pre-specified trigger event occurs

CDO: Collateralised Debt Obligations. The term CDO covers multiple means of structuring paper products for financial assets. These include bonds, loans and sometimes non-listed shares. Such derivatives enable banks to render normally non-liquid debts liquid, thus increasing the tradability of the asset. From the buyer's point of view, CDO are also supposed to reduce risk by diluting it, since there is less chance of default on a bouquet package of credits than on one single credit. In reality, the absence of clear information about the composition of CDO and the fact that they are often combined with high-risk assets make them a very risky product.

CDS: Credit Default Swaps are an insurance that a financial company may purchase to protect itself against non-payments.

Central bank: the establishment which, in a given state, is in charge of issuing banknotes and controlling the volume of currency and credit. In France, it is the Banque de France which assumes this role under the auspices of the European Central Bank (see ECB) while in the UK it is the Bank of England.

CFTC: the Commodity Futures Trading Commission is a US regulatory authority that supervises the US futures market.

CLO: a Collateralised Loan Obligation is one of the forms of securitisation of debt held by a financial institution. A homogenous portfolio of commercial loans is offered for sale to outside investors and refinanced through the issue of the most conventional securities possible in order to attract the maximum number of bids.

CMBS (see also ABS): Commercial Mortgage-Backed Securities.

Collateral: transferable assets or a guarantee serving as security against the repayment of a loan, should the borrower default.

Commodities: the goods exchanged on the commodities market, traditionally raw materials such as metals, fuels and cereals.

Common goods: in economics, common goods are characterised by being collectively owned, as opposed to either privately or publicly owned. In philosophy, the term denotes what is shared by the members of one community, whether a town or indeed all humanity, from a juridical, political or moral standpoint.

Corporate bonds: securities issued by corporations in order to raise funds on the Money Markets. These bonds resemble government bonds but are considered to be more risky than government bonds and other guaranteed securities such as Mortgage-Backed Securities, and therefore pay higher interest-rates.

Credit derivative: a financial product linked to a loan or an obligation. They are used to transfer the risk linked to a financial product while keeping, and insuring, the originating asset. One of the most common forms is the Credit Default Swap (CDS).

Debt refinancing: taking out new loans to reimburse current debts.

Deposit or commercial bank: a bank which carries out operations for individuals, companies and public bodies involving collecting deposits which are then redistributed in the form of loans or used to facilitate investment operations. The public's deposits are backed by state guarantees. A deposit bank is different from an investment bank, the bulk of whose operations concern the markets.

Derivatives: a family of financial products that includes mainly options, futures, swaps and their combinations, all related to other assets (shares, bonds, raw materials and commodities, interest-rates, indices, etc.) from which they are by nature inseparable –options on shares, futures contracts on an index, etc. Their value depends on and is derived from (thus the name) that of these other assets. There are derivatives involving a firm commitment (currency futures, interest-rate or exchange swaps) and derivatives involving a conditional commitment (options, warrants, etc.)

Emergency Liquidity Assistance (ELA): emergency funds loaned to the private banks by the Eurozone central banks.

Equity: the capital put into an enterprise by the shareholders. Not to be confused with 'hard capital' or 'unsecured debt'.

ESM: the European Stability Mechanism is a European entity for managing financial crises in the Eurozone and which since 2012 has replaced the European Financial Stability Facility and the European Financial Stabilisation Mechanism, which had been implemented in response to the public-debt crisis in the Eurozone. It concerns only EU member states that are part of the Eurozone. In case of a threat to the stability of the Eurozone, this European financial institution is supposed to grant financial 'assistance' (loans) to a country or countries in difficulty. There are strict conditions tied to this assistance.

Euro Interbank Offered Rate (EURIBOR): the interbank rate used in the Eurozone. Recalculated daily, it is the average of the transactions realised by a panel of the 57 most representative banks in the Eurozone. There are fifteen EURIBOR rates for terms ranging from one week to twelve months.

European Banking Authority (EBA): the body charged with supervising the European banking system and, along with two other authorities, the European Securities and Markets Authority (ESMA) and the European Insurance and Occupational Pensions Authority (EIOPA), part of the European System of Financial Supervision.

European Central Bank (ECB): the European Central Bank is a European institution based in Frankfurt, founded in 1998, to which the countries of the Eurozone have transferred their monetary powers. Its official role is to ensure price stability by combating inflation within that Zone. Its three decision-making organs (the Executive Board, the Governing Council and the General Council) are composed of governors of the central banks of the member states and/or recognised specialists. According to its statutes, it is politically 'independent' but it is directly influenced by the world of finance.

Eurozone: an area of Europe made up of the nineteen countries of the European Union which use the euro as their common currency: Austria, Belgium, Cyprus, Estonia, Finland, France, Germany, Greece, Ireland, Italy, Latvia, Lithuania, Luxembourg, Malta, the Netherlands, Portugal, Slovakia, Slovenia and Spain. Nine countries (Bulgaria, Croatia, the Czech Republic, Denmark, Hungary, Poland, Romania, Sweden and the United Kingdom) are EU members but do not use the euro. Before joining the Eurozone, a state must spend two years in the European Exchange Rate Mechanism (ERM II).

The Fed or Federal Reserve: (officially, the Federal Reserve System), is the United States' central bank created in 1913 by the Federal Reserve Act, also called the Owen-Glass Act, after a series of banking crises, particularly the 'Bank Panic' of 1907.

Financial contracts: also referred to as 'hedging instruments', include futures contracts on interest-rates, swaps, futures contracts on all merchandise and commodities, options contracts on the purchase or sale of financial instruments and all other futures instruments.

Financial instruments: financial instruments include financial securities and financial contracts.

Financial market: the market for long-term capital. It comprises a primary market, where new issues are sold, and a secondary market, where existing securities are traded. Aside from the regulated markets, there are Over-The-Counter (OTC) markets, which are not required to meet minimum conditions.

Financial proceeds: proceeds acquired by a company during the fiscal year that are related to financial assets (securities, bank accounts, currency, investments).

Financial securities: include equity securities issued by companies in the form of shares (shares, holdings, investment certificates, etc.), debt securities (bonds and similar securities, excluding commercial instruments and savings certificates), and holdings or shares in Undertakings for Collective Investment in Transferable Securities (UCITS).

FSB: the Financial Stability Board is an informal economic group that was created during the G20 meeting in London in April 2009. It succeeded the FSF (Financial Stability Forum) that had functioned since the G7 in 1999. The Board is made up of 26 national financial authorities (central banks and finance ministries), several international organisations and groups that devise financial stability standards. Its *raison d'être* is to enable cooperation in the fields of supervision and the observation of financial institutions.

Futures market: a market on which a product (financial instrument, currency, merchandise) is purchased or sold with payment and delivery postponed until a later date than the initial transaction that determined the price.

Futures: a futures contract is a standardised advance commitment, negotiated on an organised futures market, to deliver a specified quantity of a precisely defined underlying asset at a specified time – the 'delivery date' – and place. Futures contracts are the most widely traded financial instruments in the world.

G20: the Group of Twenty (G20 or G-20) is a group made up of nineteen countries and the European Union whose ministers, central-bank directors and heads of state meet regularly. It was created in 1999 after the series of financial crises in the 1990s. Its aim is to encourage international consultation on the principle of broadening dialogue in keeping with the growing economic importance of a certain number of countries. Its members are Argentina, Australia, Brazil, Canada, China, France, Germany, Italy, India, Indonesia, Japan, Mexico, Russia, Saudi Arabia, South Africa, South Korea, Turkey, USA, UK and the European Union (represented by the presidents of the Council and of the European Central Bank).

GDP: Gross Domestic Product – an aggregate measure of total production within a given territory equal to the sum of the gross values added. The measure is notoriously incomplete; for example it does not take into account any activity that does not enter into a commercial exchange. GDP takes into account both the production of goods and the production of services. Economic growth is defined as the variation of GDP from one period to another.

Goodwill: the difference between the assets on a company's balance-sheet and the sum of its tangible and intangible assets. When one company takes control of another company, the acquiring company generally pays a price that is higher than the value of the net assets. Goodwill generally consists of intangible elements, such as brands, which are evaluated subjectively.

Government debt: the total outstanding debt of the state, local authorities, publicly owned companies and organs of social security.

Gross debt: this concept does not include government assets. The debt in the terms of the European Stability and Growth Pact (SGP) is a consolidated gross debt, meaning that it does not take into account either public assets or debts between public administrations. To take the example of a household of several people: the household's debt, as understood in SGP terms, would be the sum of the total debt of those people but would not include any sums that they might have lent one another. Nor would the debt be reduced by the value of goods that belonged to the household, such as their car or their house.

Guarantees: acts that provide a creditor with security in complement to the debtor's commitment. A distinction is made between real guarantees (lien, pledge, mortgage, prior charge) and personal guarantees (surety, aval, letter of intent, independent guarantee).

Hard capital: the capital provided by shareholders plus the undistributed profits (retained earnings).

Hedge funds: unlisted investment funds that exist for purposes of speculation and that seek high returns, make liberal use of derivatives, especially options, and frequently make use of leverage. The main hedge funds are independent of banks, although banks frequently have their own hedge funds. Hedge funds come under the category of shadow banking.

IFRS: International Financial Reporting Standards. Accounting standards drawn up by the International Accounting Standards Board, intended for listed companies or companies who rely on investors, with a view to harmonising the presentation and ensuring the clarity of their financial statements.

Institutional investors: entities that pool large sums of money and invest those sums in securities, real property and other investment assets. They are principally banks, insurance companies, pension funds and by extension all organisations that invest collectively in transferable securities.

Interbank market: a market reserved for banks where they exchange financial assets among themselves and borrow/lend over the short term. The interbank market is also where the European Central Bank (ECB) intervenes to provide or take back liquidities (management of the money supply to control inflation).

Interest: an amount paid in remuneration of an investment or received by a lender. Interest is calculated on the amount of capital invested or borrowed, the duration of the operation and the rate that has been set.

Internet bubble: the internet or technological bubble was a speculative bubble which affected 'technological securities', i.e. the securities of sectors connected to computing and telecommunications, on the stock markets in the late 1990s. It peaked in March 2000.

Investment funds: private equity investment funds (sometimes called 'mutual funds') seek to invest in companies according to certain criteria for which they are most specialised: capital-risk, capital development funds, Leveraged Buy-Out (LBO), and which reflect the different levels of the company's maturity.

Investment or merchant bank: a finance company which carries out three types of operation: counselling (especially on mergers and take-overs), financial management of companies (increasing capital, bringing them into the stock market, issuing securities) and investments on the markets. An investment bank does not collect money from the public but is financed by borrowing from banks or on the money markets.

ISDA: International Swaps and Derivatives Association, a private entity whose members are banks who deal in derivatives.

ISDAFIX: a worldwide common reference value or benchmark for fixed-interest swap rates for swap transactions. It is a screen service providing average mid-market swap rates daily for six major currencies at selected maturities. ICE Benchmark Administration formally assumed the role of ISDAFIX administrator on 1 August 2014.

Junk Bonds: the nickname in the USA for high-risk bonds, also called High Yield Bonds, issued by a company whose solvency is considered doubtful. This type of bond is considered highly speculative by the rating agencies.

Layering: a technique involving pretending to sell before actually buying. A trader places a series of bids up to a ceiling price, thus creating layers of orders. Once the ceiling is reached, the trader sells massively and at the same time cancels all remaining orders that have been placed. The technique is based on the hope of filling competitors' sales-ledgers with offers to buy from other traders.

LBO: Leveraged Buy-Out, the purchase or takeover of a company financed by debt. Most frequently an LBO is carried out by a holding company which borrows most of the funds needed for the purchase of the target company's shares, restructures the company, then demands dividends which are used to reimburse the loans, and finally re-sells the company once it has returned to profitability.

Leverage: this is the ratio between funds borrowed for investment and the personal funds or equity that back them up. A company may have borrowed much more than its capitalised value, in which case it is said to be 'highly leveraged'. The more highly a company is leveraged, the higher the risk associated with lending to the company; but higher also are the possible profits that it may realise as compared to its own value.

Liabilities: the part of the balance-sheet that comprises the resources available to a company (equity provided by the partners, provisions for risks and charges, debts).

LIBOR: London Interbank Offered Rate. An average rate calculated daily, based on transactions made by a group of representative banks. There are several LIBORs for some ten different currencies and some fifteen duration rates, from one day to twelve months.

Liquidities: the capital an economy or company has available at a given point in time. A lack of liquidities can force a company into liquidation and an economy into recession.

Liquidity: the facility with which a financial instrument can be bought or sold without a significant change in price.

Lobby: a lobby is an entity organised to represent and defend the interests of a specific group by exerting pressure or influence on persons or institutions that hold power. Lobbying consists of conducting actions aimed at influencing, directly or indirectly, the drafting, implementation or interpretation of legislative measures, standards, regulations and, more generally, any intervention or decision by the Public Authorities.

LTRO: Long-Term Refinancing Operation. An LTRO is a mechanism whereby the European Central Bank makes large amounts of cash available to private banks via credits over three months to three years at very low rates.

Market activities / trading: buying and selling of financial instruments such as shares, futures, derivatives, options and warrants, conducted in the hope of making a short-term profit.

MBS: Mortgage-Backed Securities; see ABS.

Memoranda of Understanding: in this context, the agreements between the Greek government and the 'Troika' on financial aid.

Merger-Takeover: a merger-takeover is an operation whereby one or several companies, dissolved but not liquidated, transfer their entire holdings, including assets and liabilities, to an existing or new company.

MMF: Money Market Funds – mutual investment funds that invest in securities, including money funds.

Money market: a short-term market where banks, insurance companies, corporations and States (via the central banks and Treasuries) lend and borrow funds according to their needs.

Moral hazard: the effect on a creditor's or an economic actor's behaviour when they are covered against a given risk. They will be more likely to take risks. Thus, for example, rescuing banks without placing any conditions enhances their moral hazard.

Mortgage: a loan made against property collateral. There are two sorts of mortgages: 1) the most common form where the property that the loan is used to purchase is used as the collateral; 2) a broader use of property to guarantee any loan: it is sufficient that the borrower possesses and engages the property as collateral.

Mutual funds: see, investment funds.

Non-financial corporations: all economic agents that produce non-financial goods and services. They represent the greatest share of productive activity.

OECD: the Organisation for Economic Co-operation and Development, created in 1960. It includes the major industrialised countries and has had 34 members since 2010.

Off-Balance-Sheet: off-balance-sheet activities account for activities that do not entail disbursement or collection of funds by a company or bank, but which expose it to a certain number of risks. These are most often pending contracts in connection with which no payment has been made.

Over-The-Counter market (OTC): an Over-The-Counter or off-exchange market is an unregulated market on which transactions are made directly between the seller and the purchaser, as opposed to a so-called organised or regulated market where there is a regulatory authority, such as a stock exchange.

Payable: a sum of money that one person (debtor) or group of people owes to another (creditor).

Pension funds: investment funds that manage capitalised retirement schemes. They are funded by the employees of one or several companies paying into the scheme, which, often, is also partially funded by the employers. The objective is to pay the pensions of the employees that take part in the scheme. Pension funds manage very big amounts of money that are usually invested on the stock markets or financial markets.

PIK: a PIK (for Payment In Kind) or PIK loan is a loan characterised by the fact that the payment of interest is not necessarily made in currency. The interest can be paid, for example, in the form of another debt security, by securities issued by the borrowing company or via the issuing of stock purchase options.

Private equity: private equity or investment capital designates a specific form of institutional investment in private companies with the goal of financing their development, transformation and expansion. The most common forms of private equity are venture capital, which refers to investments in the creation and development of innovative start-ups, and Leveraged Buy-Outs (q.v.).

Profit: the positive gain yielded from a company's activity. Net profit is profit after tax. Distributable profit is the part of the net profit which can be distributed to the shareholders.

Property bubble: a property bubble is a speculative bubble on the entire property market. It is characterised by a sharp rise in the price of real-estate; this entails a significant and persistent gap between the price of property and the variation of fundamental economic determinants such as salaries and rental value.

Proprietary trading: banks trading for their own account.

Quote stuffing: a tactic of quickly entering and withdrawing large orders in an attempt to flood the market with quotes that competitors must process, thus slowing the frequency of their trading.

Rating agency: rating agencies, or credit-rating agencies, evaluate creditworthiness. This includes the creditworthiness of corporations, non-profit organisations and governments, as well as 'securitised assets' – which are assets that are bundled together and sold to investors as security. Rating agencies assign a letter grade to each bond, which represents an opinion as to the likelihood that the organisation will be able to repay both the principal and the interest as they fall due. Ratings are made on a descending scale: AAA is the highest, then AA, A, BBB, BB, B, etc. A rating of BB or below is considered a 'junk bond' because it is likely to default. Many factors go into the assignment of ratings, including the profitability of the organisation and its total indebtedness. The three largest credit-rating agencies are Moody's, Standard & Poor's and Fitch Ratings.

Recapitalisation: reconstituting or increasing a company's share capital to reinforce its equity after losses. When the banks were bailed out by the European states, they were usually recapitalised with no conditions attached and without the states obtaining the decision-making power that their participation in the banks' capital should have given them.

Secondary market: the market where institutional investors resell and purchase financial assets. Thus the secondary market is the market where already-existing financial assets are traded.

Share: a unit of ownership interest in a corporation or financial asset, representing a fraction of the total capital stock. Its owner (a shareholder) is entitled to receive an equivalent proportion of any profits distributed (a dividend) and to attend shareholder meetings.

Sovereign debt: government debts or debt guaranteed by the government.

Sovereign Wealth Fund: a sovereign wealth fund or SWF is an investment fund owned by a state. It is funded by exports of high-value raw materials or by large trade-balance surpluses. In 2013, such funds managed approximately $5.2 trillion in assets.

Speculative bubble: an economic, financial or speculative bubble is formed when the level of trading-prices on a market (financial assets market, currency-exchange market, property market, raw materials market, etc.) settles well above the intrinsic (or fundamental) financial value of the goods or assets being exchanged. In such a situation, prices diverge from the usual economic valuation under the influence of buyers' beliefs.

Stockbroker: a firm or individual that acts for clients to buy and/or sell orders on stock markets and charges a fee or commission.

Stock exchange or Stock market: the market place where securities (stocks, bonds and shares), previously issued on the primary financial market, are bought and sold. The stock market composed of dealers in second-hand transferable securities is also known as the secondary market.

Structured product: a structured product is generally a product designed by a bank. It is often a complex combination of options, swaps, etc. Its price is determined using mathematical models, which model the behaviour of the product as a function of time and the various evolutions of the market. Structured products are often sold at high margins with poor visibility for the purchaser.

Subordinated debt securities: Securities whose rights with respect to payment of interest and repayment of principal rank behind (or are subordinate to) another class or classes of debt.

Subprime mortgage crisis: this was the crisis that started in the US in 2007 involving subprime mortgages, considered to carry the highest risk. It triggered the 2007 – 2011 financial crisis. The suspicion it cast on securitised debts that included part of these loans meant that financial institutions lost confidence in one other, leading to the crisis.

Systemic banks: certain banks are known as systemic because of their size and the danger that would be incurred for the stability of the banking system globally should they fail.

Tax haven: a territory characterised by the following five independent criteria: (a) opacity (via bank secrecy or another mechanism such as trusts); (b) low taxes, sometimes as low as zero for non-residents; (c) easy regulations permitting the creation of front companies and no necessity for these companies to have a real activity on the territory; (d) lack of cooperation with the inland revenue, customs and/or judicial departments of other countries; (e) weak or non-existent financial regulation. Switzerland, the City of London and Luxembourg receive the majority of the capital placed in tax havens. Others exist, of course, such as the Cayman Islands, the Channel Islands, Hong Kong and other exotic locations.

Toxic asset: an asset that loses its liquidity when its secondary market disappears. Toxic assets represent sheer loss, as any potential buyer would pay no more than the equivalent of their initial cost. The term 'toxic asset' was coined in the financial crisis of 2008/09, referring to Mortgage-Backed Securities, Collateralised Debt Obligations and Credit Default Swaps, none of which could be sold, thus exposing their holders to massive losses.

Troika: the ECB, the European Commission and the IMF.

Transatlantic Trade and Investment Partnership (TTIP): a proposed free trade agreement between the European Union and the United States.

Universal bank: sometimes described as financial supermarkets, universal banks represent a large financial set-up grouping together and covering the activities of commercial (deposit) banks and investment banks while also providing bank insurance.

Unsecured debt: in the case of a company or bank going into liquidation there are several levels of debt guarantee: secured, preferential and unsecured. The unsecured debts are last in line to be paid after the others have been paid in full, or as fully as possible. Depending on the assets remaining, the unsecured creditors may receive a small percentage of what they are owed or even nothing at all. This justifies a higher interest-rate when the companies borrow from unsecured and/or non-preferential creditors.

Yield: the income return on an investment. This refers to the interest or dividends received from a security, and is usually expressed annually as a percentage based on the investment's cost, its current market value or its face value.

Bibliography

Aglietta, Michel and Sandra Moatti, *Le FMI. De l'ordre monétaire aux désordres financiers* (The IMF: from monetary order to financial disorder), Paris: Economica (Eyrolles), 2000.

Álvarez, Nacho, Fernando Luenzo, Jorge Uxó, *Fractura y crisis en Europa* (Fracture and Crisis in Europe), Madrid: Clave intelectual, 2013.

Artus Patrick and Marie-Paule Virard, *La Liquidité incontrôlable* (Uncontrollable liquidity), Montreuil: Pearson (France), 2010.

Artus, Patrick and Marie-Paule Virard, *Est-il trop tard pour sauver l'Amérique ?* (Is it too late to save America?), Paris: La Découverte, 2009.

ATTAC, *Le Piège de la dette publique* (The trap of public debt), Paris: Les liens qui libèrent, 2011.

ATTAC, *Leur dette, notre démocratie* (Their debt, our democracy), Paris: Les liens qui libèrent, 2013.

ATTAC, *Petit manuel de la transition* (Little handbook for an economic transition), Paris: Les liens qui libèrent, 2013.

ATTAC & Fondation Copernic, *En finir avec la compétitivité* (Doing away with competitiveness), Paris: ATTAC/Fondation Copernic, October 2012.

Avermaete, Jean-Pierre and Arnaud Zacharie, *Mise à nu des marchés financiers. Les dessous de la globalisation* (The bare truth about the financial markets. The hidden agenda of globalisation) Paris: Syllepse, Vista, Attac, 2002.

Banque de France, *La Crise de la dette souveraine* (The Sovereign-Debt Crisis), Banque de France, Documents et débats no. 4, mai 2012. https://www.banque-france.fr/uploads/tx_bdfgrandesdates/documents-et-debats-numero-4-integral_01.pdf

Berenberg Equity Research, European Banks. *Capital: misunderstood, misused and misplaced*, Wiesbaden: Berenberg, Gossler & Co., 2013. http://www.berenberg.de/fileadmin/ user_upload/berenberg2013/02_Investment_Banking/ Equity_Research/2013_06_13_european_banks.pdf.

Berruyer, Olivier, 'Solvabilité réelle des banques systémiques mondiales' (The real credit ratings of the world's systemically important banks), http://www.les-crises.fr/solvabilite-banques-systemiques/, 4 June 2013.

Bonfond, Olivier, *Et si on arrêtait de payer ?* (What if we stopped paying?), Brussels: Aden, 2012.

Bonfond, Olivier, *Il faut tuer TINA. Propositions pour rompre avec le fatalisme et pour d'autres mondes possibles* (Time to kill TINA. Proposals for breaking with fatalism and for other possible worlds), Brussels: Aden, 2015.

Braudel, Fernand, *Civilisation matérielle, économie et capitalisme. XVe-XVIIIe siècle* (see next entry), Paris: Armand Collin, 1979.

Braudel, Fernand, *Capitalism and Material Life, 1400–1800*, trans. by Myriam Kochan, New York & London: HarperCollins, 1973.

Brecht, Berthold, *The Threepenny Opera* (in German: Die Dreigroschenoper) [1928]. Trans. Ralph Manheim and John Willett, London: Penguin Classics, 2007.

Brender, Anton, Florence Pisani and Emile Gagna, *La crise des dettes souveraines* (The crisis of sovereign debt), Paris: La Découverte, 2012-2013.

Bustelo, Pablo, 'Progreso y alcance de la globalización financiera: Un análisis empírico del periodo 1986-2004' (The progress and scope of financial globalisation: an empirical analysis for the period 1986-2004), *Boletín económico de ICE*, Información Comercial Española, 2007, issue 2,922, pp. 19-22.

CADTM, *Les Crimes de la dette* (Debt crimes), Paris: CADTM-Syllepse, 2007.

CETIM-CADTM, *Let's launch an enquiry into the debt! A Manual on How to Organise Audits on Third World Debts*, Geneva: CETIM, 2006.

Chavagneux, Christian, *Une brève histoire des crises financières* (A brief history of financial crises), Paris: La Découverte, 2011.

Chavigné, Jean-Jacques and Gérard Filoche, *Dette Indigne !* (Shameful debt!), Paris: Jean-Claude Gawsewitch, 2011.

Chesnais, François, *La Mondialisation du capital* (The globalisation of capital), Paris: Syros, Coll. Alternatives économiques, 1994.

Chesnais, François, *La finance mondialisée* (Globalised finance), Paris: La Découverte, 2004.

Chesnais, François, *Les Dettes illégitimes* (Illegitimate debt), Paris: Raisons d'Agir, 2011.

CLERSÉ (Centre lillois d'études et de recherches sociologiques et économiques), *Le coût du capital et son surcoût* (The cost of capital and its extra cost), University of Lille 1, 2013. http://www.ires-fr.org/images/files/EtudesAO/RapportCgtCoutCapitalK.pdf

Cori, Nicolas and Catherine Le Gall, *DEXIA une banque toxique* (DEXIA, a toxic bank), Paris: La Découverte, 2013.

Condijts, Joan, Paul Gerard and Pierre-Henri Thomas, *La chute de la maison FORTIS* (The fall of the house of FORTIS), Paris: JC Lattès, 2009.

Duménil, Gérard and Dominique Lévy, *La grande bifurcation, En finir avec le néolibéralisme* (A major change of course: putting an end to neoliberalism), Paris: La Découverte, 2014.

Dupret, Xavier, *La Belgique endettée* (Belgium in debt), Mons: Couleur livres, 2012.

Durand, Cédric (ed.), *En finir avec l'Europe* (No more Europe), Paris: La Fabrique, 2013.

Fattorelli, Maria Lucia (ed.), *Auditoria Ciudadana de la Deuda Pública* (A Citizens' Audit of the Public Debt), Geneva & Brussels: CADTM, CETIM, 2013.

Fischer-Lescano, Andreas, *Human Rights in Times of Austerity Policy*, (Legal opinion commissioned by the Austrian Chamber of Labour), Bremen: ZERP (Centre of European Law and Politics), 17 February 2014, http://www.etui.org/content/download/13817/113830/file/Legal+Opinion+Human+Rights+in+-Times+of+Austerity+Policy+(final).pdf

Galbraith, John Kenneth, *La Crise économique de 1929,* trans. Henri Le Gallo [1970], Paris: Payot, 2008.

Galbraith, John Kenneth, *The Great Crash 1929*, London: Penguin, 2009 [1954].

Généreux, Jacques, *Nous on peut !* (Well, we can!), Paris: Éditions du Seuil, 2011.

Gibaud, Stéphanie, *La femme qui en savait vraiment trop* (The woman who really did know too much), Paris: Éditions du Cherche-Midi, 2014.

Giraud, Gaël, *L'Illusion financière* (Financial illusions), Ivry-sur-Seine: Les Editions de l'Atelier, 2012.

Graeber, David, *Debt: The First 5,000 Years*, Brooklyn: Melville House, 2012.

Green, Stephen, *Good Value: Reflections on Money, Morality and an Uncertain World*, London: Grove Press, 2010.

Greenspan, Alan, *The Age of Turbulence: Adventures in a New World*, London: Penguin Books, 2007.

Hardie, Iain and Huw Macartney, 'Too Big to Separate? A French and German defence of their biggest banks', 26 March 2015, http://www.finance-watch.org/hot-topics/blog/1067-bsr-blog-hardie-macartney

Harribey, Jean-Marie, *La richesse, la valeur et l'inestimable. Fondements d'une critique socio-écologique de l'économie capitaliste* (Wealth, value and the incalculable. Foundations of a socio-ecological critique of capitalist economics), Paris: Les liens qui libèrent, 2013.

Hilferding, Rudolph, *Finance Capital* (1910), London: Routledge, 2007.

Hudson Michael, *Killing the host: How Financial Parasites and Debt Bondage Destroy the Global Economy*, Petrolia: CounterPunch-Books, 2015

Husson, Michel, *Un pur capitalisme* (A pure form of capitalism), Lausanne: Editions Page Deux, 2008.

Husson, Michel, and Charb, illust., *Le Capitalisme en 10 leçons* (Capitalism in 10 lessons), Paris: La Découverte, 2012.

Johsua, Isaac, *Une trajectoire du capital. De la crise de 1929 à celle de la nouvelle économie* (The trajectory of capital. From the 1929 crash to the crisis of the new economy), Paris: Syllepse, 2006.

Johsua, Isaac, *La Grande Crise du XXIe siècle* (The great crisis of the 21st century), Paris: La Découverte, 2009.

Jorion, Paul, *L'Implosion* (Implosion), Paris: Fayard, 2008.

Jorion, Paul, *La Crise* (Crisis), Paris: Fayard, 2008.

Jorion, Paul, *La Crise du capitalisme Americain* (The crisis of American capitalism), Broissieux: éditions du Croquant, 2009.

Keynes, John Maynard, *The General Theory of Employment, Interest and Money* (1936), Amherst, NY: Prometheus Books, 1997.

Klein, Naomi, *The Shock Doctrine*, New York: Picador, 2007.

Laeven, Luc and Fabiàn Valencia, 'Systemic banking crisis database: an update', IMF Working Paper 12/163, 2012.

Lamberts, Philippe and Denis Gaspard, 'The Seven Deadly Sins of Banks', The Greens/EFA, 2013, http://bankingsins.eu/en/.

Lapavitsas, Costas, *Profiting Without Producing: How Finance Exploits Us All*, London: Verso, 2013.

Liikanen, Erkki, *High-level Expert Group on reforming the structure of the EU banking sector ('Liikanen Report')*, 2 October 2012, http://ec.europa.eu/internal_market/bank/docs/high-level_expert_group/report_en.pdf

Lordon, Frédéric, *Jusqu'à quand ?* (How much longer?), Paris: Raisons d'Agir, 2008.

Louçã, Francisco and Mariana Mortágua, *A Dívidura Portugal na crise do Euro* (Deep in debt. Portugal in the Euro crisis), Lisbon: Bertrand Editora, 2012.

Mandel, Ernest, *Introduction au Marxisme* (see next entry), Fondation Léon Lesoil, 2007.

Mandel, Ernest, *Introduction to Marxism*, trans. Louisa Sadler [1977], London: Pluto Press, 1992.

Mandel, Ernest, *Late Capitalism*, trans. Joris De Bres, London: New Left Books, 1977.

Mandel, Ernest, *The Second Slump: A Marxist Analysis of Recession in the Seventies*, trans. Jon Rothschild, London: New Left Books, 1978.

Marx, Karl, *Capital: A Critique of Political Economy, Volume I: The Process of Capitalist Production*, [1867], trans. Ben Fowkes, Harmondsworth: Penguin Classics, 1992.

Marx, Karl, *Capital: A Critique of Political Economy, Volume II: The Process of Circulation of Capital*, [1869], trans. David Fernbach, Harmondsworth: Penguin Classics, 1993.

Marx, Karl, *Capital: A Critique of Political Economy, Volume III: The Process of Capitalist Production as a Whole*, [1879], trans. David Fernbach, Harmondsworth: Penguin Classics, 1993.

Marx, Karl, *Economic and Philosophic Manuscripts of 1844*, trans. Moscow: Martin Mulligan, Progress Publishers, 1959.

Marx, Karl & Friedrich Engels, *La Crise* (Crisis) Paris: 10/18 (Union générale d'éditions), 1978.

Marx, Karl & Friedrich Engels, 'Crisis, prosperity, and revolutions', Journals May-October 1850,' *Neue Rheinische Zeitung*, https://www.marxists.org/archive/marx/works/1850/11/01.htm (no translator mentioned).

Medialdea, Bibiana, Antonio Sanabria, Luis Buendía, Nacho Álvarez and Ricardo Molero, *Quienes son los mercados y como nos gobiernan* (Who the markets are and how they govern us), Barcelona: Icaria, 2011.

Millet, Damien & Éric Toussaint, *La Crise, quelles crises ?* (Crisis, what crises?), Brussels: CADTM-Aden, 2010.

Millet, Damien & Éric Toussaint (ed.), *La Dette ou la vie* (Debt or life), Brussels: CADTM-Aden, 2011.

Millet, Damien & Éric Toussaint, *65 Questions / 65 Réponses sur la dette, le FMI et la Banque mondiale* (65 questions and answers on debt, the IMF and the World Bank), Liège: CADTM, 2011, available at http://cadtm.org/65-questions-65-reponses-sur-la,8331

Millet, Damien & Éric Toussaint, *AAA, Audit, Annulation, Autre politique* (AAA— Audit, Abolition and Alternative Policies), Paris: Éditions du Seuil, 2012.

Millet Damien, Daniel Munevar and Éric Toussaint, *2012 World debt figures*, CADTM, 2012, available at http://cadtm.org/2012-World-debt-figures

Morel, Thomas & Ruffin François, *Vive la Banqueroute !* (Long live bankruptcy!), Amiens: Fakir Éditions, 2013.

Peillon, Antoine, *Ces 600 milliards qui manquent à la France* (The 600 billion euros that France needs), Paris: Le Seuil, 2012.

Muižnieks, Nils, *Safeguarding Human Rights in Times of Economic Crisis*, Strasbourg: Council of Europe, 2013.

Piketty, Thomas, *Le capital au XXIe siècle* (see next entry), Paris: Éditions du Seuil, 2013.

Piketty, Thomas, *Capital in the 21st Century*, trans. Arthur Goldhammer, Cambridge (MA): Harvard University Press, 2014.

Reinhardt, Carmen and Kenneth Rogoff, *This Time Is Different: Eight Centuries of Financial Folly*, Princeton (NJ): Princeton University Press, 2009.

Sack, Alexander Nahum, *Les effets des transformations des États sur leurs dettes publiques et autres obligations financières* (The effects of the transformation of States on their public debt and other financial obligations), Paris: Sirey, 1927.

Saurin, Patrick, *Les prêts toxiques. Une affaire d'Etat* (Toxic loans: an affair of State), Paris: Demopolis, 2013.

Scialom, Laurence, *Economie bancaire* (Banking economics), Paris: La Découverte, 2013.

Smith, Adam, *An Inquiry into the Nature and Causes of the Wealth of Nations* [1776], New York: Bantam, 2003. Also available online: http://www.econlib.org/library/Smith/smWN5.html.

Soros, George, *The Crisis Of Global Capitalism: Open Society Endangered*, New York: Public Affairs, 1998.

Stiglitz, Joseph, *Globalisation and its Discontents*, New York: Norton, 2002.

Stiglitz, Joseph, *The Roaring Nineties*, New York: Norton, 2004.

Stiglitz, Joseph, *Freefall: America, Free Markets, and the Sinking of the World Economy*, New York: Norton, 2010.

Tett, Gillian, *Fool's Gold*, New York: Free Press, 2010.

Tobin James, 'A Proposal for International Monetary Reform', *The Eastern Economic Journal* 4:3-4 (July-October 1978), 153-9.

Thomas, Pierre-Henri, *DEXIA vie et mort d'un monstre bancaire* (Dexia: life and death of a banking monster), Paris: Les petits matins, 2012.

Toussaint, Éric, *Your Money or Your Life - The Tyranny of Global Finance*, trans. Vicki Briault Manus and Raghu Krishnan, Chicago: Haymarket Books, 2005.

Toussaint, Éric, *The World Bank: A Critical Primer*, London: Pluto Press, 2008.

Toussaint, Éric, *A Glance in the Rear View Mirror. Neoliberal Ideology From its Origins to the Present*, Chicago: Haymarket Books, 2010.

Toussaint, Éric, *Bank of the South. An Alternative to IMF-World Bank*, Vikas Adhyayan Kendra, 2007.

Van Hees, Marco, *Banques qui pillent, banques qui pleurent* (Banks that loot, banks that cry), Brussels: Aden, 2009.

Van Hees, Marco, *Didier Reynders, L'homme qui parle à l'oreille des riches* (Didier Reynders, the man who whispers in the ears of the rich), Brussels: Aden, 2009.

Ziegler, Jean, *Destruction massive, géopolitique de la faim* (see next entry), Paris: Éditions du Seuil, 2011.

Ziegler, Jean, *Betting on Famine. Why the World still goes Hungry*, trans. of *Destruction massive*, above, by Christopher Caines, New York: The New Press, 2013.

Zucman, Gabriel, *La Richesse cachée des nations* (see next entry), Paris: Éditions du Seuil, 2013.

Zucman, Gabriel, 'The Missing Wealth of Nations: are Europe and the U.S. Net Debtors or Net Creditors?', *The Quarterly Journal of Economics* (2013), pp. 1321–1364.

References
Non-exhaustive list of journals,
newspapers and other sources cited in the work

Newspapers, press agencies, magazines and online publications:
Agence France Presse http://www.afp.com/fr/
Alternatives économiques http://www.alternatives-economiques.fr/
BBC News http://www.bbc.com/
Bloomberg (online international business publication)
http://www.bloomberg.com/
Challenges http://www.challenges.fr/
Chicago Tribune http://www.chicagotribune.com/
The Daily Telegraph http://www.telegraph.co.uk/
L'Écho http://www.lecho.be/
Les Échos http://www.lesechos.fr/
The Economist http://www.economist.com/
El Economista http://www.eleconomista.es/ (in Spanish)
L'Express http://lexpansion.lexpress.fr/
Financial Times http://ft.com/
Financial Times' specialised site *The Banker Database*
http://www.thebankerdatabase.com
Financité (magazine du Réseau Financité) https://www.financite.be/
Forbes http://www.forbes.com/
Fortune http://fortune.com
The Guardian http://www.theguardian.com
HuffingtonPost http://www.huffingtonpost.com/
L'Humanité http://www.humanite.fr/
The Independent http://www.independent.co.uk/
International Herald Tribune (IHT) http://www.iht.com/
The Irish Independent http://www.independent.ie/
Libération http://www.liberation.fr/
Le Monde http://finance.blog.lemonde.fr/
Le Monde diplomatique http://www.monde-diplomatique.fr/
The Nation http://www.thenation.com/
The New York Times http://www.international.nytimes.com/

Le Parisien http://www.leparisien.fr/
Le Point http://www.lepoint.fr/Économie/
Reuters http://www.reuters.com/
Rolling Stone http://www.rollingstone.com/
SkyNews http://www.news.sky.com/
Le Soir http://archives.lesoir.be/
Le Temps http://www.letemps.ch/
Terra Nova http://www.tnova.fr/.../
La Tribune http://www.latribune.fr/
La Tribune de Genève http://www.tdg.ch
Vox http://www.voxeu.org
The Wall Street Journal http://www.wsj.com/

Research journals, websites and online repositories:
Boletín económico de ICE, Información Comercial Española
http://www.revistasice.com/es-ES/BICE (in Spanish)
Eastern Economic Journal http://www.palgrave-journals.com/eej/
Flash Economie
http://cib.natixis.com/research/economic/publications.aspx?lang=fr
Investopedia http://www.investopedia.com/
EurActiv (independent online media on EU affairs)
http://www.euractiv.com/
Levy Institute of Economics http://www.levyinstitute.org/pubs/
Nanex http://www.nanex.net/NxResearch/
The Quarterly Journal of Economics
http://www.mitpressjournals.org/loi/qjec
Revue Banque http://www.revue-banque.fr/
SNL Financial – ABA Banking Journal http://www.ababj.com/
Wikipedia https://en.wikipedia.org/
ZeroHedge http://www.zerohedge.com/news/

Non-government organizations:
ATTAC France https://france.attac.org/
CADTM http://cadtm.org/
Finance Watch http://www.finance-watch.org/
Fondation Copernic http://www.fondation-copernic.org/
The Greens - European Free Alliance http://www.greens-efa.eu/fr.html
Oxfam http://www.oxfam.org
Via Campesina http://viacampesina.org/en/

Institutional websites:
Banca d'Italia http://www.bancaditalia.it/
Bank of England http://www.bankofengland.co.uk/publications/
Banque de France, Documents et débats https://www.banque-france.fr/
Berenberg https://www.berenberg.de/en/berenberg.html
BIS (Bank for International Settlements) http://www.bis.org/publ/
ECB (European Central Bank) website http://sdw.ecb.europa.eu/
European Banking Authority http://www.eba.europa.eu/
European Commission Website http://ec.europa.eu/
European Parliament News http://www.europarl.europa.eu/news/en/
Eurostat http://ec.europa.eu/eurostat
Financial Stability Board
http://www.financialstabilityboard.org/publications/
GAO (U.S. Government Accountability Office) http://www.gao.gov/
ILO (International Labour Organisation) http://www.ilo.org/
IMF (International Monetary Fund) http://www.imf.org/
IRS (Internal Revenue Service) http://www.irs.gov/
OECD (Organisation for Economic Cooperation and Development) http://www.oecd.org/

Books by
Éric Toussaint
in English

The Life and Crimes of an Exemplary Man, CADTM, 2014, http://cadtm.org/TheLifeandCrimesofan
Glance in the Rear View Mirror. Neoliberal Ideology From its Origins to the Present, Chicago: Haymarket Books, 2012, http://cadtm.org/GlanceintheRearViewMirror
A Diagnosis of Emerging Global Crisis and Alternatives, Mumbai: Vikas Adhyayan Kendra, 2009.
The World Bank: A Critical Primer, London: Pluto Press, 2008, http://cadtm.org/TheWorldBankAcriticalPrimer
Bank of the South. An Alternative to IMF-World Bank, Mumbai: Vikas Adhyayan Kendra, 2007, http://cadtm.org/BankoftheSouthAnAlternative
The World Bank: a Never-ending Coup d'Etat. The Hidden Agenda of the Washington Consensus, Mumbai: Vikas Adhyayan Kendra, 2007.
Your Money [or] Your Life: the Tyranny of Global Finance, trans. Vicki Briault Manus and Raghu Krishnan, Chicago: Haymarket Books, 2005.
Globalisation: Reality, Resistance & Alternatives, Mumbai: Vikas Adhyayan Kendra, 2004.

With Damien Millet:
The Debt Crisis: from Europe to Where? Mumbai: Vikas Adhyayan Kendra, 2012, http://cadtm.org/TheDebtCrisisFromEuropeto
Debt, the IMF, and the World Bank. Sixty Questions, Sixty Answers, New York: Monthly Review Press, 2010, http://cadtm.org/Debt-theIMFandtheWorldBank
Tsunami Aid or Debt Cancellation, Mumbai: Vikas Adhyayan Kendra, 2005.

The Debt Scam - IMF, World Bank and the Third World Debt, Mumbai: Vikas Adhyayan Kendra, 2003.
Who Owes Who? 50 Questions about World Debt, trans. Vicki Briault Manus, London: Zed Books, 2004.
2012 World Debt Figures, CADTM, Damien Millet, Daniel Munevar, Éric Toussaint, http://cadtm.org/2012Worlddebtfigures

Participation in:
Capitalism – Crisis and Alternatives, Fred Leplat and Özlem Onaran (Edited by), IIRE–Resistance Books, 2011, http://iire.org/index.php?option=com_jshopping&controller=product&task=view&-category_id=1&product_id=54

Books by Éric Toussaint in French
Les chiffres de la dette 2015 with Pierre Gottiniaux, Daniel Munevar and Antonio Sanabria, CADTM, 2015, 95 pages.
Bancocratie, Bruxelles: coédition Aden-CADTM, 2014, 455 pages.
Procès d'un homme exemplaire, Marseille: coédition Al Dante-CADTM, 2013, 93 pages.
65 questions 65 réponses sur la dette, le FMI et la Banque mondiale, with Damien Millet, Liège: CADTM, 2012, 244 pages.
AAA. Audit, annulation, autre politique, with Damien Millet, Paris : Le Seuil, 2012, 177 pages.
La dette ou la vie, with Damien Millet, coédition ADEN-CADTM, Bruxelles, 2011, 384 pages.
La crise, quelles crises ?, with Damien Millet, coédition ADEN-CADTM-CETIM, Bruxelles, 2010, 285 pages.
Un coup d'oeil dans le rétroviseur, l'idéologie néolibérale des origines jusqu'à aujourd'hui, Mons : Editions du Cerisier, 2010, 95 pages.
60 questions 60 réponses sur la dette, le FMI et la Banque mondiale, with Damien Millet, Paris: coédition CADTM-Syllepse, 2008, 388 pages.
Banque du Sud et nouvelle crise internationale, alternatives et résistances au capitalisme néolibéral, Paris: coédition CADTM-Syllepse, 2008, 207 pages.
Banque mondiale: le Coup d'Etat permanent. L'Agenda caché du Consensus de Washington, Paris: coédition CADTM-Syllepse-Cetim, 2006, 310 pages.
Les Tsunamis de la dette, with Damien Millet, Paris: coédition CADTM-Syllepse, 2005, 187 pages.

La Finance contre les peuples. La Bourse ou la vie, (augmented edition of *La Bourse ou la vie* [1998], q.v.) Paris: coédition CADTM-Syllepse-Cetim, 2004, 638 pages.

50 questions 50 réponses sur la dette, le FMI et la Banque mondiale, with Damien Millet, Paris: coédition CADTM-Syllepse, 2002, 262 pages.

Sortir de l'impasse. Dette et ajustement, with Arnaud Zacharie, Paris: coédition CADTM-Syllepse, 2002, 222 pages.

Cuba: le pas suspendu de la révolution, with Yannick Bovy, Mons: Editions du Cerisier, 2001, 396 pages.

Afrique: abolir la dette pour libérer le développement, with Arnaud Zacharie, Paris: coédition CADTM-Syllepse, 2001, 272 pages.

Le Bateau ivre de la mondialisation, with Arnaud Zacharie, Paris: coédition CADTM-Syllepse-Cetim, 2000, 264 pages.

La Bourse ou la vie, Paris, Liège & Brussels: CADTM-Luc Pire-Syllepse-Cetim, 1998, 396 pages.

Participation in:
Commission pour la Vérité sur la Dette grecque. *La vérité sur la dette grecque,* Paris: Editions Les Liens qui Libèrent, 2015.

Audit citoyen de la dette publique. Expériences et méthodes, Genève: CETIM & CADTM, 2015.

Le Monde diplomatique, *Manuel d'histoire critique,* Paris, 2014.

Le Monde diplomatique, *L'Atlas 2012. Mondes émergents,* Paris, 2012.

ATTAC, *Le piège de la dette publique. Comment s'en sortir,* Paris: Edition Les liens qui libèrent, 2011.

Catherine, Lucas, *Promenade au Congo: petit guide anticolonial de Belgique,* transl. from the Dutch by Jacquie Dever, Brussels: Aden-CADTM, 2010.

Le Monde diplomatique, *L'Atlas 2009. Un monde à l'envers,* Paris, 2009.

CADTM, *Les Crimes de la dette,* Paris: CADTM-Syllepse, 2007.

CADTM, *A qui profitent toutes les richesses du peuple congolais? Pour un audit de la dette congolaise,* Liège: CADTM, 2007.

L'Autre campagne, *80 propositions à débattre d'urgence,* Paris: Editions La Découverte, 2007.

ATTAC, *Voix rebelles du monde / Rebel voices of the World,* Forcalquier: ATTAC 04 & HB éditions, 2007.

ATTAC, *Le développement a-t-il un avenir ?* Paris: Mille et une nuits, Fayard, 2004.

Husson, Michel, Isaac Johsua, Éric Toussaint & Michel Zerbato, *Crises structurelles et financières du capitalisme au 20e siècle*, Paris: Syllepse, 2002.

ATTAC, *Pour une Mondialisation à finalité humaine*, Paris: ATTAC-Syllepse-Vista, 2002.

ATTAC, *Une Autre Europe pour une Autre Mondialisation*, Brussels: ATTAC-Luc Pire, 2001.

ATTAC, *FMI : les peuples entrent en résistance*, Paris & Geneva: CADTM-Syllepse-Cetim, 2000.

ATTAC, *Contre la dictature des marchés*, Paris: Syllepse, 1999.

CADTM, *Du Nord au Sud: L'endettement dans tous ses Etats*, Brussels: CADTM, 1998.

About the CADTM, Resistance Books and the IIRE

The CADTM

Created in Belgium in 1990, the CADTM (Comité pour l'Annulation de la Dette du Tiers Monde – Committee for the Abolition of Third World Debt) is an international network run by members and local committees in Asia, Africa, Europe and Latin America.

The primary objective of the CADTM is the abolition of illegitimate public debt and the rejection of the structural adjustment and austerity policies imposed by the International Financial Institutions in complicity with governments. It is time to put an end to the infernal cycle of debt and to establish social justice and sustainable environmental development.

The CADTM's projects and activities and the resources it develops combine research and political action. We publish studies, articles, analyses and reviews; we organise conferences and debates, seminars, training sessions, international encounters, awareness campaigns, concerts and much more. The CADTM is involved in the Global Justice Movement. We are striving for a world free from all forms of oppression, respecting the sovereignty of the people, and for international solidarity, equality and social justice.

The CADTM has chosen to work in five main areas:

- Providing detailed analysis of the origins and consequences of public debt and examining the technical and political possibilities for its abolition;
- Developing alternative systems for funding human development conditioned upon the radical transformation of the international financial and institutional systems;
- Defining the stages needed to achieve a universal guarantee of fundamental human rights;
- Struggling for the abolition of illegitimate debt all over the world, whether it be public or private (illegitimate student-loans, mortgages and smallholders' debts);
- Strengthening, nationally and internationally, social movements and citizen networks and calling to account elected representatives at all levels.

CADTM
2 place de Bronckart, 4000 Liège, Belgium
Tel: 0032 (0)4 226 62 85
Email: info@cadtm.org
Web: www.cadtm.org

Resistance Books

Resistance Books is the publishing arm of Socialist Resistance, a revolutionary Marxist organisation that is the British section of the Fourth International. Resistance Books publishes books jointly with the International Institute for Research and Education in Amsterdam and independently.
Further information about Resistance Books, including a full list of titles currently available and how to purchase them, can be obtained at http://www.resistancebooks.org, or by writing to Resistance Books, PO Box 62732, London, SW2 9GQ.

Socialist Resistance is active in the trade union movement and in campaigns against austerity and in defence of public services. Socialist Resistance believes that the Labour Party and social-democratic parties have become so right-wing that we need to build new broad left parties that support workers' struggles and put forward socialist answers to the economic and environmental crisis. We are anti-racist and oppose imperialist interventions. We are ecosocialist – we argue that much of what is produced under capitalism is socially useless and directly harmful. We have been long-standing supporters of women's liberation and the struggles of lesbians, gay people, bisexuals and transgender people.

To find out more about *Socialist Resistance* or to read the organisation's magazine, go to www.socialistresistance.org. Socialist Resistance can be contacted by email at contact@socialistresistance.org or by post at PO Box 62732, London, SW2 9GQ. *International Viewpoint* is the English language online magazine of the Fourth International, which can be read online at www.internationalviewpoint.org.

The International Institute for Research and Education

The International Institute for Research and Education (IIRE) is an international foundation, recognised in Belgium as an international scientific association by a Royal decree of 11th June 1981. The IIRE provides activists and scholars worldwide with opportunities for research and education in three locations: Amsterdam, Islamabad and Manila.

Since 1982, when the Institute opened in Amsterdam, its main activity has been the organisation of courses in the service of progressive forces around the world. Our seminars and study groups deal with all subjects related to the emancipation of the oppressed and exploited around the world. It has welcomed hundreds of participants from every inhabited continent. Most participants have come from the Third World.

The IIRE has become a prominent centre for the development of critical thought and interaction, and the exchange of experiences, between people who are engaged in daily struggles on the ground. The Institute's sessions give participants a unique opportunity to step aside from the pressure of daily activism. The IIRE gives them time to study, reflect upon their involvement in a changing world and exchange ideas with people from other countries.

Our website is constantly being expanded and updated with freely downloadable publications, in several languages, and audio files. Recordings of several recent lectures given at the institute can be downloaded from www.iire.org – as can talks given by founding Fellows such as Ernest Mandel and Livio Maitan, dating back to the early 1980s.

The IIRE publishes *Notebooks for Study and Research* to focus on themes of contemporary debate or historical or theoretical importance. Lectures and study materials given in sessions in our Institute, located in Amsterdam, Manila and Islamabad, are made available to the public in large part through the *Notebooks*.

Different issues of the *Notebooks* have also appeared in languages besides English and French, including German, Dutch, Arabic, Spanish, Japanese, Korean, Portuguese, Turkish, Swedish, Danish and Russian.

For a full list of the *Notebooks for Study and Research*, visit http:// bit.ly/IIRENSR or subscribe online at: http://bit.ly/NSRsub. To order the *Notebooks*, email iire@iire.org or write to:

International Institute for Research and Education,
Lombokstraat 40,
Amsterdam, NL-1094.

www.ingramcontent.com/pod-product-compliance
Lightning Source LLC
Chambersburg PA
CBHW022137020426
42334CB00015B/929